Redcoats

Redcoats

The British Soldier of the Napoleonic Wars

Philip J. Haythornthwaite

Pen & Sword
MILITARY

First published in Great Britain in 2012 by
Pen & Sword Military
an imprint of
Pen & Sword Books Ltd
47 Church Street
Barnsley
South Yorkshire
S70 2AS

Copyright © Philip J. Haythornthwaite

ISBN 978 1 84415 958 1

A CIP catalogue record for this book is
available from the British Library.

Typeset in Ehrhardt by Phoenix Typesetting, Auldgirth, Dumfriesshire

Printed and bound in England by the MPG Books Group Ltd.

Pen & Sword Books Ltd incorporates the Imprints of Pen & Sword Aviation, Pen &
Sword Family History, Pen & Sword Maritime, Pen & Sword Military, Pen &
Sword Discovery, Wharncliffe Local History, Wharncliffe True Crime,
Wharncliffe Transport, Pen & Sword Select, Pen & Sword Military Classics, Leo
Cooper, The Praetorian Press, Remember When, Seaforth Publishing and
Frontline Publishing

For a complete list of Pen & Sword titles please contact
PEN & SWORD BOOKS LIMITED
47 Church Street, Barnsley, South Yorkshire S70 2AS England
E-mail: enquiries@pen-and-sword.co.uk
Website: www.pen-and-sword.co.uk

Contents

Dedication:
In memory of my mother,
a constant support.

AUTHOR'S NOTE

In general it has been found practical to use notes largely to identify the sources of quotations; further references appear in the bibliography.

ACKNOWLEDGEMENTS

The author extends especial thanks to: Derek Green, Alan Harrison, the late Terry Livsey, the late Edward Ryan, Dennis Sully, and Allan Wood.

Introduction

Scum of the Earth?

A number of remarks attributed to the first Duke of Wellington have passed from reportage to become military folklore: a near-run thing, stand up, Guards!, and the playing fields of Eton. Perhaps most notable of all was his description of his own ordinary soldiers as 'the scum of the earth'. This can be misinterpreted as no more than patrician disdain for those who, by the standards of the time, were his social and intellectual inferiors, disposable cannon fodder and anonymous cogs in the machinery of war. Such a perception would be profoundly in error, for most commanders recognized, like a reviewer of Napier's history of the Peninsular War, the merits of 'the patient, hard-working, brave but obscure soldier, without whom, and his rough virtues, the General would vainly hope for glory, or his country's safety.'[1]

Indeed, Wellington – who never sought to make himself popular among his followers by subterfuge and flattery as did Napoleon – said as much. Walking with Thomas Creevey on the eve of the Waterloo campaign, he pointed to an ordinary British soldier and declared: 'There, it all depends upon that article whether we do the business or not. Give me enough of it, and I am sure.'[2]

Yet to much of society, and to a relatively small number of officers ignorant of their trade, the ordinary soldier was a being apart, a faceless element in a misunderstood organization. Serving in Spain at the height of the Peninsular War, William Wheeler of the 51st Light Infantry mused on the army's published dispatches and the eulogies that accompanied the report of death or injury of some high-ranking officer: 'But who shall record the glorious deeds of the soldier whose lot is numbered with the thousands in the ranks and fight and die in obscurity?'[3]

The reason that much of society seemed to view these individuals as

1

Soldiers of the British Army in the Peninsula, before new items of uniform were introduced in 1812: left, the 4th (King's Own) Regiment; centre, the 1st (Royal) Dragoons; right, a Highlander. (Print by Goddard & Booth)

mere bricks in the red wall was described aptly some thirty years after the conclusion of the Napoleonic Wars:

> From the moment that an Englishman engages to serve . . . in the Army, he seems to become an outcast from the affections and, we would add, from the respect of civilians . . . [who regard a soldier as] a sort of necessary evil; an overpaid idler, yet always poor, because always thoughtless and extravagant; a slave of many

masters, who is flogged for getting drunk, and every other breach of discipline; a being who, in a fit of temporary insanity, or in the desperation of poverty, has enlisted, and thereby cut himself off from the society and sympathies of family, friends, and acquaintances.

Such misconceptions concealed the soldiers' true lot, as the same author continued:

> To them belong the gloom of solitude in their night-watches, the regrets of parting, the desolation of a deserted home, the miseries of exile and vain longing for a native soil; the bitter pain of separation from parents, lover, and kinsfolk; the fatigues of duty, the privations of hunger and thirst; the sad effects of the ravages of pestilence, the helplessness of the bereaved widow and orphan children far from home and friends; disappointed ambition, neglected merit, ill-requited service; the dreariness of old age ill provided for, after a youth and prime passed in turmoil and anxiety.[4]

Subsequently, Victor Hugo – son of one of Napoleon's generals and thus not unacquainted with the military condition – wrote that although Wellington was noted for his tenacity, his private soldiers were just as solid as he, and that the iron soldier is as good as the iron duke. The response to this of those iron soldiers can only be surmised, but an example of their philosophy was overheard by Moyle Sherer of the 34th during an exhausting march in the Peninsula: 'I shall never forget the speech of one of our men to his comrade, as they toiled on stumbling in the dark just before me . . . "Bill," said he, "the parliament and the great men at home, they do know all about the movements of the army and the grandè lord, but they don't know any thing about indivijals [individuals]; for instance, now, they don't know that you are damned tired, and that I hae got no pong [bread]." '[5]

Only in later years, in the afterglow of victory following the final tumultuous defeat of Napoleon, did society begin to pay attention to the more humble members of the army that had helped bring about that victory. There was a public appetite for published reminiscences of the war, but only gradually did accounts of the services and opinions of the 'other ranks' come to public notice, due in part to there being relatively few who were fully literate and with the opportunity to recount their experiences in print: for every memorialist like Edward Costello of the 95th or James Anton of the 42nd there were thousands with as good stories to tell, but no way of telling them beyond the limits of the fireside. The process of recognition was slow; those who fought in the Waterloo campaign were rewarded with a medal, the first universal issue to all ranks for a major engagement, but (to the disgust of many) those who had served in the Peninsular War and other campaigns of the period had to wait until the issue, after some grudging opposition, of the Military General Service Medal in 1848, by which time many of those qualified were no longer alive to receive it. Financial recompense for service and injury was even more parsimonious.

Perhaps a small step towards the personalization of the hitherto anonymous 'ranker' was taken by the use of the name 'Tommy Atkins' to represent the ordinary British soldier. Its origin is obscure. There was a tradition that Thomas Atkins was a member of Arthur Wellesley's own 33rd Foot who died with such stoicism in the action at Boxtel in 1794 that when, many years later, a name was required for use on the specimen of soldiers' documents, Wellesley, by then Duke of Wellington, suggested Atkins' name. This story hardly bears scrutiny, for the name appears rather earlier than this suggests; but it *was* used on the specimen documentation in 1815, when, to demonstrate how a soldier should be described officially, the mythical Thomas Atkins was quoted, as a 31-year-old native of Odiham, Hampshire, who had served in the Surrey Rangers and 4th Foot before joining the 23rd. Whatever its origin, the use of a realistic name perhaps assisted in the gradual recognition of the soldier as an individual.[6]

A reviewer of William Siborne's *History of the War in France and Belgium in 1815* (London 1844) complained about the number of names it contained, for 'very few readers have a memory capable of retaining so many names; nor can their wish be very great to remember numerous names of men whom they never heard of before . . . our heads turn dizzy with endeavouring to remember them,'[7] and he pleaded for an abridgement in which nine out of ten names were omitted. Nevertheless, the identification of ordinary soldiers by name helps bring their experiences into sharper focus; if, for example, that man there, charging his musket on the ridge of Mont St. Jean and standing fast with his comrades, ready to defeat the last attack of Napoleon's career, is seen not as just another anonymous soldier but as Private John Clarke of the 3rd Battalion 1st Foot Guards, a 38-year-old cordwainer from Middleton, Suffolk, 5 feet 9½ inches tall, of dark complexion, with dark hair and grey eyes, who will be wounded in the left thigh and neck before nightfall. For that reason, in this work many aspects of the life of the 'ranker' are exemplified by cases involving named individuals.

Despite the passage of time, the experiences of the rank and file can be resurrected, even if sometimes these are only glimpses of the sort they would themselves have had through the shifting smoke of battle. The author of the Anglo-Saxon poem *The Wanderer* wrote of warriors whose time had departed, vanished under the darkness of night as if it had never been, but sufficient records remain to recount the experiences of the ordinary soldiers of the Napoleonic Wars. These are not merely Gray's 'short and simple annals of the poor' – though in very many cases their paths of glory did lead but to the grave – but they concern participants in great events, whose deeds were just as significant in their own way, as were those of the leaders who directed them:

'They shall not die, while tongue can raise
Their monument – a nation's praise,
To all who've ever fought, and won,
A laurel 'neath proud Wellington!'[8]

1

'In Arms We Rise':
The Military Establishment

Our Country calls, in arms we rise
To guard fair Britain's isle

Defiance to Bonaparte:
A New Martial Song, by Morva , 1804[1]

From a position of government parsimony and a lingering mistrust of the very concept of a standing army, a legacy of the consequences of the English Civil War, the needs of the war against France led to military and naval affairs becoming the overriding concern of the state. War dominated national finances: in 1803, almost 60 per cent of the entire annual expenditure went on the army and navy; by 1814, including military subsidies to allies, this had risen to about 68 per cent. This was reflected in the strength of the armed forces: on New Year's Day 1804, some 236,112 men were in full-time military service; by September 1813, this figure had risen to 330,663. The 1811 census revealed that there were 5,693,587 males in Great Britain; even when Ireland is included, it is obvious that the 319,033 soldiers serving in January of that year represented a considerable proportion of the entire population. The maintenance of such numbers involved the replacement of casualties; with deaths in battle and incapacitation from injury and disease, the average loss between the resumption of war in 1803 and the end of 1813 was about 20,500 per annum, with a total during this period of 225,796, the high point being the 25,498 men lost to the service in 1812.

It is against this background that the career of the Redcoat should be considered, though his own perception of the military establishment was restricted largely to his own regiment. The regiment was the army's principal administrative unit, and it was with the regiment that the ordinary soldier most identified. The military force of the state was divided into the army, comprising the infantry and cavalry regiments, controlled by the Commander-in-Chief at Horse Guards; and the ordnance services, the artillery and engineers, under the jurisdiction of the Board of Ordnance, headed by the Master General. To the ordinary soldier, this division of responsibilities was of little consequence; nor was he much concerned with the commissariat, which was controlled by the Treasury, beyond the fact that on campaign his rations were often late in arriving.

The ethos of the regiment has always been regarded as one of the greatest assets of the British military establishment, a golden thread running down the centuries that connected soldiers with their forebears. It is more than a focus for emulation of the past, important though that is; the regiment can provide an alternative family to the soldier's blood kin, and a vital bolster to morale in time of trial. The regimental system has matured over the centuries; although a number of regiments that served in the Napoleonic Wars dated only from the beginning of that period, many were already of considerable antiquity with a distinguished past. For example, excluding the King's German Legion, of the 39 regiments present at Waterloo, seventeen had been raised in the seventeenth century, ten in the first half of the eighteenth century and nine between 1755 and 1780. Regimental longeivity was not the only significant factor, however; the most junior regiment at Waterloo, the 95th Rifles, formed in 1800, had one of the strongest regimental identities and esprit de corps, arising from their elite status, unique mode of operation and distinctive uniform.

Regimental identity was marked and fostered not only by history but by insignia and even by nicknames, so that most soldiers identified with their regiment much more than with the army in general, which had a marked effect upon morale. A writer who interviewed many officers who had fought at Waterloo stated that many had expected to be beaten and that other regiments would give way, but 'certainly not my own corps'. 'Such was the universal answer; and this is the true English feeling: this indignancy of being even supposed to be likely to be the first to give way before an enemy is the true harbinger of success . . . . Our regiments, accustomed to act and live alone, are not taught to dread the failures of adjoining corps in combined operations; they cannot readily yield to the belief that the defeat of a corps in their neighbourhood can license themselves to flee; penetrate an English line, you have gained nothing but a point; cut into a continental line, even a French one, and the *morale* of everything in view, and vicinity, is gone. The English regiment will not give way, because the English regiment of the same brigade has done so, but will mock the fugitive, and in all likelihood redouble its own exertions to restore the fight – a true bull-dog courage against all odds – if well led.'[2]

This belief in the superiority of an individual's particular regiment would be recognized by many generations of British soldiers; but at the time it was not an entirely positive emotion. While some corps maintained unusually cordial relations with others that had shared in some great event (for example the relationship between the 1st Foot Guards and 15th Hussars, dating from the Netherlands campaign of the French Revolutionary Wars), others bore grudges. A case was quoted of a regiment moving into a shared camp in Ireland, and almost immediately launching into an attack on the neighbouring encampment, first with fists and then bayonets; because the aggressor corps could not forgive the other for supposedly deserting them in an action during the Seven Years War, almost half a century earlier, when hardly any of the soldiers involved would even have been born.

Similarly, regimental pride could overflow into unjust criticism, such as that which fell on the 4th Foot after the French garrison had been allowed to escape from Almeida in 1811. Regiments that attracted much public attention discomfited equally worthy corps that felt themselves overlooked; in some quarters this applied to the Highland regiments whose distinctive dress and traditions attracted much attention. An extreme example of this bias was articulated by Joseph Donaldson, who declared the 42nd Royal Highlanders guilty of 'egotism and gasconading', with their reputation as doughty fighters arising from the fact that they had 'got into scrapes by want of steadiness' and then having to fight desperately to save themselves. What had they done to warrant their great reputation? 'Nothing – absolutely nothing: they are a complete verification of the proverb, "If you get a name of rising early, you may lie in bed all day."'[3] It might not be unreasonable to suggest that at least some of Donaldson's unfair prejudice arose from the fact that his own regiment had not attracted the public plaudits that its perfectly respectable career deserved.

Although no regiment would have admitted it, some were fairly undistinguished at times. Among well-known cases, Wellington threatened to send home the 18th Hussars from the Peninsula if they did not improve, and it was stated that one of the causes of the failure of the attack on the American positions at New Orleans was because the 2/44th, carrying ladders and fascines to overcome the enemy defences, was badly led and either threw down their burdens or turned tail, and it was after attempting to halt them with cries of 'For shame! recollect that you are British soldiers!'[4] that the British commander, Sir Edward Pakenham, was mortally wounded. Nevertheless, the members of such regiments would still have averred that *their* regiment was superior to all others.

The infantry's principal tactical element was the battalion. A regiment comprised one or two battalions, occasionally up to four, with the 60th (Royal

Americans) eventually maintaining eight. Any intention that a regiment's 1st Battalion would go on service, leaving the 2nd Battalion at home to provide reinforcement drafts, was negated by the pressing need for troops, so that many 2nd Battalions also went on campaign. At the conclusion of the Peninsular War, for example, the field army comprised forty-two 1st Battalions or single-battalion regiments, thirteen 2nd Battalions, four 3rd Battalions and the 5th Battn. 60th. Each battalion comprised ten companies, eight 'battalion' or centre companies and two 'flank' companies, these terms

INFANTERIE

The classic 'redcoat': a private of the light company of the 5th (Northumberland) Regiment in the uniform of 1812-15. The green plume was indicative of light infantry and the regimental identity is emblazoned on the knapsack. (Print by Genty)

deriving from their position when the battalion was drawn up in line; the flank companies consisted of one of grenadiers, in theory the battalion's most stalwart, and one of light infantry, trained in skirmishing. Each company had a notional strength of 100, so that each battalion was nominally 1,000 strong, but these numbers were hardly ever attained: on the day of Waterloo, for example, excluding those that had suffered severe casualties at Quatre Bras two days earlier, including the four detached at Hal but excluding the 3/95th, which had only three companies present, the average battalion strength was 752. At the outset of the Vittoria campaign, another case in which there had been no reduction in numbers from the attrition of campaign, the average strength was 680. This attrition could be profound; in 1814 it was remarked of the men who began its Peninsular service (it was 778 strong in its first battle at Talavera), only seven 'other ranks' of the 1/61st were still serving, including the brothers Robert and William Hogg. Not only did they survive a combined total of fifteen battles, but both lived to be awarded the Military General Service Medal in 1848.

The infantry comprised three regiments of Foot Guards, traditionally the monarch's bodyguard, and consecutively-numbered 'line' regiments, the numbers in 1815 running from the 1st (Royal Scots) through to the 104th, although in the French Revolutionary Wars the number had extended to the 135th (Limerick), the higher-numbered corps of only brief existence. From 1782 most regiments had been allocated a county affiliation, with the intention of enhancing morale and aiding recruiting, but for many the connection with a specific county was tenuous. Of the regiments existing in 1815, fifteen had Scottish titles (and three more had been 'Highland' until 1809), eight were Irish and two bore Welsh titles. The latter exemplify the diverse nature of recruiting: the 43rd (Monmouthshire) Light Infantry was never an overtly Welsh corps despite its title (when county titles were allocated the regiment had expressed a desire not to have one and had declared that its primary recruiting ground was Cleveland); while that most Welsh of corps, the 23rd (Royal Welch Fuzileers) at Waterloo comprised less than 27 per cent Welshmen, with 8 per cent from both Lancashire and Norfolk and 7 per cent from Ireland. The Scottish regiments generally retained a regional identity more than the English, although those officially 'Highland' could not draw sufficient recruits from that area to reflect their title, a principal reason why a number lost their 'Highland' designation and costume in 1809. For example, arguably the most famous of the Scottish regiments, the 42nd (Black Watch), between 1807 and 1812 enlisted about 87 per cent Scots, almost 9 per cent Irish, and the remainder English, while in 1811, the 93rd Highlanders was almost 97 per cent Scottish. Conversely, the 3/1st (Royal Scots) during its

Heavy cavalry: a dragoon in the uniform worn until the introduction of a French-style helmet and short-tailed jacket from 1812.

existence appears to have recruited only 18 per cent Scots, but 42 per cent Irish and 37 per cent English. The dilution of regional identity became much more marked when volunteers were accepted from the county militia regiments, who rarely joined the line regiment associated with their own county.

While identifying most readily with his regiment, it was with his company, with its familiar complement of officers and NCOs, that the soldier would feel closest. Officially there was no lower sub-unit, but in May 1809 for his army in the Peninsula, Wellington instituted the formation within each company of 'as many squads as there are Non-Commissioned Officers' in an attempt to check looting by the closer supervision of the NCOs, there being 'no description of property of which the unfortunate inhabitants of Portugal have not been plundered by the British soldiers.'[5]

Each cavalry regiment was divided into a number of squadrons, each of usually two troops, with each regiment commonly of ten troops, two of which formed the depot and the remainder went on service. The number of 'service' troops was reduced to six in 1811, with light regiments maintaining ten, increased to twelve in 1813. Strengths varied considerably on campaign; for example, at the beginning of the 1809 campaign average regimental strength was 385; at the beginning of the Vittoria campaign, 412, and at Waterloo, 441. The cavalry comprised two regiments of Life Guards and the Royal Horse Guards, together forming the Household Cavalry (though the status of the Royal Horse Guards was not confirmed until 1820); the heavy cavalry comprised seven regiments of Dragoon Guards, six of Dragoons (reduced to

Gunners of the Royal Artillery in the uniform of 1812. (Print by J.C. Stadler after Charles Hamilton Smith)

five in 1799 when the 5th Dragoons was disbanded following infiltration by Irish rebels). The Light Dragoons were numbered consecutively after the 6th Dragoons, 7th–33rd, the later-numbered corps of ephemeral existence, so that the 25th was the highest number in use by 1815. The 7th, 10th, 15th and 18th Light Dragoons were granted the additional title (and uniform) of Hussars. In general, cavalry regiments had no county affiliation, though the 2nd Dragoons was predominantly Scottish and the 5th and 6th Dragoons Irish.

The Royal Artillery was also organised in battalions, but never served as such; each six-gun unit was manned by a company (sometimes styled a 'brigade'), or by a troop in the case of the Royal Horse Artillery. These were autonomous units, usually including a detachment from the Corps of Drivers, so that the focus of the gunner's existence was not his battalion but his company or troop.

Other types of regiment competed with the regular army for recruits. During the French Revolutionary Wars there were corps of infantry and cavalry Fencibles (their name derived from 'defencible'), which were regularly recruited but liable for service only within the country in which they had been raised unless they volunteered to serve elsewhere; none survived beyond the Peace of Amiens. More substantial was the Militia, battalions of infantry raised on a county basis for service at home, especially valuable in releasing regular troops for overseas service. This was the only category of regiment not raised entirely by voluntary enlistment, as men could be compelled to serve by ballot, a form of selective conscription; but it was possible to obtain exemption by paying for a 'substitute', so that only a small number of militiamen were 'principals' or conscripts. The hiring of such substitutes took away many potential recruits from the regular army, but when militiamen were allowed to volunteer for regular service, the regular army gained a priceless resource of new recruits who were already inured to military discipline and trained in the use of arms.

There was in addition a huge force of part-time volunteers formed for the defence of their own localities – in December 1803 no less than 380,193 in mainland Britain plus 82,941 in Ireland – who drilled once or twice a week and who acted as a form of security force in times of civil disturbance; but they had little bearing upon the regular army beyond giving some men a taste for a military life.

2

'Come 'List and Enter Into Pay': Recruiting

Come 'list and enter into pay,
Then o'er the hills and far away

Anon

The Duke of Wellington's most notorious remark arose largely from a comparison of the British system of voluntary enlistment with the conscription utilized by some European armies, and without the closing phrase, often omitted, the remarks seem savagely critical:

'... our friends [the ordinary British soldiers] are the very scum of the earth. People talk of their enlisting from their fine military feeling – all stuff – no such thing. Some of our men enlist from having got bastard children – some for minor offences – many more for drink; but you can hardly conceive such a set brought together, and it is really wonderful that we should have made them the fine fellows they are.'[1] On another occasion he used the same term, and repeated his thoughts on what they had become: 'the scum of the earth – the mere scum of the earth. It is only wonderful that we should be able to make so much of them afterwards. The English soldiers are fellows who have all enlisted for drink – that is the plain fact – they have all enlisted for drink.'[2]

There was an element of truth in this assertion, but it was far from being as universal as the Duke suggested. Motivations for enlisting in the army were many and varied, although it is difficult to construct a balanced picture from the writings of the rank and file themselves, for those who left an account of their services were generally among the exceptional proportion who were literate.

Army service must be seen against the perception of the military prevalent in some parts of society: a refuge for the indigent, criminal or those unwilling to shoulder the responsibility of civilian family life. This attitude was summarized by the 15th Light Dragoon who published his memoirs anonymously as *Jottings from my Sabretasche* (1847): 'Whoever "listed for a soldier" was at once set down among the catalogue of persons who had turned out ill.' The

Recruiting: to the despair of his wife, a countryman has his head turned by a drummer and sergeant of a recruiting party. (Print by G. Keating after George Morland)

attitude was reinforced by the use of the army in suppression of civil disorder, and the hostility of part of society towards the army could even overflow into violence, as at Holborn in July 1795, when two men of the 12th Light Dragoons recognized a deserter:

> They very properly went up to the man to apprehend him. He immediately attracted a mob, by calling out that they wanted to

kidnap him. The mob, taking part with the deserter, began to ill use the soldiers, who drew their swords in their defence, and one of them, in the act of defending himself from the acts of the furious populace, cut off the nose of one of them, which so irritated them, that the lives of the two men became seriously endangered. They were knocked down, and beat very severely; and the populace had proceeded so far as to have laid one of them down in the street that a cart might run over his neck; but, fortunately, the high constable, with proper assistance, coming up, the unfortunate soldier was rescued from immediate death, though he suffered so much while in the power of the mob, that it was reported that he died last night.[3]

This was no unique case of an attack upon soldiers attempting to arrest deserters; for example, at Canterbury in August 1810 men of the Queen's Bays were set upon: 'Two of the soldiers were dreadfully wounded with a large knife: the one received two severe cuts in the left breast, and the other in the abdomen. They were both conveyed to the hospital, where they lie without hope of recovery.'[4] At Leatherhead Fair in October 1803 as trivial an event as the demonstration of the sword exercise by men of the 10th Light Dragoons 'drew on them the displeasure of the crowd, who attacked them; and, driving them into a field, assailed them with stones. The soldiers charged the people with drawn swords, but the crowd stood firm, and proved victorious. One soldier was severely wounded in the face and eyes. A poor woman received a cut across her arm and breast, but supposed not dangerously; and a man had his hand or fingers nearly cut off.'[5]

Prejudice against the ordinary soldier extended to the higher level of society; many would have concurred with Lord Erskine's well-known remark about 'the uncontrolled licentiousness of a brutal and insolent soldiery' and to the Secretary at War's reference in the House of Commons in November 1795, concerning the process of recruiting, to 'men of a very low description'.[6] In that context, Wellington's 'scum of the earth' remark, even had it not been qualified, would have been seen as not surprising.

The process of attracting men to enrol in an organization so mistrusted by part of society depended largely upon recruiting parties sent out by each regiment, for not until 1812 was every recruiting district formed into subdivisions, headed by an experienced officer to superintend the process. Operating on the strength of a 'beating order', recruiting parties usually consisted of one or two loquacious sergeants, a few smart privates and a drummer or trumpeter to announce their presence (hence the term 'drum-

Recruiting: clearly against the wishes of his sweetheart, a countryman considers life as a light dragoon. The regiment's black trumpeter sounds a call to attract potential recruits. (Print by C. Turner after John Eckstein, 1803)

ming up support'), usually with an officer who tended to remain in the background. Recruiting parties were an almost universal sight at fairs and markets; for example, no less than 1,113 parties were operating in 1806-07, and despite the territorial affiliations of infantry regiments, they could extend their efforts beyond any such specific region. Some areas were fertile grounds for recruiting, notably if a particular local trade were especially depressed, but others were notably barren: one recruiter quoted the example of Kirbymoorside (mid-way between Pickering and Helmsley) where, he claimed, the inhabitants had never heard a drum and only rarely seen a red coat.

The presence of recruiting parties might be announced by the posting of notices that emphasized the joys of a military life and the fame of the regi-

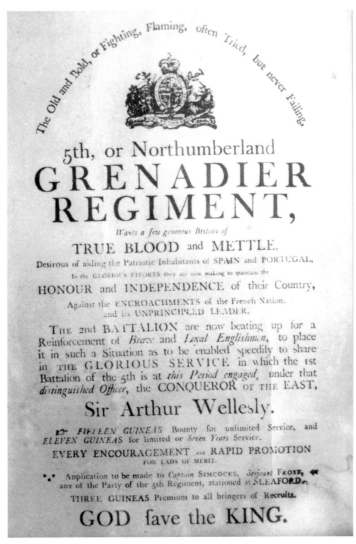

An advertisement for the 5th Foot produced by a recruiting party led by Captain John Simcocks at Sleaford. The text is typically overstated: the 5th was not a 'Grenadier regiment' but it sounded impressive!

ment, often wildly exaggerated: 'Five Shillings a Day and a Black Servant'[7]; 'luxurious living, an hospitable table and capacious bowl of punch'[8] and similar untruths. A typical example advertised for recruits for the 81st in 1793: 'Those Loyal Heroes, who, ambitious of gaining Glory in the Honourable Profession of Arms, have now an opportunity of entering a Regiment, where Honor and Happiness, will be sure to reward their noble exertions for their King and Country, and a liberal pension will soften the sorrows of declining life, and procure a more comfortable competence than can be acquired by many years of hard labour. Every Hero will be provided with genteel clothing, fit for a Gentleman Soldier.'[9] An appeal to patriotism could also figure: 'surely every Man of Spirit must blush to remain at Home in Inactivity and Indolence, when his Country and the best of Kings needs his Assistance.'[10]

The principal incentive for enlisting was the 'bounty', a sum in cash; not the proverbial 'king's shilling' but to a pauper on subsistence wages a huge sum. In 1805 the bounty was twelve guineas, paid to the recruit on his enlistment. This was not the entire expense to the government: a person who brought a recruit to the army received £2 12s 6d and the recruiting party £1 11s 6d (bringing the total cost to 16 guineas), though one sergeant claimed the recruiters never made a profit as the money they received was spent on the drink used to soften up potential recruits so that their cash 'melted awa' like snaw off a dyke.'[11] One recruiter recalled how his sergeant handed out cheap watches to recruits, an emblem of gentrification irresistible to an uneducated pauper.

Competition for recruits was intense, between various parties and the Royal Navy, which in 1796 was offering a bounty of up to forty guineas. This could be exploited, as in Edinburgh in April 1794: 'Yesterday, the Grass-market was crowded with recruiting parties. A stout young countryman, being determined to enlist, collected the recruiting parties together, and fairly set himself up for public auction, but he would not admit of any offer less than a guinea. The bidders were many; and he was at last knocked down at twenty guineas.'[12] Other enterprising recruits are recorded as selling themselves much as butcher's meat, at so much a pound or an inch in height. Sharp practice had long been forbidden, for example, as in recruiting instructions issued to the 17th Foot: 'You are not to suffer your party to use any Villanies or low practices to trapan [sic] recruits, but to punish such as are guilty thereof'[13] (this also forbade the enlistment of miners and Welshmen!), but many 'low practices' existed. The worst offenders were the 'crimps', shady publicans or criminals who enveigled the gullible by cash, or made them insensible with drink and then sold them to the army. The worst of these excesses occurred in the mid-1790s, when there was an acute shortage of men, and even involved

Recruiting: a sergeant of the 33rd Foot attracts recruits by flourishing a havercake (oatcake) on his sword, representing the regular food offered to soldiers. Bunches of ribbons were customarily worn by members of a recruiting party and by those they enlisted. (Print by R. Havell after George Walker)

kidnapping: alerted by the breaking of a window by an imprisoned pot-boy, when the authorities entered a house in St. George's Fields in 1795, eighteen men were found in shackles, awaiting sale.

Less downright illegal ploys were used to attract the unwary. Recruiters were always smart, with bunches of ribbons in their headdress, which would be given to those who enlisted; alcohol flowed, and stranger attractions included the recruiting sergeants of the 33rd displaying havercakes (oatcake) on their swords, symbolizing the plentiful food available in the army (hence the old nickname 'Havercake Lads' bestowed on the Duke of Wellington's Regiment). Thomas Plunkett, rogue and champion marksman of the 95th, once danced a jig on top of a cask of ale to attract recruits until the top gave way and he fell in; soaked through, he ran into a nearby dwelling and poked his head up a chimney, emerging caked in soot and claiming that it matched his regiment's dark green uniform. More bizarre still was the employment of a previous member of a freak show, the 42-inch-high John Heyes, 'the Yorkshire dwarf', who performed the sword drill to attract the crowd.

One recruiting sergeant described how to ensnare various types: weavers, he claimed, were always discontented and could be lured by claims that the textile trade was doomed and that a soldier's life was much easier; conversely, a ploughboy or 'bumpkin' would respond best to tales of wealth and promotion. The easiest was the 'sentimental chap': 'You had only to get into heroics, and spout a great deal about glory, honour, laurels, drums, trumpets, applauding world, deathless fame, immortality, and all that, and you had him as safe as a mouse in a trap.'[14] If all else failed, a man could be rendered insensible with drink, slip a shilling in his pocket, and when he came round marshal a crowd of (soldier) witnesses to swear that he had enlisted voluntarily. This was perhaps not uncommon; for example, a generation earlier, in March 1760, a drummer named Clayton of the 94th (Royal Welsh Volunteers) attempted to ensnare two stocking-frame knitters in London by dropping a shilling onto the floor of a public house; when one of his intended victims picked it up and passed it to the other, Clayton claimed that both had taken the 'king's shilling'. They went before Justice Palmer of Islington, who uncovered the truth, released them and reprimanded the drummer.

Not all recruiters were happy with subterfuges, like Sergeant Thomas Jackson of the Coldstream Guards, who recalled how distasteful he found the recruiting service when sent to fairs to swagger about, waving his sword, to persuade the gawping 'clodpoles' to enlist. (He only had limited success, for most of those inclined to enrol failed to meet the high standard demanded by this exclusive corps.) A sergeant major of the 95th described by Benjamin Harris seems to have no such scruples; he was 'quite a beau, in his way; he had a sling-belt to his sword like a field-officer, a tremendous green feather in his cap, a flaring sash, his whistle and powder-flask displayed, an officer's pelisse over one shoulder, and a double allowance of ribbons in his cap . . . we made as much of ourselves as if we had both been Generals.' Harris described how, at Rye, they enlisted a chimney sweep named John Lee, who was covered with soot:

> "Damn your black face," said the Serjeant Major; "the Rifles can't be too dark [the regiment prided itself on its very dark green uniform and black equipment]: you're a strong rascal, and if you mean it, we'll take you to the doctor tomorrow and make a Giniril of you the next day." So we had the sweep that night into a large tub of water, and scoured him outside, and filled him with punch inside, and made a rifleman of him. The Serjeant Major, however, on this night, suspected . . . that Lee was rather a slippery fellow, and might repent. So after filling him drunk, he said to me – "Harris, *you* have caught this bird, and *you* must keep him fast.

You must both sleep tonight handcuffed together in the same bed,
or he will escape us"; which I actually did . . . .[15]

The most beguiling inducement to enlist was that reputedly deployed
when the Marquess of Huntly was recruiting his 100th Foot (subsequently
re-numbered 92nd) in 1794. Huntly was the son of the Duke of Gordon
(who had offered to raise the regiment, hence its title 'Gordon Highlanders'),
and his mother, the Duchess, a noted beauty known as 'Bonnie Jean', dressed
in uniform and 'rode from farm to farm, from hamlet to hamlet of her extensive estates – by an eloquent tongue rousing the martial ardour of her
tenantry, and in rare cases, where this failed, offering the bribe of a kiss from
her own lips. Such a bribe always proved irresistible.'[16] Versions of the story
have her holding a shilling, or a guinea, in her lips and transferring it to the
recruit by way of the kiss, and some stories make clear which was thought the
most valuable: one man was said to have taken the shilling and immediately
paid a pound 'smart money' to release him from his undertaking, remarking
that it was worth the expense for a kiss; another took a proffered guinea and
threw it into the watching crowd, showing that it was not for gold that he had
signed on.

This story of Scottish recruiting recalls how vestiges of the old clan system
have been quoted as reasons why Highland regiments were able to recruit
from the tenantry of their colonel or officers: that men were prepared to follow
their clan chiefs despite there being among the Highlanders 'a deep dislike,
or, more properly speaking, a bitter hatred of the "red army", of the King's
troops, as associated with all the sad and savage scenes that followed
Culloden.'[17] The raising of the Strathspey Fencibles in 1793 by Sir James
Grant of Grant would appear to demonstrate how a colonel could exploit such
connections: no less than eighty of his 'other ranks' bore his name, and of
seventy-six officers who served in the regiment, thirty-six were named Grant.

Not even a kiss from a beauty like 'Bonnie Jean' could disguise the fact that
by taking the shilling, a man was essentially signing away his life, for he was
bound to the army for as long as he was physically able to perform his duties,
or until his services were no longer required. The concept of this lifetime
service was criticized: in 1794 Sir Robert Wilson published a pamphlet that
stated: 'It is strange that in a free country a custom so repugnant to freedom
as enlisting for life, and to the particular character of the British constitution,
should ever have been introduced . . . .The independence of an Englishman
naturally recoils at the prospect of bondage, which gradually produces discon-
tent even against the bent of inclination,' while Sir Samuel Romilly described
it as 'repugnant to the principles of the British constitution' by binding men

to an occupation without the opportunity of readily changing their employment.[18]

Consequently, in 1806 'limited service' was introduced, by which a man could enlist for a period of seven years in the infantry, with the opportunity of extending his service by two further periods of seven years each. In the cavalry the first period was ten years, the other two of seven years each, and in the artillery the first period was twelve years, the other two five years each. This was intended 'to improve the trade of a soldier, and to bring it into fair

Having changed his mind and deserted, the unwilling recruit is apprehended and takes leave of his wife. (Print by G. Keating after George Morland)

competition with a sufficient portion of the habits and callings of the lower orders,'[19] and as a largely unsuccessful attempt to reduce the rate of desertion. Even so, the majority of recruits still opted for lifetime service, though the new system did find some favour; for example, Thomas Morris of the 73rd recalled that 'They wanted me to go for life, but I thought the term I had selected quite long enough for a trial.'[20] Limited service enlistment was discontinued on 18 April 1829.

Enlistment was often unpopular with a recruit's family, given the common perception of the military. Probably a typical reaction was that of Joseph Donaldson's mother: 'Now you are lost to us and yourself,' while his father exclaimed, 'God forgive you! . . . the first news I hear of you may be that your corpse is bleaching on the Continent – a prey to wolves and eagles.'[21] Some kinfolk resorted to more drastic measures than just discouraging harangues, for the following was not an isolated occurrence: 'The following circumstance of Sunday se'n-night occurred at Wellington, in Shropshire: a man on the evening preceding enlisted; his wife in vain remonstrated, but determining to effect her purpose, while he lay asleep, she cut two of his fingers quite off, and thereby disqualified him for his new avocation.'[22] (This was clearly a more serious affair than that described in military terms by the contemporary collo-quialism that held that a man dragged from the alehouse by his wife had been 'arrested by the white sergeant'!) Parents could go to extraordinary lengths to 'rescue' their offspring; when John Collinge, a young gardener from Rochdale, enlisted in the Foot Guards, his widowed mother made the long journey to London and secured an interview with the Duke of York, in which she begged her son be allowed to return home; in a typically kind gesture the Duke not only arranged his discharge but gave the woman a guinea to sustain them on their return journey. (Sadly, Collinge was a drunkard who thereafter lived off his mother's meagre earnings.)

Having agreed to 'take the shilling', the recruit was escorted to a magistrate within four days, but officially not within twenty-four hours (to prevent the attestation of a man still incapably drunk; indeed, when Captain Mortimer published recruiting advertisements for the York Fencibles in the *Hull Packet* newspaper in 1794 he specifically asked that none should apply 'but those that are sober'). Presented to the magistate or justice of the peace (providing this functionary was not also an army officer), the recruit could withdraw his offer to enlist providing he returned any money he had received and pay twenty shillings 'smart money' in addition to defray any expenses. Those unable to pay had to stand by their original intention, desert, or take the ultimate route of escape, like a young wheelwright named Pearce who in October 1807 so regretted having enlisted in the Foot Guards, leaving a wife and two children, that he blew out his brains in the unfortunately-named Cut-throat Lane, Lambeth.

The magistrate then read the 'articles of war' relating to mutiny and desertion, and upon oath the recruit declared his name, age, place of birth, that he was not already in the army or navy, 'and that he has had no Rupture, and was not troubled with Fits, and was no ways disabled by Lameness, Deafness, or otherwise, but had the perfect Use of his Limbs and Hearing, and was not an Apprentice.' The declaration regarding physical fitness was important, for there were no regulations about medical inspections, and in time of need recruits were accepted even though infirm or aged. An extreme case was claimed by an MP named Hussey in Parliament in 1795 when he stated he had seen a newly-formed Irish regiment 'filled up with decrepid [sic] men from 70 to 80 years of age, and of boys little more than 12,' and that in his own constituency an aged man had been enlisted who had been discharged ten years earlier as wholly unfit for any service.[23]

The clause regarding ruptures was especially significant as it was estimated in 1814 that ordinary manual labour was so arduous that one in eight of the male population was affected by a rupture. In 1806 it was ordered that no man should be enlisted who had symptoms of scurvy, sore legs or 'scald head' (scurf on the scalp), but not until 1821 were flat feet prohibited. Perhaps the best-known soldier to be accepted with a physical disability was the memorialist Benjamin Harris, who had maimed a forefinger in childhood. It is perhaps a measure of the rigour of medical inspections that a number of women are known to have served in the ranks, masquerading as men; indeed, there seems not to have been much surprise that a woman could enveigle herself into the army: when a soldier of the 13th Foot was discovered to be female, it was only thought 'remarkable she learnt her Exercise surprisingly quick'![24]

Apprentices were among the few who could not be enlisted legally, though many runaways did, the memorialist William Lawrence of the 40th being among the most notable, an apprentice builder who left a harsh master, while another, John Shipp, was an orphan who enlisted in the 22nd at the age of twelve to escape a brutal farmer to whom he had been bound by the parish officers.

The reasons why men enlisted as soldiers are many. The popular concept that all were men of bad habits or shady repute was refuted by Henry Marshall, Deputy Inspector General of Army Hospitals: 'The folly or inconsiderateness of youth, and the difficulty of procuring the means of subsistence, are the real causes which fill the ranks of the British Army . . . . Great delinquents, or criminal offenders, rarely become soldiers; and, when persons of this class do enlist, they commonly soon desert.'[25] As he suggested, economic hardship was a powerful incentive, and as depressions affected various trades, their practitioners entered the army. At times during the French wars there was great hardship and decline in prosperity; in 1807, for example, a petition was submitted to parliament on behalf of the weavers of Lancashire, Yorkshire and Cheshire asking for the fixing of a minimum wage at a time when some weavers earned only 9s per week; and in the following year a similarly un-successful petition stated that the average wage had fallen to just 6s per week, from which a married man might have to support not only himself but his family. As described by the song *John's Ramble from Grinfelt*, men tired of 'clemming and starving, and never a farthing' might decide to 'feight for old England as hard as I con', for set against such civilian wages, the soldier's pay was not outrageously low.[26]

The drudgery of civilian life must also have had an effect. Henry Marshall thought that many recruits never considered the consequences of enlisting for life because 'the labouring or poorer classes of the population, appear to think little on the subject; or, at any rate, they seem to contemplate a permanent loss of personal liberty without concern or with great indifference. Folly and misery, the usual precursors of enlistment, are almost incompatible with prudence and consideration . . . . The lower we descend the social scale, the greater is the recklessness of conduct, and the less is the regard to future consequences,'[27] presumably because if their civilian life was so wretched a military vocation could hardly have been worse.

Despite Wellington's strictures against the idea that 'fine military feeling' played a part, apparently in many cases it did. Thomas Morris of the 73rd, an employee of the noted gunmakers Brander & Potts, joined the St. George's Volunteers (Middlesex) at the age of sixteen, after reading 'the heart-stirring accounts of sieges and battles, and the glorious achievements of the British troops in Spain [which] created in me an irrepressible desire for military service'; feeling 'almost ashamed at being only half a soldier,' he then followed his brother into the 73rd.[28]

The writings of some soldiers do indeed display a level of patriotism that transcends the fairly general disdain of all things foreign, and found expression in the glamour of uniform and the idea of a military life.

Domestic circumstances were another motivation. A sergeant of the 43rd who published his memoirs anonymously stated that his reason for enlisting was to escape parental control, and being unduly influenced by a wild friend; he exemplified, perhaps, those to whom a recruiting poster of the 14th Light Dragoons was aimed, which extolled the military life to all 'with too little wages, and a pinch-gut Master – all you with too much wife, or are perplexed with obstinate and unfeeling parents.'[29]

The fact that some relatively trivial domestic disagreements may have provided the impulsion to abandon civilian life may be suggested by the 18th-century Cumbrian poet Susanna Blamire in her poem *Barley Broth*, in which a man's disagreement with his wife over the contents of her soup leads him to declare, in exasperation, 'I'll sarve my king, An' niver, niver mair come heame,' which presumably must not have seemed an impossible circumstance to contemporary readers. More drastic domestic friction led Thomas Wheatley to enlist in the 23rd Light Dragoons, after trying to shoot his father for being a strike-breaker in the stocking-weaving trade. (Wheatley was one of the 'Cossall heroes' from that place in Nottinghamshire, and the only one to survive: the others, both killed at Waterloo with the 2nd Life Guards, were the famous bare-knuckle prizefighter John Shaw, who enlisted to further his pugilistic career, and Richard Waplington, who sought refuge from the coal mines where he had laboured from childhood.)

Shortages of recruits led to the enrollment of very young men, as reported in 1798, concerning boys 'from 13 to 18 years old. They are to be well fed, and for some time to be mere walking drills; after which they are to be exercised with light fusees, one hundred of which have been sent to each of the six regiments' (selected for the experiment).[30] Although this was a policy not deliberately repeated, very young men continued to be enlisted; it was remarked, for example, that the 91st was such a 'young' battalion in the Netherlands in 1814 that they were equipped with fusils, lighter than the ordinary musket and easier for youths to carry. Unlike subsequent practice, there was no hesitation in committing such young soldiers to action; for example, the youngest member of the 73rd to be killed at Waterloo was Edward Spink, who was only sixteen, having enlisted on his fifteenth birthday, and even he was not the youngest member of his battalion. Even younger children could be enlisted if they were the offspring of serving soldiers. One remarkable 'child of the regiment' was Thomas Mackerell, whose father was drum major of the 44th. Young Thomas was enrolled as a drummer; he was the last serving member of the regiment to have served in the Egyptian campaign when, being so young, he was unable to march through heavy sand and had to be carried on his father's shoulders. He was commissioned into the same regiment in September 1804 and in 1841, as lieutenant colonel, was mortally wounded in Afghanistan, having spent his entire life in the regiment.

Another very important source of recruits was the militia. Its relationship with the regular army was not always easy, for though its presence released regular troops for service abroad, it provided stiff competition for the army's recruiting parties, for purely financial reasons. The Earl of Rosslyn articulated this in Parliament in April 1811: 'What man of sense could expect that persons would inlist [sic] for general service for ten guineas, while a sum so much larger was to be had for inlisting in the Militia?'[31] and he stated that a man offering to serve as a militia substitute could get £50. Nevertheless, recruiting from the militia brought in men who were already trained and used to the military life, though it was originally an emergency measure, with limits on the numbers taken, requiring separate Acts of Parliament in 1798, 1799, 1805 and 1807, until in 1809 regular volunteering from the militia was authorised. The cost to the government of such recruits was substantial, with the bounty paid to voluntary recruits to the militia being supplemented by another when they joined the regulars; for example, it was reported in December 1807 that enlistees to the Wexford Militia were receiving a fourteen-guinea bounty, to the Dublin Militia fifteen guineas, with ten guineas to a militiaman who transferred to the regulars, so that in place of the ordinary twelve-guinea bounty, such militiamen were costing twenty-four or twenty-five guineas.

It was, however, worth the cost to the exchequer, because from 1805 to the end of the war some 100,000 militiamen joined the regular army, a period that witnessed a great improvement in standards, leading to the excellence of the Peninsular army, militia recruits in general being much superior to those enrolled from civilian life. Indeed, one experienced commentator stated that without volunteering from the militia, 'there would have been no army at all – at least, not more than sufficient to garrison the colonies . . . this too, when all the roads in England were covered with sturdy vagrants, who would rather beg than work, or enter the Army.'[32]

Various expedients were used to persuade militiamen to join the regular army in addition to the cash bounty. Some militiamen reckoned that as they were soldiers already, they might as well go the whole way, and were seduced by the glamour of a uniform like that of the 95th, while alcohol continued to be the universal incentive. Benjamin Harris recounted a typical effort to recruit from the Leicestershire Militia: 'We worked hard in this business. I must say that for three days and nights we kept up the dance and the drunken riot. Every volunteer got ten guineas bounty, which, except the two kept back for necessaries, they spent in every sort of excess, till all was gone. Then came the reaction. The drooping spirits, the grief at parting with old comrades, sweethearts, and wives, for the uncertain fate of war . . . and our attempts to give a fillip to their spirits as we marched them off from the friends they were never to look upon again; and, as we termed it, "shove them on to glory."'[33] That many militiamen were not immune from the realization of the dangers of regular service seems proven by claims that if insufficient volunteered, mildly coercive measures were adopted such as long drills and field exercises, so annoying the militiamen that they enlisted in the regulars just to escape!

A stranger method was recounted by George Napier of the 52nd who recalled how he and his brother William (from the 43rd) attempted to secure militia recruits at Limerick; they were met by 'ten very handsome militia soldiers, six feet high, who said they would volunteer with which officer of the line . . . could beat them in running and jumping. Of course, in order to get these fine fellows, we all tried and exerted ourselves to the utmost. [William] and I were the two most active of all the officers, and we had a hard struggle with Pat; but I was beat by them. Not so [William]; with his cursed long legs he beat the men both in running and jumping, and they, being honourable fellows, as most Irishmen are, kept their word, and he took them all ten to the 43rd, and probably most of them found their graves in Spain, poor fellows!'[34]

The enrolment of drafts of militiamen had a marked consequence upon the nature of regiments, in that many no longer had even a pretence of an attachment to the area indicated by their county title, undermining the intention to connect regiments to particular regions. For example, of those who volunteered for regular service from the 3rd West York Militia between 1805 and 1814, only 15 per cent went into Yorkshire regiments, and only 8 per cent into a regiment from their own Riding.

From whatever route had carried him into the army, the final stage in the process of enlistment was for the recruit to sign (or commonly make his mark upon) the attestation document and swear an oath before the magistrate:

> I swear to be true to our Sovereign Lord King George, and serve Him honestly and faithfully in Defence of his Person, Crown, and Dignity, against all His Enemies or Opposers whatsoever: And to observe and obey His Majesty's Orders, and the Orders of the Generals and Officers set over me by His Majesty.

From that moment the man was officially a soldier.

3

'All Free-Born Sons': The Soldier

All free-born sons, they Freedom's Rights defend,
And each to each secures a steady Friend!

The Patriot Volunteers, or *Loyalty*
Display'd, by Clarinda, July 1795[1]

When the recruiting party had assembled a sufficient quota of men, it marched them to a rendezvous point or the regimental depot. The departure was often tearful as the recruits parted with their kinfolk, sometimes with some ceremony; indeed, the Farewell Inn at Rochdale was named from such occasions as local people shared a last drink with their newly-enrolled friends and relations. The march to the depot could be an adventure, especially if the recruits still had their bounty money: 'a perfect military saturnalia, all discipline and restraint were at an end, and it was "hail fellow well met" throughout; glorious times for the publicans on the road' as the men competed in committing 'the oldest kind of folly in the newest kind of way'.[2] Benjamin Harris described escorting a party of recruits from Dublin to Ashford, just a drunken spree, 'every now and then stopping for another pull at the whiskey decanters. Thus we kept it up till we had danced, shouted, and piped thirteen Irish miles, from Cashel to Clonmel . . . before we embarked we were nearly pestered to death with a detachment of old Irish women, who came from different parts (on hearing of their sons having enlisted), in order to endeavour to get them away from us . . . they hung to their offspring, and dragging them away, sent forth such dismal howls and moans that it was quite distracting to hear them. The Lieutenant, commanding the party, ordered me (being the only Englishman present) to endeavour to keep them back. It was, however, as much as I could do to preserve myself from being torn to pieces by them, and I was glad to escape out of their hands.'[3] The disorder turned to conflict at sea, when 'having nothing else to do' the Catholics laid into the Protestants, and fighting continued along the way, including a drunken rampage at Andover that had

30

to be quelled by the local volunteer corps. It is hardly surprising that soldiers in general had a bad reputation with the civilian population.

Perhaps to prevent similar disorder by keeping his recruits amused, in June 1813 Corporal Henry Wood of the 2nd Foot took six of them on a boat trip on the Severn; the hired boatman rocked the boat to frighten the recruits, causing it to capsize, and five were drowned, including the boatman, who was pulled under by the corporal.

The bounty money, usually more cash than the recruit had ever seen, generally lasted but a short time, either squandered or duped out of him by older soldiers and the recruiters. A song from *Wit and Mirth: or Pills to Purge Melancholy* by Thomas D'Urfray (1653-1723) included lines concerning sergeants:

> 'They will free you from duty and all other trouble,
> Your money being gone, your duty comes double,'

which was confirmed by a soldier who joined the llth Light Dragoons in 1808: 'Non-commissioned officers are in an especial manner to be shunned, whenever they profess to hold you in favour, or seem to relax the bonds of discipline, in order that you may not be distressed by them. These harpies desire only to make a prey of you. They will suck you dry, and then grind you to powder.'[4] Recruits were expected to be generous with their bounties; when a member of the 18th Light Dragoons refused to treat his comrades with his bounty near Chichester in July 1809 he was tossed in a blanket as a punishment and died from a broken neck when they dropped him. Payment of the bounty in small amounts at intervals would have prevented much trouble, but this could not be contemplated; when bounties were not paid on the nail in late 1797 it was said to be the cause of disturbances at Mansfield and Nottingham, though the recruits were said to have been encouraged in their refusal to march by 'some disaffected persons'.[5]

On reaching his regiment the soldier was subject to what little bureaucracy existed, his name added to the muster rolls of his company or troop and battalion or regiment. Soldiers' individual numbers had not been introduced at this time, so to distinguish men of the same name, a number was appended on the regimental roll, for example, 'John Smith 1st', 'John Smith 2nd' and so on. The necessity may be gauged from extreme cases like that of the Strathspey Fencibles, in which the original complement of privates included sixteen John McDonalds and twelve named John McDonell. In the published roll these men are listed with a number in parentheses after their name so that, for example, John McDonald (1), a labourer from Urquhart, could be distinguished from John McDonald (16), a weaver from Aberdeen.[6] A further complication arose from the fact that many were totally illiterate, and many of those just able to sign their own name could probably do no more than that. It is likely that well over half the recruits were unable to read. Such illiteracy led to a complication in the rolls when names were recorded phonetically, perhaps by clerks themselves only semi-literate. This was the case of a man whose forenames were Tubal Cain (from the father of metalworkers in Genesis iv, 22), who was recorded as 'Two Ball Cane', and this may also have been a factor in the recording of unusual names like that of Henry Urine of the 28th. Other details might also be recorded inaccurately; John Swift, who fought at Waterloo with the 51st, told of a fellow Lancastrian unaware of his own date of birth but stated that it was a Pancake Tuesday, so the authorities could calculate it from that!

A considerable number of men enlisted under a false name, perhaps to evade the law or their family; this was the case of Captain Galbraith Joynt of the 43rd, later 103rd, who rose from the ranks. He had enlisted under the name of William Faulkland, and when a sergeant in the 43rd, revealed his real identity and submitted a memorial to the Duke of York that henceforward he should be known by his real name. Perhaps the most famous to enlist under an alias was the poet Coleridge, who enrolled in the 15th Light Dragoons in 1793 as Silas Tomkyn Comberbatch; he was rescued from a miserable existence in the ranks by his brother, who arranged his discharge.

In considering who the soldier really was, account should be taken of the contemporary belief that various nationalities possessed certain national characteristics. English recruits, some believed, were not naturally 'warlike' but exhibited 'a praiseworthy courage, a boldness of character, a coolness of judgment and decision under the most trying circumstances'.[7] The Scot came from a background involving habits 'more frugal and less luxurious; he is brought up from infancy on coarser and less nutritious diet, accustomed from an early period to hardships, fatigue and privation, which neither the English peasant or artisan care to endure; he is thus presumtively better calculated to submit to the toils and wants incident to the profession of soldier.' He also possesed the martial spirit 'cherished and handed down to successive generations,' and a religious education that 'gave to their character that firmness and undaunted courage which may be said to be characteristic of the people.' The Highlander was regarded as unique, not merely because his first (and sometimes only) language was Gaelic, but 'remarkable for courage at the most trying moment, the sound of the national instrument calling forth all his energy and independence under circumstances of despondency or retreat.' Highlanders were also supposedly much better behaved; one officer recalled that with Highlanders he had been able almost to dispense with corporal punishment, but had to reinstate it when men from other regions joined his regiment.

Ireland provided a huge resource of manpower out of proportion to its size; it represented about 27 per cent of the population of the United Kingdom but a considerably higher proportion of the infantry, quite apart from the few regiments that officially bore an Irish title. Henry Curling, best known as the editor of Benjamin Harris's memoirs, described the Irishman as 'a creature, at present, unprepared, unmeet for civilized life [yet] with all his natural wild ferocity, he possesses many of the finest qualities of human nature . . . the poor half-starved fellow will run for miles and miles before your horse's head to guide your path – nay, fight for you, die for you; but let him once suspect you are spying upon his way of life, or looking with a longing eye upon his land, and he brains you from behind a dyke.'[8]

Another experienced officer wrote of the Welsh, generally shorter but sturdier than the others – he stated that the Carmarthenshire Militia was the shortest but most broad-shouldered corps in the army – and, 'Will any man say that a Merthyr miner of five foot two would not outrun in light, outmarch in heavy marching order, or outfight . . . any Manchester weaver or Cockney counter-jumper of six feet three, without chest, loins or sinews?' He claimed that the Welsh were more religious, 'stern and grave' than the others, and while the Irishman might be best able to resist wet and hunger and was better tempered, 'the Welshman is very generally the stouter made and more able to bear up against the pack.' However, 'The Welch hate a *red* coat,' so that 'the Welch peasantry . . . think their children lost if they enter the Line,' but there was no prejudice against blue or green, leading to many Welsh recruits to the green-clad rifle corps; while the lack of religious instruction in the army 'renders a Welch parent averse to his son's enlistment.'[9]

Similarly, there were contemporary views on the merits of members of various civilian occupations. One early assessment stated that the rural outdoor worker was 'of firm constitution, robust frame, active, healthy in his aspect, energetic in character, habituated to the vicissitudes of heat and cold, courageous and determined. Proud of the soil on which he was reared, he is independent in spirit often to rudeness; confident of his powers, he is apt to be overbearing and ungracious.' Conversely, the urban or indoor worker 'is generally deficient in physical strength . . . of stunted growth, often emaciated and unsound in condition – his aspect is neither healthy nor pleasing; he is, however, frequently superior in intelligence to the peasant, more dextrous in the motions of his body, and thus, is an apt scholar for military exercise.'[10]

It is difficult to describe the appearance of the 'average' soldier as accept-able physical standards varied according to the availability of recruits, standards being lowered as the demand grew. Approximate physical appear-ance may be gauged from existing statistics. For the 3rd West York Militia, for example, between the years 1803 and 1813, the average height was just over 5 feet 6 inches, with only 1.85 per cent of men being 6 feet or taller. As the war progressed the number of short men increased: the proportion of those of 5 feet 5 inches and below rose from 8.3 per cent in 1806 to 31.6 per cent in 1811. (Thirty per cent were aged under twenty-five years and only 5.8 per cent over forty.)

For the period just after the Napoleonic Wars, when the demand for men was not so urgent, an analysis of 1,000 men recruited in London revealed that 47.6 per cent were between 5 feet 6 inches and 5 feet 7 inches in height; just over 7 per cent shorter than that, 40 per cent between 5 feet 7 inches and 5 feet 10 inches, and less than 4 per cent taller, with just two men over 6 feet. The average chest measurement was 32.66 inches, that of 'country' recruits being three-quarters of an inch greater than that of urban recruits. (Some men were actually not as tall as they appeared; tricks played by those desperate to be accepted included increasing their height by pasting buff-leather pads onto the soles of their feet, or concealing lumps of wood in their hair to add an inch or so.) More than one-third of these applicants were rejected as unfit (though during the war many of them would have been accepted), the proportion of unfit men increasing with their height. Indeed, some officers believed that small men were more hardy, though the famous memorialist John Kincaid of the 95th thought there was no difference, except that big men were more noticed when they broke down with fatigue. Even in wartime some regiments attempted to maintain an exclusive standard; for example, in 1812 it was reported that the 10th Hussars was preparing to discharge all men below 5 feet 7 inches in height.

Henry Marshall remarked that only about 5 per cent of line soldiers were over forty years of age, for most had become 'worn out' – unfit for service – before that age. He believed that twenty-five or twenty-six was the maximum age at which a man should be enlisted, for those older 'are habitually dissi-pated and profligate characters, broken-down gentlemen, discharged soldiers, deserters, &c.,[11]' whose health might fail after only a short period of service. Although the army might be expected to get more years out of a younger man, in time of need older recruits were taken. One who seems to disprove Wellington's comment on the lack of 'fine military feeling' was Robert Eadie, who had a good occupation in the wine trade as a cork cutter but first enlisted when drunk. Discharged when his regiment was disbanded, he returned to civilian life but must have missed the military and in 1806, aged forty-two, decided to re-enlist and, impressed by their tartans and feather bonnets, enrolled in the 79th Highlanders. He only took his final discharge at age fifty-seven. The value of experienced men may be demonstrated by the career of George Ryston, a veteran of Dettingen, Culloden and Belleisle. At his death in 1808, aged ninety-four, it was recalled that he had twice given up a pension to re-enlist, and had had thirteen wives, of whom six were alive at one time; his stamina and survival were attributed not only to the iron constitution of a veteran but to living on a mixture of gin, rum and water.

With lifetime service meaning exactly that, age was no barrier to active duty providing a soldier remained fit. Thomas Stobo of the 2nd Dragoons was the oldest man in his regiment at Waterloo, where he was wounded, and had the unusual distinction of participating in Britain's first and last campaigns of the French Wars, having been in the Netherlands in 1793-94. His regiment had not been on campaign between these two episodes so Stobo must have been one of the very few Scots Greys at Waterloo who had previously been under fire.

Soldiers no longer fit for field service could be retained for garrison duty: barrack sergeant Durham, who died at Plymouth in 1813, aged eighty-eight, had served seventy years in the army and had fought at Culloden with Barrell's Regiment (the 4th King's Own); Bombardier Richard James of the Royal Artillery served in the Quebec campaign and was still on duty as part of the garrison of Carlisle Castle when he died in March 1812, after sixty-five years' service. Even more remarkable was W. Anderson, also of the Royal Artillery, who died at Woolwich in 1809 aged 102, having served more than eighty years in the regiment.

Virtually every trade or profession was represented within the army, although the majority of recruits appear to have had no particular skill beyond their physical strength, and were described as labourers. In the case of the 23rd Foot at Waterloo, for example, some 51 per cent of the 'other ranks' were unskilled labourers; some 15 per cent were textile workers, metalworkers and shoemakers each represented about six per cent, and tailors five per cent. Depressions in particular trades brought in more skilled men at times, not always manual workers: for example, the 23rd's sergeant major mortally wounded at Waterloo, David Morrissey, was an optician.[12]

The civilian skills of some soldiers were of use to the army, notably shoe-makers, like Benjamin Harris, and tailors. Wellington's headquarters in the Peninsula made good use of Corporal Buchan of the 3rd Foot Guards, who acted as printer for the Adjutant General's department, and trained gunsmiths were invaluable as battalion armourers, like Armourer Sergeant

One of the few 'other ranks' to be the subject of an engraved portrait: Trumpet Major William Weldon of the 13th Light Dragoons, wearing his Waterloo Medal. He served in the Peninsula from spring 1810 and was Lord Hill's orderly trumpeter. (Engraving by J. Godby after I. Renton)

John Taylor who served at Waterloo with the 2/73rd, a professional gunsmith from Birmingham.

Possession of a skill could elevate a craftsman to a level above the ordinary soldiers, occasionally to a remarkable degree. Thomas Bennett was the son of a Kent tenant farmer who trained as a saddler to such a level of proficiency that he was appointed master saddler to the 13th Light Dragoons, which he entered with the rank of sergeant. In addition to regimental duties he must have done private work, for he could afford to pay 160 guineas to have a carriage built to carry his kit when the regiment marched, and when he accompanied the 13th to the Peninsula he took not only his plate but hired an Italian cook, a level of luxury to which few officers could aspire. A different type of skill was discovered when, in the Peninsula, Wellington needed to produce coinage to pay the army's way; the army produced the necessary coiners to do the job, most of whom had probably learned their trade by counterfeiting. (This was rather too late for Private Robert Langton of the 40th, who in Portugal in 1809 was sentenced to 600 lashes for being absent from his regiment and for having in his possession 'instruments for coining', though he was acquitted of actually counterfeiting.)

There were also a small number of 'gentlemen rankers', men of good birth escaping their families, responsibilities or debts. Their relations with the rest varied, as suggested by a story concerning Joseph 'Gentleman' Roach of the 28th's light company on the retreat to Corunna. His incessant chatter, usually concerning his exalted ancestry, led one night to a comrade exclaiming: 'Hould your jaw, and let us lie quiet a bit before the day comes, for we can hardly hould up our heads with the sleep.' 'Gentleman' Roach replied that his antagonists 'personify all the dispositions of a vulgar cabbage plant,' and after further heated exchanges in which Roach's conduct in action was criticized (for taking cover, 'squeezed up behind a tree, like the back of an ould Cramona fiddle'), a soldier respected by all calmed everyone down and the company was able to sleep.[13]

A considerable proportion of the British Army was not of British nationality. From the time of the early French Revolutionary Wars, large numbers of 'foreign corps' were formed to accommodate refugees and mercenaries who wished to continue the fight after their own states had capitulated. Most were disbanded after the Peace of Amiens, but others existed throughout the period so that by 1813, including 'colonial' corps, about one member in eight of the British military establishment was a foreigner. Most notable was the King's German Legion, created after the king's Hanoverian possessions had been overrun by the French in 1803. Motivated by loyalty to their joint sovereign, large numbers of Hanoverians fitted fairly seamlessly into the British Army regiments created for them; subsequently other nationalities were accepted into the German Legion, which came to be regarded as one of the army's elite corps, with a most distinguished reputation. The Brunswick 'Black Legion' was another, which in 1809 marched across Germany after the defeat of Austria, to be evacuated from the North Sea coast by British ships, continuing their fight in British pay as the Brunswick Oels Corps, with rifle companies deployed as specialist sharpshooters in the Peninsula. The record of some 'foreign corps' was mixed: the Brunswickers and a largely French corps, the Chasseurs Britanniques, fought well in the Peninsula but were notably prone to desertion, while a few were a disgrace, like the rabble of largely Greeks and Albanians duped into enlisting by an unscrupulous colonel whose name was carried by his regiment, Froberg's, which was disbanded after they mutinied at Malta in April 1807, in the course of which they shelled Valetta.

Foreigners also served in regiments of the British Army proper, especially in the 60th (Royal American) Regiment, which included battalions armed with rifles and trained as skirmishers, overwhelmingly German in composition; and the regiment originally named as Stuart's Minorca Regiment. Its members were mainly Germans and Swiss who had formed part of the Spanish garrison of Minorca, ex-Austrian prisoners of war given to Spain by France. The regiment served with such distinction that it was taken into the line as the 97th Queen's Germans. Its most distinguished member was Antoine Lutz, born in Alsace and conscripted into the French army, from which he escaped to join the French Armée de Condé; subsequently he served in five national armies in five years, and with the Queen's Germans performed

A regimental band, including the percussion section, illustrating the practice of enlisting very small children as musicians, usually the sons of serving soldiers. (Print by M. Skelt)

the deed that made him famous, capturing a colour of the French 21st Demi-Brigade Légère at Alexandria.

Most regiments contained a few foreigners, some of similarly diverse backgrounds, like Corporal James Aldenrath of the 24th Foot, who died at Norwich in March 1804, aged fifty-two, having served seven sovereigns in the Netherlands, Austria, Spain, France and finally Britain; appropriately, he was given a huge funeral attended by almost the whole of his regiment.

European bandsmen were much in demand as having a rather higher level of competence than British musicians, and were enrolled for their professional skills irrespective of nationality. Even prisoners of war were enlisted; in 1804, for example, Major General Alexander Mackenzie-Frazer was permitted to enlist Germans from the prison hulk HMS *Sultan* to form a band for his 2nd Battalion 78th Foot. Good musicians were even enrolled on campaign, like the French deserters in the Peninsula who taught the 31st's band a tune known as *Bonaparte's March*. The 10th Hussars was among the regiments that employed a considerable number of foreign musicians (and others: in February 1812 Lord Folkestone claimed in the House of Commons that the regiment included no less than 108 foreigners, and 'he reprobated the practice altogether, in the strongest terms'[14]). A number of these served at Waterloo, including the Hungarians Sergeant John Uckrowitch and Private Peter Shaoskie – the latter a sailor who had served in the Queen's Germans – Privates Thomas Haslam and Ernest Lehe, both Dutch, and the Hanoverian Corporal Henry Mayer.

A noted contemporary fashion was to employ black percussionists in a regimental band, often dressed in pseudo-oriental costume, as part of the popularity of so-called 'Turkish music' that included the use of small kettle drums, tambourines, cymbals and the 'jingling johnny' (a set of bells affixed to a decorative staff). A wider use of black musicians included cavalry trumpeters and the drummers of the 29th, the latter a tradition originating in 1759 when after the surrender of Guadeloupe Admiral Boscawen acquired ten black men who he presented as a gift to his brother, then colonel of the 29th; this regimental practice lasted until 1843. Although black trumpeters and musicians gave a regiment an air of the exotic, it is possible that some officers regarded black soldiers as inappropriate for service in the ranks; for example, when some African percussionists from the 78th's band were no longer required in that function, they were made pioneers rather than serving in the ranks, and it is conceivable that this was also a factor in other cases. William Affleck from St. Kitts served twenty-one years as a trumpeter in the 10th Hussars (he received a Military General Service Medal with clasps for Sahagun & Benavente, Vittoria, Orthes and Toulouse, and served at

John Frazer, a tambourine player in the Coldstream Guards, wearing oriental-style uniform characteristic of percussionists in regimental bands. (Mezzotint by Mrs Ross)

Waterloo), but one reason for his discharge was the loss of his front teeth, which made it impossible to play his trumpet, and perhaps he was thought unsuitable because of his colour to serve in the ranks. A similar case may have involved another black musician in the same regiment, Thomas Collins, discharged when the regiment was reduced in size and deemed 'ineligible' to continue.

Such factors apart, there seems to be little evidence of discrimination against black soldiers because of their ethnic origin, although it is not impossible that this was a factor in the murder of one of the 29th's black drummers in 1807, attacked by a party of soldiers in a 'house of bad fame' in Aberdeen.[15] It was certainly possible for a black soldier to prosper, like the Jamaican-born George Rose, described as being of 'copper colour' with black hair and eyes and of exemplary conduct: he was shot in the arm as a private in the 73rd and subsequently became a sergeant in the 42nd, serving for almost twenty-eight years.[16]

A final type of hired professional were the pipers maintained in most Highland (and a few Lowland) regiments. They were not officially permitted on the strength until 1856, so were usually hired by the officers, and their superior nature is exemplified by the story of one who objected to a company drummer taking precedence, saying to his captain, 'Oh, sir, shall a little rascal that beats a sheepskin take the right hand of me that am a *musician*?'[17]

4

'My Humble Knapsack': The Soldier's Kit

My humble knapsack all my wealth,
A poor but honest sodger

The Soldier's Return, Robert Burns

As soon as the recruit joined his regiment he received his kit and uniform, usually his sole possessions for his entire service. Only part of his equipment was provided at government expense: in 1800, for example, he received annually a coat, a waistcoat, a pair of breeches, two pairs of shoes (which if they cost more than 5s 6d per pair, the soldier had to pay the difference); and every two years a cap or shako, with a new crown, cockade and plume every year. Everything else – known as the soldier's 'necessaries' – had to be paid by deductions from his pay: annually, two pairs of black cloth gaiters, extra pairs of shoes and breeches, three shirts, three pairs of socks, a forage cap, worsted mittens, a stock, hair ribbon and queue leather, spare shoe soles (and cost of repairs), pipeclay, blacking, two combs and three shoe brushes; a clothes brush every two years and a knapsack every six years. This represented an annual deduction of £3 16s 1½d, or more than two months' pay for a private. The financial burden was increased by additional items: the soldier even had to pay for the straps to carry his greatcoat, if such an item were issued, and 17s 4d was deducted annually for washing. Some items were restricted to certain regiments: in Highland corps the soldier was issued with four pairs of hose annually and 6 yards of plaid every two years in lieu of the breeches, but his 'necessaries' included a kilt in place of the extra breeches, plus a 6s deduction for feathers for his bonnet and additional hose. An even greater burden was reported in the November 1804 Inspection Return of the 13th Light Dragoons, which reported that the men were very much in debt after having to purchase overalls at the extraordinary sum of 28s per pair.

The coat, worn initially by all save light cavalry, was based on a civilian style, with long skirts, a standing collar and lapels cut open at the front to expose the waistcoat. The lapels were removed in 1796 and the coat took on an entirely new appearance, in a vaguely Austrian style considerably more practical for campaigning, single-breasted and with short tails. For all but artillery and light cavalry the coat was of the red colour – actually a dusky brick-red for the rank and file – that had characterized British soldiers from the second half of the seventeenth century and had given rise to the common nicknames of 'redcoat' and 'lobster'. The use of red was so associated with the common soldier that some thought it vaguely common, so that when units of middle-class or gentlemen volunteers were formed during the French Revolutionary Wars, many chose 'genteel' blue uniforms instead. The coat also identified the regiment: collar, cuffs and lapels were in the 'facing colour', the principal regimental distinction, and the collar and buttonholes were bound in white tape or lace, which had a woven coloured design specific to each regiment. The flank companies were distinguished by worsted-tufted 'wings' carried on the shoulders of the jacket.

Legwear in the infantry consisted of white fabric breeches (buff-coloured for regiments with buff facings), worn with knee-length black gaiters held in place by garters, which a contemporary medical opinion held to be hazardous: in October 1803 Thomas Milner of the Wakefield Volunteers was adjudged to have died 'of a compression of the brain' caused by his garters being too tight, 'whereby the circulation of the blood was mortally obstructed.'[1] Other styles included one-piece 'gaiter-trousers' worn in hot climates, and short gaiters favoured by light infantry. Long trousers worn over or instead of the breeches were far more practical on campaign but were unregulated until 1812, when the different regimental styles were replaced by universal grey trousers, worn over short gaiters.

Excluding the light cavalry and horse artillery, initially the army's head-dress was a cocked hat based on the civilian style, with small caps for light infantry and fur caps for grenadiers and fusiliers, the latter generally restricted to parade dress. In 1800 the shako was introduced, a cylindrical, peaked construction with a large brass plate, initially largely leather but felt from 1806. It was not a very practical head covering but presumably was intended to help frighten the enemy by increasing the soldier's height, and in changing patterns remained in use until 1878. Its unsuitability was demonstrated by George Bell, a Peninsular veteran, when as an experiment while commanding the 1st Royals in the Crimean War he fried a slice of bacon on the flat top of his shako to demonstrate how little protection it provided from the sun.

Given the greater chance of hand-to-hand combat, the cavalry needed a more protective head covering, and light cavalry wore the handsome, fur-crested 'Tarleton' helmet, though it was prone to warp in the sun and in

1812 was replaced by a shako. The heavy cavalry bicorn hat was replaced at the same time by a leather helmet with a metal crest supporting a horsehair mane, which was unpopular partly from its imitation of a French style. Most impractical of all was the fur cap favoured by hussars, which Sir Robert Ker Porter described as 'muff-like appendages . . . by being constructed partly of pasteboard, [it] soaks up a great quantity of wet . . . and so becomes unbearably heavy and disagreeable, while it affords no protection to the wearer. At all times they can be cut down to his skull with the greatest ease.'[2] Similar criticism was made of the braided hussar jacket and pelisse: 'That the ingenuity of our army milliners . . . should be exercised for the purpose of rendering the appearance of our brave fellows ridiculous instead of promoting health and comfort and security, is much to be lamented . . . the fribbling ornaments with which they are attired would better become an equestrian performer on one of our inferior stages, than a hardy veteran, when equipped for the field.'[3]

A case regarding 'health and comfort' was also argued at the time concerning the traditional dress of Highland regiments, notably the kilt (commonly the 'philabeg' or 'little kilt', which generally replaced the more ancient and much more voluminous 'breacan-an-fheilidh' or 'belted plaid'). As an expression of Highland identity, following the defeat of the Jacobite Rebellion in 1746, the kilt, plaid and trews were prohibited (officially until 1782 but the restriction seems not to have been enforced long before then), but they were permitted for those serving in Highland corps. The ability to wear the kilt may have had some effect in encouraging Highlanders to enlist, but the government decided subsequently that the kilt was an obstacle to the recruitment of non-Highlanders when it was obvious that there were insufficient genuine Highlanders to fill the Highland regiments. Opinions on the kilt varied; Sir John Sinclair of Ulbster, Bt., a prominent figure in a number of fields and commander of the Rothsay and Caithness Fencibles, declared that 'the usual Highland dress is liable to some objections. I thought it necessary, therefore, in my two battalions of Fencibles, instead of the Philabeg and the belted Plaid, to adopt the *Trews*, which . . . seemed to be particularly convenient for a soldier.'[4] (He also believed trews to be the traditional Highland dress, with bare knees being a Roman fashion!)

In 1804 the Adjutant General proposed the replacement of the kilt by trews, 'better calculated to preserve the health and promote the comfort of men on service.' Alan Cameron, Colonel of the 79th, was scathing in his reply: that the kilt permitted 'free congenial circulation of that pure wholesome air (as an exhilarating native bracer) which has so peculiarly benefited the Highlander,' and had the 'exclusive advantage, when halted, of drenching his kilt in the *next brook*, as well as washing his limbs, and drying *both*, as it were, by constant fanning'; whereas the 'buffoon tartan pantaloon' was difficult to pull on or off when wet and the cause of rheumatism and fevers. Furthermore, stated Cameron, the sight of the kilt struck terror into the enemy and that 'if anything was wanted to aid the rack-renting Highland landlord in destroying that source which has hitherto proved so fruitful in keeping up Highland corps, it will be that of abolishing their native garb.'[5]

The abolition of the kilt was only deferred, however, for in April 1809 it was ordered that most existing Highland regiments should no longer wear Highland dress, which by being 'objectionable to the natives of South Britain' discouraged recruiting, leaving only the 42nd, 78th, 79th, 92nd and 93rd as kilted corps. James Anton of the 42nd recalled another drawback: during the attempt to repel d'Erlon's great attack at Waterloo, the Highlanders found it difficult to pass through the hedges lining the Ohain road at the front of Wellington's position: 'our bare thighs had no protection from the piercing thorns' and had they advanced immediately, without waiting to cut gaps in the hedgerow, it would have been 'self-inflicted torture.'[6] Ironically, even kilted corps used trousers at times, often in hot climates, and during the Peninsular War trousers had to be adopted as kilts wore out. It is indicative of the nature of some of the Highland recruits that they had never worn trousers; when they were first issued it was thought a great joke to persuade the young men to put them on back-to-front for their first inspection!

A notable item of kit never encountered by the recruit in civilian life was the stock, a high, thick leather collar worn inside the jacket. Unyielding and uncomfortable, it was intended to make the soldier keep his head upright, and to afford a measure of protection to the throat; one soldier described it as 'like a top-boot scrubbing the very sowl [sic] out of a fellow's chin if he dared look round,'[7] while John Shipp remarked that it felt as stiff as if he had swallowed a ramrod. On campaign soldiers might be permitted to remove their stocks for greater comfort in action, and cloth stocks were ordered in 1795 for troops in the West Indies, as more suitable for the climate, but some soldiers seem not to have objected to them. Writing of the war in Burma, subsequent to the Napoleonic campaigns, Viscount Wolseley recalled how permission to remove stocks was declined by the more experienced soldiers, who believed that the stock protected the back of the neck and kept them cool.

Another facet of soldiering alien to the recruit was the dressing of his hair. The soldier's hair was worn long and pulled back into a pigtail or 'queue', or folded back upon itself to form a 'club', a process involving immense trouble and discomfort. Harry Ross-Lewin described the process as it existed in 1793:

'each had a huge false tail attached by means of a string that passed round the upper part of his head, and over it the hair was combed and well thickened with powder or flour; a plastering of pomatum or grease was then laid on; a square bag of sand was next placed at the extremity of the tail, rolled up with the assistance of a small oblong iron until it touched the head, and tied with a leathern thong and rosette so as to confine it in a proper position.' This process took an hour, and one grenadier remarked to him that 'I can't turn my head without moving my body along with it, an' I'm afraid to eat after my hair is dressed, for fear of it getting creased.'[8]

John Gaspard Le Marchant recalled how, serving in the Netherlands in 1794-95, 'he went in to look at his troop of heavy cavalry, the night previous to the general action. They were in a Flemish barn, lying on the hay; but to preserve the form of their clubs for the next day, they were all prone on their faces, trying to sleep in that pleasant posture. The hair at the side of the head was plastered into two flat divisions, that looked something like the lee-boards of a Dutch dogger; and the whole was dusted over, or rather basted with flour.'[9] In the words of an Irish soldier, 'every head and tail looked like a snow-ball with a handle to it,'[10] and soldiers trying to sleep in such conditions are known to have encountered rats trying to eat the flour off their heads.

The use of hair powder in civilian life must have declined with the imposition of a powder tax (though soldiers below the rank of captain, like clergymen not possessed of an income of £100 per annum, were exempt), and the military use of hair powder was suspended in July 1795. Queues continued in use until abolished by a General Order of 20 July 1808, so that henceforth commanding officers had to 'take care that the men's hair is cut close in their necks in the neatest and most uniform manner, and that their heads are kept perfectly clean by combing, brushing, and frequently washing them.' The abolition of the queue and the labour it involved was greeted with joy; a report concerning a regiment at Southampton described how when 'receiving the order for cropping off their pig-tails previous to embarkation: so eager were the men to obey the order, that they instantly dispersed, and ran into the nearest houses to procure scissars [sic], knives and even saws to get rid of an incumbrance, which cost them much daily trouble to dress, besides a very grievous expence for ribbons, &c.'[11] The 28th received the order aboard ship at Spithead, collected all the severed queues and ceremonially threw them overboard with three cheers. There was, however, bizarre trouble within the 23rd in Canada, as the soldiers' wives had competed with each over over who could best dress their husbands' hair, and were loath to see the queues abolished. The commanding officer had

A sense of regimental identity was encouraged by the decoration of soldiers' accoutrements. The amount of polishing evident on this belt plate of the 27th (Enniskillen) Regiment shows that such items remained in use for many years. The representation of the castle of Enniskillen exemplified the significance of regimental tradition in 1751, although it was used before then and is still used today by the Royal Irish Regiment.

each company assembled and the queues cut off en masse, to the curses and mutterings of the wives.[12]

Although mounted troops wore boots of various height, the most common footwear was the shoe worn by dismounted troops. It was a sturdy construction of uniform shape with no rights or lefts, and it was noted that the men should swap the shoes between feet every day, to prevent them becoming crooked.

The infantryman carried all his possessions on his back. Over each shoulder was a leather belt, crossing on his chest and hooked together there by his belt plate (styled at the time a 'breast-plate'), an oval or rectangular metal badge on which regimental devices were inscribed, thus contributing to his identity and to regimental esprit de corps. Its central position on the chest could save

The soldier's knapsack, his principal possession: an early example made of painted canvas, bearing a typically elaborate regimental device, in this case that of the 10th North British (Edinburgh) Militia.

lives; this was the case with Joseph Brown of the 45th, who was struck on the plate at Vittoria by a volley that killed the man next to him. One of the belts supported his bayonet, the other a leather pouch or cartridge box that contained his ammunition. The pouch contained a wooden block with holes drilled in, each accomodating a single cartridge, and more were held in a tin container. Usually each man carried sixty rounds, but before battle he was expected to stow more about his person, notably in his pockets, a practice seemingly sanctioned officially despite the danger of carrying so haphazardly cartridges filled with gunpowder, which could explode if touched by a stray spark. (When the Cheshire Militia was turned out by a nocturnal alarm in 1778, one grenadier leaped from his bed wearing not a stitch, and fell in wearing just his belts; he was reprimanded not for indecent exposure but because he had no pocket in which to put spare cartridges.) At Toulouse a party of 45th Foot was alarmed by a nearby explosion, which they took to be a shell; but it was one of their number who had stowed cartridges in his shako, which, ignited by the flash of his musket, had blown his cap to pieces and singed off his hair but had otherwise left him unharmed.

The soldier's personal goods were carried in his knapsack. Made of canvas,

The reverse of the knapsack, showing the shoulder straps with the constricting, buckled strap carried horizontally across the chest.

painted to make it waterproof (and sometimes bearing elaborately-painted devices until about 1812, when plain black knapsacks with just the regimental number began to be introduced), it was carried on the back by leather straps around the shoulders, connected by a strap across the chest that further restricted the soldier's breathing and movement. The knapsack contained spare clothing and any personal impedimenta, such as prizes picked up on campaign or even mementos from home: one soldier is recorded as carrying a dessicated ham, a parting gift from his mother, which for sentimental reasons he had never been able to bring himself to eat. Strapped to the knapsack was a blanket, and often a greatcoat when these were issued universally, though both together was 'more than [a man] can carry. The Duke of Wellington tried it in the year his army entered France, but it distressed the troops greatly.'[13] Previously, companies had maintained a number of communal greatcoats or 'watch-coats' to be used by sentries in bad weather. Slung over the soldier's shoulder was a canvas haversack for his rations and a barrel-shaped wooden canteen for water, while a mess tin was sometimes strapped to the knapsack.

While the cavalryman could carry part of his kit on his horse, the infantryman's burden was enormous. John Cooper of the 7th itemised what he carried during the Peninsular War, with weight in pounds in parentheses: pouch and sixty rounds (6), full canteen (4), mess tin (1), knapsack (3), blanket (4), greatcoat (4), dress coat (3), white undress jacket (½), two shirts and three ruffles (2½), two pairs shoes (3), trousers (2), gaiters (¼), two pairs stockings (1), two tent pegs (½), pipe clay (1), three days' bread (3), two days' beef (2), musket and bayonet (14); plus, as a sergeant, pen, ink and paper (¼), with the orderly sergeant of each company also carrying the orderly book. Small wonder that he remarked that 'the government should have sent us new backbones'[14] to bear the weight. This load was not exceptional: Sergeant Major Murray of the 3rd Foot Guards stated that the kit carried by a private of his regiment in the Peninsula in 1812 weighed in excess of 75lbs, inclusive of the shared duty of carrying each section's bill hook and camp kettle, while Edward Costello of the 95th, supposedly the lightest and most mobile corps in the army, calculated that on the famous forced march to Talavera each man carried between 70 and 80lbs. The burden of a battalion's pioneer squad was even greater: usually comprising a corporal and ten privates, they carried in addition a leather apron and billhook each, and between them eight spades, five axes, three saws, three picks and three mattocks. At least their commander was acutely aware of the soldier's plight: as a young officer Arthur Wellesley had a soldier weighed so as to appreciate the burden of the rank and file.

The infantryman's most constant companion was his musket, commonly styled a 'firelock' and known by the affectionate term 'Brown Bess'. This is said to derive from the colour of the stock or the rustproofing of the barrel, with 'Bess' either an alliterative term of endearment or from the German *Buchse* (gun). (The term 'to hug Brown Bess', meaning to serve as a private soldier, was recorded by Francis Grose in 1785.) The nickname was used irrespective of the actual pattern of musket, of which a number existed; at the beginning of the war the 'Short Land Service' pattern with 42-inch barrel was the standard weapon, but after large quantities were purchased in the national emergency from the East India Company, the 'India Pattern' became the standard infantry weapon, with 39-inch barrel.

The musket was a single-shot, smoothbored flintlock firing a lead ball weighing 14 to the pound. Though it could inflict a dreadful injury it was inefficient in the extreme by modern standards, with an unreliable system of ignition. Conflicting data was provided by contemporary trials, but the overall performance is clear. Tests in 1841 established the range of the musket at between 100 and 700 yards (91 and 640 metres), though at every elevation there could be a difference of between 100 and 300 yards (91 and 274 metres).

The only technology employed by the ordinary soldier: the lock of an 'India Pattern' Brown Bess musket, here with the pan closed and the hammer drawn back onto 'half-cock'.

Generally it was held that musketry was most effective when delivered at 200 yards or much less, and while it was unlikely in the extreme that a man would be hit by a shot aimed at him at 200 yards, usually the only accuracy needed was the ability to hit any point on the massed ranks of men utilised in contemporary tactics. Opinions varied on its effectiveness in combat (as different from controlled tests) but a fair comment was made by Richard Henegan, head of the Field Train in the Peninsula (and thus responsible for munitions), who calculated from the ammunition expended that at Vittoria one enemy casualty was inflicted for every 459 shots, but this takes no account of casualties inflicted by artillery fire; and that this was the same for every Peninsular action except Barrosa.

In the flintlock mechanism, on the side of the musket stock, above the trigger, was the lock, a metal plate attached to a small dish or 'priming pan', alongside the 'touch hole' that communicated to the interior of the barrel, in which the propellant charge and projectile had been placed. A small amount of gunpowder was placed in the pan, which was then closed by a hinged lid attached to an upright metal plate ('steel' or 'frizzen'); the spark of ignition was provided by a lump of flint held in the spring-loaded jaws of a 'cock' or 'hammer' attached to the lockplate. Having been drawn back, the cock was released by pressure on the trigger, the flint crashed into the frizzen and forced it back, striking sparks that ignited the power in the pan, creating a flame that passed through the touch hole in the barrel and set off the propellant charge inside. The projectile and charge were supplied in the form of a cartridge, a waxed paper tube containing both ball and gunpowder; loose powder and balls were generally only used by troops armed with rifles, and then only occasionally.

To load the musket, the soldier held it horizontally and drew back the cock one notch, allowing the pan to be closed, but at this stage pressure on the trigger would have no effect unless the mechanism were faulty and 'went off at half-cock.' The soldier then extracted a cartridge from his pouch, and bit open the top; separating the ball (which he might hold in his mouth), he poured a small amount of powder into the pan and closed it by moving the frizzen into an upright position. He then grounded the musket butt and with the barrel vertical inserted powder, ball and cartridge paper, ramming them down with the ramrod he had removed from its position on the underside of the barrel. He then returned the ramrod, raised the musket to his shoulder and pressed the trigger; as the 'flash in the pan' communicated a spark to the charge in the barrel it went off with a loud report, a cloud of smoke and a fero- cious recoil. The firing of the musket impacted upon the soldier's body and senses: the biting of the cartridge caused a severe thirst as gunpowder entered the mouth and faces became 'as black as if we had come out of a coal pit', and the recoil caused severe bruising: 'the recoil against my shoulder and breast had blackened them, and rendered them rather painful, and the middle finger of my right hand was completely blackened and swoln [sic] from the same cause.'[15] The smoke not only stung the eyes but could lie so thickly around the troops as to block out any sight of the enemy beyond their answering gun- flashes, so that the 'fog of war' prevented any knowledge of what was occuring beyond the soldier's most immediate vicinity.

Misfires were a perpetual hazard, whether from degraded flints, blocked touch holes or soldiers' negligence. To clean the pan and unblock the touch hole each man carried a wire brush and needle-like 'picker', sometimes suspended from the shoulder belt, but if the barrel became completely clogged with burnt powder the only way of clearing it in action might be to urinate into it. One test under ideal conditions produced a mis-fire rate of one in every 6½ shots.

The musket could be dangerous to the firer and his comrades around him. Over-priming – putting too much powder in the pan – could project a shower of burning powder like that which hit William Lawrence of the 40th in the face at Waterloo, when the man next to him over-primed, which 'made me dance for a time without a fiddle.'[16] In the confusion of battle a man might ignore a mis-fire and continue to load and snap his musket until it blew up, and this could occur in the relatively stress-free environment of training, as occurred in 1803, 'while the Bromley Volunteers were this day going through the platoon firing, one of the muskets burst, and shattered to pieces the head of one of the corps, since dead, and knocked down two other persons. The piece had, from the inattention of its owner, six cartridges in it at the time it was discharged.'[17] The same thing occurred in the following year with a member of the Tower Hamlets Militia, who had loaded five times; he was killed and seven others wounded. Some accidents were truly bizarre, like that

The 95th Rifles, whose distinctive dark green uniform with black facings and equipment was perfectly attuned to their role as skirmishers. (Print by Genty)

which befell Lieutenant Joseph Strachan of the 73rd, who had hurried to join his regiment in 1815 in fear of missing the action. Only hours after his arrival, during the retreat from Quatre Bras, Private Jeremiah Bates (a nail maker from Worcester with a penchant for pilfering) must have kept his loaded musket on full-cock, for a stalk of corn became entangled in the trigger and it went off, dropping poor Strachan dead on the spot.

Unless he belonged to the light infantry, once the infantryman attained the rank of sergeant he exchanged his musket for a straight-bladed sword and a spontoon or half-pike, a relic of the seventeenth century that also served as a mark of rank. Some 7 feet in length, it had a wooden shaft, a spear point and a metal crossbar below the blade to prevent it becoming wedged by penetrating too far in an enemy's body. Its use was criticized for depriving some of the steadiest men of a firearm, and Stephen Morley of the 5th Foot may have expressed a common view when recalling how at Salamanca he was called to carry the battalion colours, which 'served as a good pretext for throwing away my pike: a useless piece of military furniture.'[18] Nevertheless, the spontoon could be an effective weapon: at Busaco Sergeant Pat Brazil saved the life of his captain by killing a French officer with his pike, and at Waterloo Sergeant Christopher Switzer of the 32nd ran his spontoon through a French officer who had tried to seize the regiment's colour.

Single combat: Corporal Logan of the 13th Light Dragoons engaged and killed Colonel Vital Chamorin of the French 26th Dragoons at Campo Mayor on 25 March 1811.
(Print by M. Dubourg after Denis Dighton)

Conversely, John Cooper recalled how in Spain in 1809 a sergeant of the Foot Guards was chasing a pig at full speed, when 'the point of his pike ran into the earth and stuck fast, causing the butt-end to pass through his body. 'Twas reported that he recovered, was discharged, and afterwards kept a public-house in London.'[19]

The rifle was a very superior form of firearm, with which a trained man could achieve remarkable feats of marksmanship. Although the system of ignition and projectile were like those of the ordinary musket, the rifling of the barrel imparted a spin onto the ball, making it much more accurate. The Baker rifle (named after the gunmaker Ezekiel Baker) was the standard weapon used by the regular army, though it was restricted largely to the three battalions of the 95th Rifle Corps, the rifle-armed elements of the 60th Royal Americans and the light battalions of the King's German Legion. Its proper-ties were most suited to skirmishing, when riflemen could take aim at a particular target (notably the enemy's officers and NCOs), and to maximise the abilities of trained marksmen, in the Peninsula the riflemen of the 60th were deployed in individual companies at brigade level to supplement the skirmishing facility of the light companies of the other regiments.

Proficiency with firearms was not a necessity for the average cavalryman, whose principal weapon was his sabre. It was a brutal weapon, re-designed in 1796 after the previous pattern, that of 1788, had proven somewhat ineffec-tive on service. Some of the 1788 sabres were so heavy that the blade twisted in the hand, striking the enemy almost harmlessly with the flat of the blade, and so unwieldy that some riders injured their horses, or even their own feet, by the uncontrolled swinging of the sword. The new heavy cavalry sabre of 1796 was a heavy, straight-bladed weapon with a 'hatchet' point, modified prior to the 1815 campaign by being ground to a spear point in an attempt to combat the armoured French cuirassiers, while the 1796 light cavalry sabre had a broad, curved blade. Both were intended primarily for the cut or slash, rather than the thrust favoured by French heavy cavalry, and neither had a particularly efficient guard to protect the hand.

Despite the improvements, the sabre was not regarded as especially effec-tive by some of those who used it; one described the heavy cavalry sabre as 'a lumbering, clumsy, ill-contrived machine. It is too heavy, too short, too broad, too much like the sort of weapon with which we have seen Grimaldi cut off the heads of a line of urchins on the stage,' while the light dragoon sabre was best suited 'in making billets for the fire.'[20] Nevertheless, the sabre could inflict a horrific injury, and if the cut favoured by the British was potentially less fatal than the French thrust, what mattered was to incapacitate the enemy, so a non-fatal injury was as good as a lethal blow; and, it was stated, the dreadful appearance of a slash was more likely to undermine the enemy's morale than a more unobtrusive injury caused by a thrust.

Cavalrymen were also armed with a pistol, and most with a carbine, intended for skirmishing, but generally they had little effect; and with the exception of the Uhlans Britanniques, an ephemeral emigrant corps in the French Revolutionary Wars, lances were not carried by British cavalry until 1816.

5

'At the Sound of the Fife':
Aspects of Everyday Life

At the sound of the fife, and the roll of the drum,
Come away, my lads, come, come away my lads come

British Bounty, or *Beauty's Donation*, Charles Dibdin

Dibdin's song, celebrating a patriotic subscription to provide flannel for warm clothing for the army, represented one aspect of the soldier's life; but those with experience of campaigning might have been more attuned to the reference to the fife in a song in Charles Lever's *Charles O'Malley*:

'To the tune of a fife
They dispose of your life,
You surrender your soul to some illigant [sic] lilt,
Now I like Garryowen,
When I hear it at home,
But it's not half so sweet when you're going to be kilt.'

Before experiencing the hazards of campaigning, however, the recruit had to become used to other aspects of the military life. A great difference from his civilian life was in his living arrangements. Initially, barracks were relatively few, troops being housed in tents in summer and billeted upon innkeepers in winter, but the great enlargement of the army from the time of the French Revolutionary Wars made this impractical. Some were suspicious of the number of barracks being constructed from this time, regarding them as a potential threat to liberty, as articulated by the radical MP Sir Francis Burdett, who in May 1812 declared that the creation of barracks was so that the government 'might use the troops paid by the people to subdue the people.'[1] A more practical objection to the establishment of barracks near civilian residences was the annoyance that troops could cause when off duty. An extreme case concerned the 83rd Foot when stationed at Chelmsford Barracks in 1803, when an official investigation was established into 'disgraceful instances of Indiscipline'. The enquiry found that not only had the officers made no attempt to check the 'enormities' and 'licentiousness'[2] of their men, but had tried to prevent the discovery of offenders. Three officers were dismissed and put on half pay, including the lieutenant colonel, John Byrne Skerrett, who survived the disgrace to hold commands in the Peninsula (without distinction) and who was killed as a major general at Bergen op Zoom in 1814.

In truth, a greater objection was the state of the barracks themselves, which must have shocked recruits used to anything above the most basic standards in civilian life. Most were cramped and squalid, with beds that often had to be shared, and sanitation in the form of open tubs in the dormitories. One experienced officer (Lieutenant Colonel Wilkie) wrote of 'miseries and indecencies' in barracks permeated with an 'indescribable odour arising from vitiated air': 'The barrack-rooms, insufficiently ventilated, are never vacant long enough to get rid of the foul air, and they remain constantly tainted with this heavy smell . . . . This serves as a sort of matrix to unhealthy miasma, and where infectious diseases find a secure asylum . . . . One of the infantry barracks at Canterbury had been occupied by a regiment returned from Egypt; it became tainted by opthalmia, and all the regiments that succeeded were equally infected.' Cavalry barracks, he averred, were even worse, and when the cavalryman escaped their stale air it was to work in hot stables, 'where he breathes at second-hand the air already inhaled by the horses, and the effluvia arising from their excretions.'[3] (It was believed that maladies could linger within a living space; for example, one Royal Navy frigate became known as an unhealthy ship after conveying French prisoners of war, who had so impregnated it with their 'foreign nastinesses and abominations' that even repeated fumigations 'could not eradicate the unhealthy taint.'[4])

Some attempts were made to clean barracks, with regular sweeping and even taking the beds outside to air in fine weather, and some of the worst ills could be averted easily: in Sicily in 1807 one officer improved the condition of barracks markedly by the simple expedient of knocking loopholes in the walls, which could be closed by wooden plugs in cold weather, permitting a circulation of fresh air. There remained, however, a complete lack of privacy; if sharing a bed with a comrade was not bad enough, married soldiers had no separate quarters, and all they might expect was to have their bed space separated from the rest by a blanket hung over a cord; small wonder that one officer described barracks as 'wretched rooms, wherein were huddled together a crowd of soldiers, and a number of hideous female savages, called soldiers' wives, with their ragged and abominable brats.'[5]

A soldier's wife could escape these horrors by lodging privately outside the barracks, but that demanded money, and soldiers' pay was meagre. It varied according to rank and corps and was slightly enhanced during the period. In 1797 the pay of an infantry private was increased by 2d, bringing it to 1s per diem, in the cavalry 1s 3d (but 1s 11¼d in the Life Guards), with more for higher ranks: in the infantry, for example, a corporal received 1s 2¼d and a sergeant 1s 6¾d. An additional 1d per diem was granted in 1800 to compensate for the discontinuance of the official allowance of free beer, and another addition was made in 1806 according to length of service, 1d per diem after

Light Dragoons on the march halt at an inn. (Print by J. Hill after J.A. Atkinson, 1806)

seven years in the infantry, ten in the cavalry, and 2d per diem after fourteen and seventeen years respectively. At the same time the pay of sergeants was increased to 1s 10d, that of corporals to 1s 4d, and in 1813 the new rank of colour sergeant was accompanied by an extra 6d per diem, so that holders of that rank received 2s 4d per diem.

These sums, however, were not all disposable income; from it, there were deductions for 'necessaries' and laundry, so that very little was left if the soldier wanted to supplement his rations. In barracks the soldier's bed, coal, candles, cooking utensils and five pints of small beer per diem were provided. The official daily food ration consisted of 1½lbs of bread, 1lb of beef or ½lb of pork, ¼ pint of pease, an ounce of butter or cheese and an ounce of rice, but variations were permitted according to circumstances and availability. Thus, a complete daily ration might be 1½ lbs of flour or bread and 1½lbs of beef or 10oz of pork; or 3lbs of beef; or 2lbs of cheese, and on campaign it could also include local foodstuffs.

Troops on the march, or in garrison where no barracks existed, were billeted upon inns and private houses. At inns they might encounter a service less than that accorded to civilian travellers and might be greeted, as in one recorded case, with the news that the innkeeper and his wife were abed and that the cook could not be roused as 'she sleeps like a porpus.'[6] On the march the soldier received 6d per diem, which with 4d out of his subsistence went to the innkeeper for three meals; in quarters there was an allowance of 2d to the innkeeper for bed, five pints of small beer or cider, salt, vinegar, fire and cooking utensils. With the consent of his commanding officer, a man could receive 2d per diem if he wanted to make his own lodging arrangements. Billeting on private individuals was probably unpopular with the house-holders, as suggested by an incident in 1813 in which Private Andrew Shaw of the 71st forged ninety billeting orders and extorted 1s 6d from each house-holder involved to excuse them from having to take in a soldier; he was sentenced to six months' imprisonment.

James Anton of the 42nd remembered one reception after an exhausting march on wet feet, when a kindly landlady provided whisky to rub into his swollen ankles; conversely, when he remarked to another that his meal had been presented on a dirty plate he was told 'it taks a deal o'dirt to poison sogers.'[7] Another hazard was exemplified in 1804 when the Black Boy inn at Chelmsford burned down when full of troops, quartered there for the night; twelve men of the German Legion were found in the ashes next morning, and one who had been rescued died later that day. It was remarked that Hanoverians smoked continually, but the cause of the conflagration was unknown.

The Girl I Left Behind Me: *as a drummer beats the 'assembly', in* The Billeted Soldier's Departure, *an infantryman takes leave of a sweetheart acquired during a period of being billeted in the community.* (Print after George Morland)

Unless their meals were prepared by innkeepers, soldiers did their own cooking. 'Messing' was the approved practice, in which several men pooled their rations and cooked them together, ensuring a fair distribution and that no man received only the bone that was included in the daily meat ration. Beef and mutton were regarded as most nutritious, while fish and pork were thought to induce fluxes. Boiling with oatmeal and potatoes was thought more healthy and less thirst-inducing than roasting or baking, and it also provided broth. Vegetables – which might be purchased privately out of the bread allowance – were cooked separately. Soldiers usually took turns in cooking, for 'a soldier capable of doing his duty, would never agree to [being a cook] but in turn,'[8] although more formal cooking arrangements may have been adopted regimentally. When the Sussex Militia was in camp in 1796, for example, some men were trained as cooks and received a shilling for eight days' work, less fines for justified complaints about their handiwork. (This regiment used boilers devised by the great inventor – and Minister of War for Bavaria – Benjamin Rumford.) Soldiers' meals were usually superintended, to prevent the men from starving themselves to buy drink or gamble, or (especially in Highland regiments) to send food money home to their families.

Efforts to ensure the soldier was adequately fed were part of a wider concern about his health, for losses from sickness greatly outweighed casualties suffered in battle; yet statistics concerning overall losses from illness are grossly distorted by those concerning regions that were notoriously unhealthy, notably the West Indies. Between 1796 and 1805, for example, 24,916 troops died of sickness in the Leeward and Windward Islands, and this figure does not include all those who had to be invalided with their health broken. Between 1796 and 1828 an average of 13.4 per cent of the garrison died each year (in 1796, 6,585 men, 41.3 per cent), while in Jamaica and Honduras the rate was even worse, with an average mortality of 15.5 per cent between 1810 and 1828; it was, for example, ten times greater than the mortality among troops stationed in Ireland.[9] Battalions sent to the West Indies could be destroyed more comprehensively than in any battle, while West Africa was so deadly a posting that it was garrisoned largely by penal corps, of men sent there as a punishment.

Some overseas service was notorious for a particular malady, like the opthalmia (inflammation of the eyes) prevalent in Egypt. A curious fever afflicted the 13th Foot in Gibraltar in 1805, which led to the hair falling out; it was treated by a daily application of rum and oil rubbed into the scalp, under strict supervision, presumably to prevent the sufferers from drinking it instead. Outside the West Indies, the greatest scourge was the 'Walcheren fever' that decimated the expedition to that part of the Netherlands in 1809, a malarial infection against which there was little effective remedy. Benjamin Harris recalled how 'I beheld whole parties of riflemen in the street shaking with a sort of ague, to such a degree that they could hardly walk; strong and fine young men . . . seemed suddenly reduced in strength to infants, unable to stand upright – so great a shaking had seized upon their whole bodies from head to heel.'[10] The dire effects of this fever are difficult to overstate: following the landing in August 1809, for example, the 81st Foot, which had embarked on campaign with 656 fit men, had just forty capable of duty by the end of September. By February 1810, from just over 39,000 troops involved, 4,066 had died, of whom only 106 had been killed in action, and 11,513 were still sick and incapable of duty. Regiments returned from Walcheren mere skeletons, like the 20th Foot, withdrawn from Walcheren after about six weeks' service: 'The appearance of the regiment on its return to Colchester was lamentable: about three hundred men, and those weak and sickly, with barely sufficient strength to walk, was all that it could muster,'[11] while a further 600 were in hospital. The consequences of Walcheren fever were enduring, and not just in cases like that of Private Thomas Green of the 43rd who, just returned from Walcheren, cut his throat at Colchester barracks while in the grip of the fever's delirium. The recurrent nature of the fever affected units long after, notably among those sent to the Peninsula whose members were so sickly as to render the corps almost ineffective.

Battalion or regimental surgeons (to whom it was usual for each private and NCO to pay 2d per month to defray any medical expenses forthcoming) probably had more expertise in treating battle injuries than illnesses (when the army's Physician General was asked to investigate Walcheren fever he declined on the excuse that he was unacquainted with the diseases of soldiers!), but in one aspect military medical care was in the forefront of innovation. Smallpox was a scourge that killed thousands; in the year commencing 15 December 1801, for example, it was the cause of 1,579 deaths in London, more than those who died of old age and almost 8 per cent of the total causes of mortality. Innoculation had been used from the mid-eighteenth century, but even in the most expert hands could prove fatal: Carolina, the infant daughter of William, Duke of Gloucester, and thus a niece of the king, had died in 1775 after innoculation. Furthermore, even successful treatment caused those innoculated to feel ill and required isolation. Edward Jenner's development of vaccination revolutionised treatment, and in June 1800, only four years after his first experiment and two years after he published his work on the subject, he personally vaccinated the 85th Foot, including wives and children, with no ill-effects. Consequently, in November 1803 the Duke of York ordered commanding officers to 'use their best endeavours' to persuade any of their men not bearing smallpox scars 'to be immediately innoculated with the Vaccine Matter; the process of which, experience has shewn to be perfectly safe; and which, as it does not require confinement, is attended with little or no inconvenience to the individual or the service.'[12] Six months later the order was repeated and officers exhorted to do more to persuade their men to be vaccinated, and it is interesting that this was not a compulsory order but required willingness of the part of the soldiers.

Sergeant Samuel 'Big Sam' Macdonald was one of the most renowned 'other ranks' in the army, by virtue of his size and matching strength: he was 6ft 10ins tall and served in the 1st Foot, Sutherland Fencibles and 93rd Highlanders. A native of Sutherland, until he re-enlisted upon the outbreak of war, he was employed as porter at the Prince of Wales's residence at Carlton House. He looked so out of place in the ranks that he was often employed as a recruiter; he died at Guernsey, serving with the 93rd, of inflammation of the lungs, at the age of forty.
(Print after John Kay)

Men were also lost to the army by injuries sustained away from the battle-field; falls from and kicks by horses accounted for many, and trips, falls and feet crushed by cartwheels or artillery pieces were not uncommon. The physical effort of manhandling artillery was another source of injury, notably ruptures and to a lesser extent hydrocele (fluid in the scrotum), for few gunners were as powerful as the famous giant 'Big Sam' McDonald of the Sutherland Fencibles and 93rd. One bitter night he was posted as sentry over a large cannon; he escaped the cold by hoisting the huge mass of iron on his shoulder and carrying it into the warmth of the guardhouse.

In addition to genuine illness, medical officers had to be aware of malingerers attempting to escape duty, like one W. Reginauld of the 7th Fuzileers who had suffered from an ulcerated leg for 3½ years until the afflicted limb was locked into a boot-shaped iron box. This prevented him from applying the corrosive substance that had kept the wound open, and it healed in twelve days; he received 500 lashes for his fraud. More extreme measures were taken by soldiers endeavouring to obtain a medical discharge, some of which were extremely dangerous. Frauds to simulate eye problems included rubbing lime, snuff, tobacco ash or gonorrheal discharge into the eye, placing silver nitrate on the eyeball to simulate blindness, or piercing the eye with a needle or table fork. Other known ploys included drinking vinegar to simulate consumption, and cutting the mouth to produce bloody saliva; the insertion of garlic or tobacco into the anus to fake heart disease, 'simulated to a great extent in the army'[13]; drinking chalk and vinegar to produce a swollen stomach; and creating ulcers by the application of nitric acid, yellow arsenic and quicklime among a number of preparations. Some men actually maimed themselves, as shown by two cases from 1813: Thomas Beckwith of the 45th cut the tendons in his heel, for which he was sentenced to 1,000 lashes, while Gilbert Kane of the Buffs chopped off a finger; he also got a flogging rather than the discharge he sought.

The most drastic escape from the army was by suicide. It was stated that a far higher proportion of suicides occurred in the army than in civilian life; statistics (albeit some two decades later than the Napoleonic Wars) showed an annual rate of one suicide per 1,274 soldiers, as against one in more than 15,000 civilians. Fear of punishment was one cause attributed at the time, and another suggestion was the realization that even discharge from the army would only result in a life of unemployment. Not all military suicides were related to the service, like the case of a corporal named Green who on recruiting duty at Radstock in 1812 had his advances towards a young woman spurned by her parents, whereupon 'the villain, in a fit of desperation, took out a double-barrelled pistol, the contents of one of which he discharged at the unfortunate young woman, and with the other shot himself through the head. He died on the spot, but his intended victim survives.'[14] Some suicides were simply unaccountable, like that of Sergeant Walsh of the 77th who assiduously paid the wages of his company at Winchester barracks in June 1809, then went into a locked room and using a string tied to his foot shot himself through the head, 'and by the explosion his brains were blown up the cieling'[sic]. He was found a shocking spectacle.'[15]

Although efforts were made to keep the soldier healthy, there were few attempts to keep him occupied off duty, which had far-reaching consequences. One soldier directly blamed the prevalence of drunkenness on the absence of anything else to do unless, like himself and his friends, they were literate and keen to improve themselves with books or music, even pleasantly passing the time on guard duty by discussing philosophy or history. Had the officers shown any encouragement, he thought, many drunks could have been directed towards a more profitable way of passing their idle hours. Some regiments did make efforts, and on rare occasions a commanding officer might mark a holiday with such intellectual diversions as running after a greased pig, though there is little evidence of organized sports beyond a few mentions of football or cricket, and perhaps the latter may have been restricted to officers or those men from areas where that sport was strongest, like Kent or Hampshire. According to James Smithies of the Royal Dragoons, in his regiment in the Peninsula efforts were made to keep the men amused when off duty, diversions including the organization of prayer meetings, bouts of skill with sword or bayonet, and discussion groups. The latter were especially popular, but usually ended in fights. A more productive recreation was gardening, which was so encouraged among the men of the 100th (later 92nd) when in garrison in 1797 that the King himself sent a present of seeds for the soldiers' gardens.

Although a few individuals believed that teaching the poor to read and write only made them 'proud, idle and discontented . . . and [to] scorn handling ploughs and spades, scrubbing brushes or mops,'[16] the military authorities recognized the merits of literacy. Lieutenant General Viscount Molesworth had written as much in his *A Short Course of Standing Rules for the Government & Conduct of an Army* (Dublin 1745): 'by making your Army Better Men, you make them Better Soldiers,' even though this related primarily to religious education.[17] There was certainly a need for education; statistics published some two decades after the end of the Napoleonic Wars suggested that 33 per cent of men in England were so unlettered that they had to sign the marriage register with a cross, while Henry Marshall stated that of persons charged with offences in England in 1836, 33 per cent were unable to read and 52 per cent able to read and write only imperfectly (and only 30 per cent in Ireland properly literate).

There was a practical dimension to this problem, for sergeants, and to a lesser extent corporals, needed a basic understanding of letters and numbers to enable them to perform their duties (which helps explain why a steady man who was literate could achieve fairly rapid promotion after enlistment). To this end, schools were established in garrisons and individual units from a fairly early date (there was, for example, a garrison school at Tangier in 1675), for the education of a regiment's children and any aspiring soldier. Such improvement of the individual was not unconnected with theories of light infantry training that emphasized initiative and self-reliance, enabling the soldier to operate effectively even when not under the close scrutiny of his officers and NCOs, so the establishment of a regimental school by Lieutenant Colonel Robert Barclay of the 52nd Light Infantry in 1807 was entirely in keeping. In 1808 instructions were given for the establishment of schools to educate a regiment's children, and in August 1811 the Duke of York recommended that a school be established in each battalion to instruct any boys in receipt of pay and soldiers' children, believing that the service would benefit from a more educated rank and file. (The Duke's concern for education had already led to the creation of the Royal Military Asylum at Chelsea, which opened in 1803, as a free boarding school for the orphans and other children of NCOs and privates; inmates received basic conventional education plus (for boys) instruction in drill, physical exercise, gunnery and trades, of use should the children subsequently join the army.)

There was no requirement that teachers in regimental schools should have received any formal training; not until 1846 was the Corps of Army Schoolmasters founded to provide proper instruction. In 1813 it was forbidden for army schoolmasters to go on active service, but this was frequently ignored; for example, the schoolmaster sergeant of the 2/73rd, Charles Collins, was killed at Waterloo. A framework knitter from Nottingham, he had been appointed to his post and must have been a very young man, as he joined from the Royal Military Asylum.[18] Students of regimental schools were expected to pay for tuition, in the case of the 52nd a weekly fee that also covered the purchase of books, pens, ink and paper. In the 25th Foot in 1804 the fee varied according to rank, from 3d per week for a sergeant to 1d for a private. Expenses might also be defrayed by charitable funds; the 54th, for example, had one in 1813 specifically to further the education of the regiment's children. Some regiments awarded prize medals, presumably to outstanding students; the 17th Foot had one of the earliest recorded, dated 1816, utilising a die for the obverse, which originally probably commemorated a campaign in India.[19] Regimental schools certainly had an effect, for many learned to read and write during their army service, like John Biddle, an uneducated labourer from Worcestershire, who on his enlistment in the Coldstream Guards in 1806 signed his name with a cross; yet at Waterloo he was the colour sergeant of the light company of the 2nd Battalion, responsible for keeping the company roll and writing a clear and educated hand.

With education, religion might have been expected to provide a check upon excesses, though spiritual comfort appears not to have been a priority with the military authorities. Until 1796 each regiment was supposed to have had a chaplain (though for some it was a sinecure appointment), but in that year they were replaced by the Army Chaplains Departments, which provided a small number of clergymen for service abroad, with civilian chaplains in the vicinity of barracks acting at home. There was not complete unanimity among the religious establishment concerning the level of support that should be accorded to troops, even at the time of the danger of invasion; the rector of Matlock, for example, dismissed his curate for preaching against drilling on a Sunday. In 1798 the Bishop of Winchester authorised the whole of his clergy to take up arms in person, presumably a stance that would have been approved by the Reverend Joseph Bradshaw, an officer in the Belper, Shottle and Holbrooke Volunteers (Derbyshire), who read prayers in uniform, and on horseback, on a Sunday. Others just provided encouragement, like the Reverend M.H. Luscombe, curate of Clewer, Berkshire, chaplain to the Windsor garrison, who in August 1803 preached a vehement sermon to the troops based on Nehemiah 4, 14 ('fight for your brethren, your sons, and your daughters, your wives, and your houses').

The religious support provided to the military was exclusively Protestant; strictures against Roman Catholics still existed, even prohibiting them from holding military commissions (though this rule was not infrequently circumvented). Indeed, until the Roman Catholic Relief Act of 1791 (and the Scottish Catholic Emancipation Act of 1793), the soldier's declaration on his attestation document began: 'I, ------, do make Oath, That I am a Protestant, and by Trade a ------, and to the best of my Knowledge and Belief, was born in the Parish of ------.' Statistics concerning the proportion of Roman Catholic recruits are elusive, but an estimate of 1794 suggested that at least three-quarters of Irish militiamen were Catholic,[21] and only units from Ulster might have been expected to be largely Protestant. Conversely, Roman Catholics and Quakers were officially prohibited from militia service in England.

The fact that many recruits were Roman Catholic, especially from Ireland, was accepted; for example, in February 1810 Henry Grattan presented a petition to Parliament appealing for an end to discrimination: 'Where the military and naval strength of the Empire is to be recruited, the Catholics are eagerly solicited . . . to bear their full share in the perils of warfare, and in the lowest ranks; but when preferment and promotion . . . are to be distributed as rewards of merit, no laurels are destined to grace a Catholic's brow, or fit the wearer for command.'[22] Nevertheless, the religious dimensions of the Jacobite rebellions, and notably the Irish rising of 1798, gave rise to a little disquiet concerning the enrolment of Roman Catholics, especially at the prospect of a wholly Roman Catholic regiment upon the formation of the Glengarry Fencibles in 1794, in which its Catholic chaplain, Father Alexander MacDonell, had played a leading role. (He was unique in being the only Catholic clergyman in the army, contrary to the existing law.) Discrimination continued to decrease, however; in 1806 it was ordered that under no circumstances should Roman Catholics, and all other sects, be prohibited from attending their own divine service, which was to be respected exactly as that of the 'Established Church', providing that it did not interfere with military duty; and in 1811 a further regulation forbade the punishment of Catholics who declined to attend Church of England services.

Whether Protestant or Catholic, most soldiers seem to have been not unduly concerned with religious matters. Despite the strong Roman Catholicism of the Iberian Peninsula, Wellington once remarked that he had not seen a single act of worship by his Catholic soldiery except in making the sign of the cross to induce the local people to give them wine. At the time it was believed, evidently with some justification, that certain categories of men were inherently more pious than others, notably Scots. (In the Scottish 26th Foot there was the only case of a regiment with a religious origin, in the Cameronian sect that gave its name to the regiment, which retained the practice of conventicles – open-air services with sentries posted around – until the regiment was disbanded in 1968.) For example, it was remarked that when Scots were quartered at Tenterden, those who attended local services 'on giving out of the Lessons each drew out his Bible as at a word of command.'[23] One such religious individual was William Young, a young Scottish private killed at Orthes. He had asked that in the event of his death his Bible should be returned to his mother, who had given it to him, in which he had written for her comfort passages suitable for a soldier and his family: 'Refrain thy voice from weeping, and thine eyes from tears: for . . . thy children shall come again to their own border' (Jeremiah 31, 16-17); and 'Call upon me in the day of trouble: I will deliver thee' (Psalm 50, 15). Young had come from a respectable family and had enlisted after being cruelly treated by his sweetheart, and had been ridiculed by the cruder members of his battalion for his regular Bible study.

There are not many accounts of soldiers seeking spiritual solace at time of battle, but the general reaction might have been similar to that accorded a pious Reay Fencible, who in the attack upon an Irish insurgent force at Tara Hill in May 1798, under fire for the first time, took shelter in a ditch and began to pray. His sergeant prodded him with the butt of his spontoon and said (in Gaelic), 'Get up with you; how can you lag behind while your comrades are gaining glory in front? Go and acquit yourself like a man; there will be time enough for prayer when the fight is finished, and every devil's son of those rebel Irishers killed!'[24]

Few chaplains served on campaign; at the conclusion of the Peninsular War, for example, there were only sixteen in the entire field army, and one of those (the worthy Samuel Briscall) was with Wellington's headquarters. Some of the others seem to have been neither inspiration nor comfort, but among the truly outstanding individuals, admired by the whole army, was Reverend Edward Frith, known as 'the fighting parson', who was always in the front of the action and who at Maya saved three or four casualties by carrying them out of danger on his back. In the first religious service after Waterloo he preached a sermon to the troops on the text 'go to your tents and rejoice, and return thanks to the Lord for the mercies He has granted you,' so that 'there was hardly a dry eye in the whole division, and it had an excellent effect on the men.'[25]

There was a degree of suspicion over attempts to evangelise soldiers, for though the Naval and Military Bible Society had been founded in 1780, a proposal to form a society for promoting religion and morality among soldiers was criticized in the press, which feared that such organizations could be 'perverted into a means of overthrowing our establishments, civil, political and ecclesiastical.'[26]

With so little religious support in the army, there was scope for the growth of nonconformity, which was also viewed with some suspicion. In February 1811 Wellington complained about the absence of chaplains in some formations that had led to a growth of Methodism, 'spreading very fast in the army.' In the Foot Guards, 'The men meet in the evening, and sing psalms; and I believe a serjeant (Stephens) now and then gives them a sermon. Mr Briscall has his eye upon these transactions, and would give me notice if they were growing into any thing which ought to be put a stop to.' Nevertheless, he admitted that 'The meeting of soldiers in their cantonments to sing psalms, or hear a sermon read by one of their comrades, is, in the abstract, perfectly innocent; and it is a better way of spending their time than many others to which they are addicted; but it may become otherwise.'[27]

Suspicion about such practices arose from the fear that it might undermine discipline, though the interaction between officers and other ranks was slight (as it was in Freemasonry, which existed to a limited degree, in which officers and men enjoyed a level of parity). As Wellington described, lay preaching was almost entirely restricted to the rank and file, some of whom carried the practice into civilian life: Sergeant Joseph Mackay from Strathalladale, for example, gained a commission and was wounded as an ensign in the 1st Royal Scots at Waterloo; he was granted half pay in 1816 and spent the next four decades as an evangelist in the Highlands. Some officers were not so forgiving of overt and unorthodox religious practices; Colonel Robert Kingscote of the North Gloucestershire Militia, for example, issued an order informing his regiment that participation in meetings purporting to be religious, which might conceal darker motives, could be subject to the civil law concerning unlawful assemblies, with the threat of both imprisonment and military punishment. Captain Richard Drewe of the 73rd was more blunt when ordering a member of his company to burn his Bible, declaring that the man's musket was his Bible and that he, Drewe, was his God Almighty.

There were a few cases where religion had a deleterious effect, possibly arising from the absence of professional spiritual guidance, though the worst cases were the consequence of mental unbalance. Joseph Donaldson told of a man who suffered from 'religious melancholy' and got into trouble for knocking down an innkeeper. While under arrest he borrowed a hatchet, cut off his right hand and threw it out of a window, following the instruction in Matthew 5, 30: 'And if thy right hand offend thee, cut it off, and cast it from thee; for it is profitable for thee that one of thy members should perish, and not that thy whole body should be cast in hell.'

One way of breaking the monotony of military life was a practice known as 'working out', by which soldiers when not on duty could follow a trade or hire themselves out as labourers. Those with a skill could profit considerably – Benjamin Harris of the 95th accumulated the huge sum of £200 from shoe-making, most of which he spent on private treatment for Walcheren fever – but control was exercised over these occupations. For example, a Horse Guards circular of June 1808 permitted soldiers of good character, who were fully trained and not exceeding one quarter of a battalion to help in haymaking and gathering the corn harvest, but they were not allowed to go more than two days' march from the battalion's quarters. By law a soldier honourably discharged was allowed to follow a trade without membership of a guild or trade association, but in 1812 there was a legal action between Sergeants John Brash (a tailor) and Robert Bird (a wright), both serving, and the respective trade associations of Linlithgow, which prosecuted them for trading without the associations' consent. The sergeants contended there was no difference between an ex- and serving soldier who followed his trade in off-duty hours, but they lost their case.

Soldiers engaged in public works, like the construction or repair of public roads or military buildings, received a wage on top of their normal pay: in summer a day's work was ten hours, in winter eight, for which they received a penny an hour, while NCOs acting as overseers received an extra shilling a day, and subalterns in charge of a working party, four shillings ('summer' commenced on Lady Day and 'winter' on Michaelmas Day). Soldiers were expected to act as labourers on campaign, notably in the construction of siege works, 'when the Use of the Spade, Pick-Axe, and Barrow, are as essential for the Defensive, as that of the Musquet and Bayonet are for the Offensive Operations of the Army.'[28] In such tasks, it was observed that those who had hired out as labourers at home were the most efficient in the siege trenches.

Private work was not without its hazards; for example, Samuel Barnes of the 3rd Foot Guards was drowned in July 1806 while repairing the brickwork of a sewer in Pimlico. In the following year Privates John Hodge and William Stock of the 3rd Dragoons died descending a foul well at Canterbury, and in that October Private Robert Potter of the North York Militia was loading wood onto a cart when it slipped: 'his head was crushed between the timber, and he expired in half an hour.'[29]

Troops could be called to support the civil authorities at times of unrest, but this was a wholly distasteful task and was generally assigned to the local volunteers. One very unfortunate incident occurred in April 1810 during the disturbances arising from the arrest of Sir Francis Burdett for breaching parliamentary privilege. A mob of his supporters so pelted a detachment of Life Guards with stones that 'they could endure the assault no longer, but charged the multitude sword in hand. The firing of the carbines became now pretty general,'[30] in consequence of which three citizens were killed. Inquests found that one had been slain justifiably but a verdict of wilful murder against unknown Life Guardsmen was returned on the other two.

Military assistance in civil emergencies was less contentious, but still hazardous. Troops were not infrequently called out to help fight fires, or at least to cordon the area to prevent looting while civilian firemen fought the blazes. In October 1800, however, the 2nd Dragoon Guards helped tackle a huge fire at a paper mill in Exeter, using the fire engine from the local barracks, and two months later the 10th Light Dragoons helped save Oriel College, Oxford, when a fire started there. The dangers were exemplified by the death of Sergeant Poole of the 2nd Foot Guards in March 1800, who broke his neck falling through a skylight obscured by smoke when rescuing furniture from the Hole-in-the-Wall Inn in Panton St., London, to which fire had communicated from an adjoining brothel (he received a ceremonial funeral attended not only by his own regiment but the Life Guards and some sixty Freemasons). In the famous destruction of Covent Garden Theatre in September 1808, not only were eight firemen killed but three members of the 1st Foot Guards and one of the Bloomsbury Volunteers who had been called in to help.

Further interaction with civilians occurred when troops were permitted out of barracks unsupervised, soldiers granted furlough to visit their homes being permitted to make their own way. Disquiet arising from the reputation of soldiers was often groundless as Dorothy Wordsworth discovered in 1801 when she was nervous of two soldiers, one extremely drunk, that she encountered on the road between Rydal and Grasmere, but they proved to be very civil. Conversely, a carter who gave two soldiers a lift in January 1798 at Stratford had cause to regret his kindness as they made off with his wagon containing more than £1,000 worth of linen. Roaming unsupervised around the country was not without hazards for the soldiers, as shown by two incidents involving the West Middlesex Militia. In April 1800 a soldier walking from Sunderland to Durham was gored to death by an angry cow, despite being armed with his bayonet, while in January 1814 several men became so drunk that they lay down to sleep by the roadside and froze to death.

A notorious example of the hazards of ill-intentioned soldiers loose in the community was a case in 1800 when two members of the Tarbert Fencibles, John Diggens and Richard Pendergrass (or Prendergast), adopted a sideline of highway robbery while the regiment was stationed in Hampshire. They attacked an old man named Thomas Webb, a traveller in wooden ware, at Botley, who crawled for more than a mile with a 6-inch length of broken bayonet stuck in his neck, and gave an account of the assault before he died. Diggens admitted the crime and was hanged, his body gibbeted near the scene of the attack, but Pendergrass (who it appears actually committed the attack) was discharged for lack of evidence, though his regiment perhaps thought he had escaped justified punishment, for he received 600 lashes for disobedience of orders and was drummed out. The regiment was so incensed at the besmirching of their reputation that every man subscribed half a day's pay for the relief of Webb's family, and Sergeant Major William Blaney published a letter in the press deploring the conduct of their villainous comrades and stating their 'full determination always to prove ourselves good soldiers and peaceable citizens.'[31] The murder had been committed for only seven pence and six eggs, all that poor Webb possessed.

Not all soldiers were supportive of the civilian victims of crime. When in 1795 some members of the Somerset Militia, quartered at Barham Down

*'Shoulder arms': the pose in which much drill, and most
marching, was performed. The uniform shown is that worn
prior to the abolition of the lapels in 1797.*

camp, were discovered stealing vegetables, the owner of the garden let fly and
winged one of the soldiers with his shotgun. When two of the aggrieved
gardeners went to the camp to complain, 'They were soon recognized, and as
soon pursued; one of them was knocked down, jumped upon, and most cruelly
kicked and bruised'[32] before officers intervened. Three of the assailants were
sentenced to between 200 and 300 lashes.

A constant in the soldier's everyday life was training, which commenced as
soon as he joined his regiment. The first thing learned by the recruit was how

to stand like a soldier; in the words of Sir David Dundas's infantry manual, adopted universally in 1792: 'The heels must be in line, and closed. The knees straight, without stiffness. The toes a little turned out, so that the feet may form an angle of about 60 degrees. Let the arms hang near the body, but not stiff, the flat part of the hand and little finger touching the thigh; the thumbs as far back as the seam of the breeches. The elbow and shoulders to be kept back; the belly rather drawn in, and the breast advanced, but without constraint; the body upright, but inclining forward, so that the weight of it principally bears on the fore part of the feet; the head to be erect, and neither turned to the right nor left'; in short, to 'banish the air of the rustic,'[33] although the varied physiques that would have been brought in when recruits were at a premium perhaps influenced Sir John Moore to believe that 'A little more or less round-shouldered is of little importance' provided the soldier remained square to his front.[34]

The recruit was taught how to march, at first in small groups, then as part of a company, the principal and lowest manoeuvre element. Dundas specified that only three speeds of march be employed: 'ordinary time' of 75 paces to the minute, each pace of 30 inches (76.2 cm) from heel to heel; 'quick march'

A company assembled: although this depicts an auxiliary unit, the Cornhill Volunteers, the scene is typical; formed in a two-deep line with most men in the 'stand at ease' pose, with weight on the right leg and the left knee slightly bent, and 'the hands are shut in front with the thumbs turn'd in.' (Engraving by C. Grinion after Edward Dayes, 1799)

of 108 paces to the minute, and 'wheeling step' of 120 paces, used for changing formation or passing obstacles. There were, however, other ways of marching that had to be mastered: 'stepping out' for a temporary increase in pace in which the pace was extended to 33 inches (83.8 cm); 'stepping short', in which the pace was drastically reduced when a unit needed to slow down but still to maintain some forward momentum, perhaps to permit an adjoining formation to catch up; 'back step' for a temporary move to the rear, 'side or closing step' to move to left or right, and 'oblique step', in which the soldier moved diagonally at an angle of about 25 degrees.

Having learned to march, the soldier was schooled in operating in formation. A company customarily assembled in line, initially three ranks deep according to the regulation, but by about 1800 a two-deep line was the usual formation for combat, having been found to be more effective. It was in line that the soldier most often fought, but for movement columns were the best method of maintaining cohesion. The column employed on the battlefield was very different from that used on the march: for action a column might have a frontage of about 20 yards, with the battalion's companies ranged one behind the other, whereas for marching on a road the column might have no more than four men abreast.

The soldier was drilled until the movements expected of him became

Training: infantrymen at drill, wearing their white undress jackets or sleeved waistcoats. The soldier a few paces in front of the main body is a 'fugleman', an experienced man whose drill movements were copied by the remainder. (Print by J. Hill after J.A. Atkinson, 1807)

second nature. Drill was no simple thing to learn; in the 'manual and platoon exercise' (weapons-handling and the most basic movements in formation) there were no fewer than 45 words of command and 109 distinct motions to be learned by rote, which disproves any perception that the troops were ignorant, mindless automata herded sheep-like into position: a trained

The sergeant major: probably the most famous drill instructor of the period was Patrick Gould, a native of Clackmannanshire who had served as a drill sergeant in the Foot Guards and Argyllshire Fencibles before appointed to instruct the Royal Edinburgh Volunteers in 1794. (Mezzotint after George Watson)

battalion, confident in its aptitude, was instead as flexible and formidable a formation as existed.

Nonetheless, the training was directed towards the production of a unit that would act like a machine on the day of battle, that would move, change position, load and fire as a single entity, the drill so ingrained that the men would continue to perform their duty despite the unimaginable horror occurring around them, when winnowed by enemy musketry or raked by artillery fire that would decapitate and dismember. The complexity of the drill was perhaps partly directed towards imbuing this attitude, and it was emphasized to the men that only by remaining in their formation, only by performing their tasks with cool detachment, could they be safe, for a unit that shook or scattered was defenceless.

To inculcate this sense of order, initiative was often deliberately discouraged. One officer claimed that 'The soldier was treated as an unruly child in a workhouse – fed, clothed, and flogged, but never instructed, never reasoned with. "You have no business to *think*, Sir," was a sentence often addressed to him, "but to do as you are bid."' He also remarked that officers often swore at the men, as they swore at each other, so that 'it has often been asserted that a British soldier never thought his officer in *earnest* with him unless he swore at him.'[35] (This seems to have been a tradition: Lawrence Sterne, who knew army life from his soldier father, had his character 'Uncle Toby' remark, 'Our armies swore terribly in Flanders,' and this explains why the nickname 'goddams' was applied by foreigners to British soldiers for generations.)

The conventional attitude was expressed by one of the most famous sergeant majors of the period, Patrick Gould, who was appointed to instruct the 1st Royal Edinburgh Volunteers, formed in 1794, whose rank and file included many members of the professions and gentry not used to obeying orders. They gave Gould much trouble by questioning *why* certain manoeuvres were necessary, which caused the sergeant major to explode to the effect that there was nothing in the King's orders about *reasons*; they were to obey orders and nothing more, because a soldier was a 'mere machine' and that no one below the rank of field officer was permitted to think. Gould declared, no doubt with feeling, that he would prefer to drill ten clowns than one philosopher.

With his customary perception, Wellington identified the real value of teaching the complex drill: 'Subordination and habits of obedience are more necessary than mechanical discipline . . . . The object of all drill must be to practice and form individuals to perform that which is thought expedient they should perform when part of a body before an enemy.'[36] In other words, knowledge of complex drill on the parade ground was useful on campaign only

Dogged resilience was one of the British soldier's defining characteristics, leading to a French opinion that he was not intelligent enough to know when he was beaten. Never was this attitude more essential than when standing under attack in square, as in this view of Waterloo. (Print after P. Jazet)

as a basis for a few vital manoeuvres; as one officer observed, the 'absurd minutiae' of the drill 'were unknown or disregarded by the veterans of the Peninsula, and which must again fall into disuse at the first sound of the enemy's guns,'[37] while William Grattan of the 88th, one of the finest regiments in the Peninsular army, stated that their drill was 'chiefly confined to line marching, echellon [sic] movements and the formation of the square in every possible way; and in all those we excelled.'[38]

To these relatively few, vital manoeuvres was added the ability to deliver a crushing volume of musketry, one of the cornerstones of the British infantry's success in battle. Despite the parsimonious supply of live rounds for training, the soldier was taught to fire his musket in a number of systems, from a single, devastating volley along an entire line, to various 'rolling vollies', in which sub-units fired in succession, or by rank, to 'file-firing', in which the two or three men in each file fired together and re-loaded as the next file along fired, and so on down the line, so that a fairly continuous fire was delivered.

Among the most important manoeuvres on the battlefield was the ability to form square, virtually the only salvation for infantry when attacked by cavalry. Formed from line or column, the square – often actually an oblong – was a four-sided formation, usually hollow in the centre, each side several ranks deep, facing outwards, the front ranks kneeling with muskets and bayonets braced at horse's breast height, the rear ranks standing and firing. It thus presented an all-round defence against which horses could not be made to charge. As Lieutenant Colonel Alexander Wallace of the 88th told his men: 'Mind the square; you know I have often told you that if ever you had to form it from line, in the face of the enemy, you'd be in a d---d ugly way, and have plenty of noise about you; . . . by G-d, if you are once broken, you'll be running here and there like a parcel of frightened pullets!'[39] It is a measure of the army's discipline and esprit de corps that there were no complete collapses of squares in action as sometimes occurred in other armies.

The noise of battle was so overwhelming that verbal commands could often not be heard – one soldier compared it to 'the roll of a hundred thousand drums, of all sizes and shapes'[40] – in which circumstances the ingrained nature of drill became increasingly important. Orders could be given by drum beat, requiring the soldier to recognise a number of calls, though in action most of a battalion's drummers would be employed in assisting the wounded. Orders for light infantry and cavalry could be given by bugle or trumpet call respectively, which again demanded an ability to recognize the calls; Thomas Cooper's light infantry manual of 1806, for example, included fourteen calls for use in barracks and thirty-seven in the field, though he stated that only those for advance, retreat, halt, cease firing and assemble were really necessary.

Light infantry drill was the most advanced aspect of the system, demanding much more from the soldier. Their essence was the ability to fight in 'open order', not in the usual compact blocks, to skirmish and scout, accomplished without the minute supervision of officers and NCOs, demanding a high degree of initiative on the part of the solder. Having declined in efficiency following the American War of Independence, light infantry tactics had to be redeveloped during the French Revolutionary Wars, and were perfected by the training of the 43rd, 52nd and 95th Regiments at Shorncliffe camp under the command of Sir John Moore. Moore was crucial in disseminating the theory that discipline and obedience were derived from pride, comradeship and encouragement rather than from the threat of punishment, from which grew esprit de corps, confidence and self-reliance. The result was probably the best and most flexible infantry units that had ever existed, and it was with reason that the Light Division was regarded as the elite of the Peninsular army, and it might be said that it was a direct forerunner of modern infantry service.

6

'Fifty I Got For Selling My Coat': Discipline

Fifty I got for selling my coat,
Fifty for selling my blanket;
If ever I 'list for a soldier again,
The devil shall be my sergeant

The Rogue's March, played when a soldier
was dishonourably discharged

Among the common perceptions of the soldier of this period is the use of the
lash, the ultimate sanction to enforce discipline. Although important, it is an
aspect of the soldier's life that can be overstated.

When presenting colours to the 93rd Highlanders in 1834, the Duke of
Wellington explained the necessity for discipline and good order:

> It is not by your native gallantry, it is not by the bodily strength of
> each of you alone . . . that bodies such as you can contend effectu-
> ally for any object . . . bodies of men so numerous as you are must
> get into confusion unless regulated by discipline; unless accus-
> tomed to subordination, obedient to command. I am afraid that
> panic is the usual attendance upon such confusion. It is then by the
> enforcement of the rules of discipline, subordination, and good
> order, that such bodies as yours can render efficient service to their
> King and Country; and can be otherwise than a terror to their
> friends, contemptible to their enemies, and a burthen to the State.
> The rules of discipline, subordination, and good order teach the
> Officers their duties towards the soldiers . . . they teach the soldiers
> to respect their superiors the non-commissioned Officers and
> Officers; and to consider them as their best friends and protectors
> . . . . There may be some whose youth, indiscretion, or bad habits
> may lead into irregularities. These must be restrained: discipline,

subordination, and good order must be established among all. The very nature of such an institution as yours requires it.[1]

A popular belief was that only the brutal enforcement of discipline could keep soldiery in check. Moyle Sherer, an experienced officer, sought to state what he regarded as the true situation:

> . . . the world is ever too forward to characterise [the soldier's conduct] as barbarous and licentious. My opinion of the moral excellence of soldiers is very superior to that generally entertained; and I think that we should find as much virtue, and as many amiable qualities, among ten thousand soldiers, as among a similar number of individuals taken, without selection, from the bosom of civil society. It will be remarked that those who live among soldiers, that they are charitable and generous, kind to children, and fond of dumb animals: add to this, a frequent exposure to hardship, privation and danger, makes them friendly, and ready to assist each other. Nor are they without a just and laudable pride. The worthless characters who are to be met with in every regiment (and society) are generally shunned; nor have I ever seen an expression of discontent on their countenances at the just punishment of a moral offender.[2]

He also commented that 'the British army must not be made responsible for the folly and ignorance of many, who have been too honoured by admission into her ranks. We must not look to all who have fought our battles in the vain hope of meeting heroes; we shall find *but men*.'[3]

Nevertheless, the fact that there were 'worthless characters' in the army led to draconian measures for the enforcement of good order, even though the more enlightened officers recognized that more could be achieved by the instillation of an ethos of pride, high morale and comradeship. As early as 1760 advice to officers stated that they should 'Look upon the soldiers under your command as servants to the same Royal Master with yourself, and not as slaves . . . . Consider that without them you would be of no consequence . . . an affable, courteous behaviour, from an officer to his soldiers, cannot fail of gaining their love and confidence, which is certainly more eligible than their hatred and disesteem.'[4] There was, however, a small core of individuals immune to such an approach, for whom other methods had to be applied.

The almost universal punishment for serious offenders – and, sadly, some who committed relatively minor misdemeanours – was flogging. This terrible

Corporal punishment: a soldier tied to a 'triangle' of spontoons with his unit formed into a hollow square to witness the consequences of misbehaviour. In the rear of the triangle are the drummers, taking duty in turn, supervised by the drum-major (left), identifiable by his long cane. At right, an NCO keeps a tally of the number of strokes inflicted.

sanction was always carried out with ceremony, usually in view of the culprit's entire regiment or battalion, assembled to witness the punishment, which thus acted not only as retribution for a crime but as a warning and example to others. In essence, the ceremony was simple; the culprit was tied to a pyramid formed of three or more sergeants' spontoons, often still known by the archaic term 'halberds', hence the expression 'being sent to the halberds' as a euphemism for being flogged. The victim was then beaten upon his bare back with a cat-o'nine-tails, generally wielded by a relay of drummers, until either the prescribed number of blows had been inflicted, or until the regimental surgeon in attendance decreed that to proceed further would threaten life.

The number of lashes that could be inflicted for a single crime was limited by a General Order of 30 January 1807, in response to a sentence of 1,500 lashes awarded to a private of the 54th for mutinous conduct: 'It appearing to His Majesty, that a punishment to the extent of one thousand lashes, is a sufficient example for any breach of military discipline, short of capital offence;

and as even that number cannot be safely inflicted at any one period, His Majesty has been graciously pleased to express his opinion, that no sentence for corporal punishment should exceed one thousand lashes.' In 1812 the number of lashes that could be imposed by a regimental, rather than 'general', court martial, was limited to 300, though this was sometimes exceeded.

The nature of crimes that warranted corporal punishment may be gauged by some of those ordered in the 10th Hussars in 1813-14, with the number of lashes actually inflicted in parentheses if different from the sentence: Alexander Brown, asleep at his post, 400 lashes (360 inflicted); Thomas Syer, drunk at stables, 400; William Pettit, absent from quarters and parade, 200 (160); John Robinson, drunk on the march, 400 (200); Thomas Weston, insolence, 400; John Hickman, suspicion of theft, 300 (200). Simple statistics convey no idea of the barbaric nature of the punishment. Sir Charles Napier, a noted humanitarian, provided a clue: 'I . . . have always observed, that when the skin is thoroughly cut up or flayed off, the great pain subsides. Men are frequently convulsed and screaming during the time they receive one lash to three hundred lashes, and then they bear the remainder, even to eight hundred or one thousand lashes, without a groan; they will often lie as if without life, and the Drummers appear to be flogging a lump of dead raw flesh.'[5]

A drummer who on many occasions had administered a flogging recalled that after about 100 lashes blood 'would fly about in all directions with every additional blow of the cat, so that by the time he had received three hundred, I have found my clothes all over blood from the knees to the crown of the head. Horrified at my disgusting appearance, I have, immediately after parade, ran into the barrack-room, to escape from the observations of the soldiers, and to rid my clothes and person of my comrade's blood.'[6]

After punishment had been stopped on medical grounds before a sentence had been completed, it could be resumed as soon as the injuries had healed, though if two-thirds of the punishment had been completed, it was customary for the remainder to be remitted, though it was sometimes allowed to 'hang over', so that a commanding officer could have the man flogged again whenever he chose. If the victim's back were thought incapable of sustaining another flogging, it was not unknown for him to be lashed on the backside or thighs instead. Completion of sentence by repeated floggings was abolished in 1815.

The sight of a flogging could have a profound effect upon the victim's comrades, usually drawn up in a hollow square around the ceremony so that all had a clear view. Charles Napier recalled that 'accustomed as I was to such scenes, I could not on these occasions bear to look at the first blows; the feeling of horror that ran through the ranks was evident, and all soldiers know the frequent faintings that take place among recruits when they first see a soldier flogged.'[7] He believed that most soldiers concurred with a flogging they regarded as deserved, until it became excessive, when 'the faces of the spectators assumed a look of disgust; there was always a low whispering sound, scarcely audible, issuing from the apparently stern and silent ranks [even] when the soldiers believed in its justice, and approved of the punishment . . . . This low and scarcely audible sound spoke aloud to my mind, that punishment had become excessive, that the culprit had disappeared and the martyr taken his place.'[8] Henry Marshall concurred, describing the low murmur as 'sniffing', a loud inhalation through the nose.

John Cooper of the 7th remarked that 'It required strong nerves to look on,' and that 'many were lashed into insensibility' and in one case of which he knew, a Brunswicker, into insanity. He recalled the nature of one flogging injury: 'A man of ours was flogged for breaking into a church and stealing some silver candlesticks. By some neglect his back festered. Being in hospital one morning, I saw the poor fellow brought in to have his back dressed. He was laid upon the floor, and a large poultice taken off the wound. O! what a sickening sight! The wound was perhaps eight inches by six, full of matter, in which were a number of black-headed maggots striving to hide themselves. At this scene those who looked on were horrified.'[9]

Some corps did have a reputation for bad conduct or dishonesty – the Royal Waggon Train, the transport service, for example, was nicknamed 'The Newgate Blues', from Newgate prison – but it is likely that those that acquired a reputation for corporal punishment were as much victims of poor leadership, from officers who showed no compassion, as from the felonies of their men. (For example, while quartered in Glasgow it was said that a battalion of the Inniskillings became known as 'the whipping 27th', and the traditional nickname of what became the Northamptonshire Regiment, 'The Steelbacks', had the same origin.)

The extent to which a commanding officer could become infamous is shown by the case of the 28th Foot in the expedition to Germany in 1806, where daily parades flogged as many as twenty-five men at a time for the most trivial reasons. One stalwart old soldier of spotless character, attending parade in winter with a heavy cold, coughed in the ranks; the tyrannical officer ordered an immediate fifty lashes with no formal trial, and it was said that the shame ruined the man and led to his discharge. Another story recounted an officer who flogged a man by mistake during the Peninsular War; when the error was brought to his attention he remarked that it didn't matter, as although the man might be innocent of that transgression, he would be guilty some other time.

One commanding officer criticized for use of the lash was Colonel George Quentin of the 10th Hussars, a man of Hanoverian birth and a friend of the Prince of Wales. In 1813-14 he ordered sixty-two floggings in his regiment, and when the matter was raised in the House of Commons in 1815 an ex-10th officer, Colonel Charles Palmer, stated that previously the regiment had been in a good state, so that few floggings were necessary, but that Quentin had altered the system, increasing indiscipline. (Almost all Quentin's officers revolted against his regime and petitioned for his removal; he was almost entirely exonerated by a court martial and all the dissenting officers were transferred from the regiment, which may well have been something of a travesty.)

Quentin was probably an exception, for many officers viewed corporal punishment with extreme distaste, though most acknowledged its necessity in some cases. On one occasion a reluctant commanding officer asked a man before he was tied to the halberds if he would volunteer to serve in Africa rather than suffer a flogging. '"No, sir," replied the man, "I've been a long time in the regiment, and I'll not give it up for three hundred lashes; not that I care about going to Africa. I deserve my punishment and I'll bear it; but I'll not quit the regiment yet, Colonel."' Biting his lip, the officer reluctantly ordered the punishment to begin, but after fifty-five lashes could stand it no more, and after a word with the surgeon had the prisoner released on the pretext that his life was in danger. He told the prisoner that he was a good man despite his transgression and would remain in line for promotion, whereupon the soldier burst into tears. 'The lash could not force one from his burning eyelid; the word of kindness – the breath of tender feeling from his respected Colonel, dissolved the stern soldier to the grateful and contrite penitent.'[10] It was, observed the author, worthy of being remembered by every commanding officer: that improvement might be achieved more effectively by humanity than by the lash.

Sir Robert Wilson, an experienced if somewhat mercurial officer, stated the same thing in the House of Commons: 'He never knew an instance where a man was severely punished by flogging, who did not by that means become a bad man . . . a system of encouragement, and stimulating men by impressing notions of self-respect, would . . . go farther to produce subordination and good discipline than any system of severe corporal punishment.'[11]

Wilson was not alone in Parliament in expressing disquiet at the system of enforcing discipline; another Member stated in 1815 that 'There was no man at Charing-cross who would dare to treat an animal as we treated those unfortunate persons who had braved death in the face of battle.'[12] On 18 June 1811 – somewhat ironically four years to the day prior to the Battle of

Waterloo – Sir Francis Burdett, perhaps the most famous dissident Member of Parliament, spoke at length on the subject in the House of Commons, emphasizing the nature of the instrument of punishment, that 'severe instrument of torture the cat-o'nine-tails. Every lash inflicted by it was, more properly speaking, nine lashes. These were pieces of whipcord, not such as Gentlemen used to their horse-whips, but each of them as thick as a quill, and knotted.' He quoted some dreadful cases, including that of a young soldier unjustly flogged for malingering about whom, when his innocence was proven, an officer remarked: 'Well! what signifies a hundred lashes to a man of his description?'[13]; and of two soldiers at Gibraltar who each cut off a hand to escape the service, and who were punished for it.

Similar desperation was experienced by some of those sentenced to a flogging; John Lloyd of the North Gloucestershire Militia was sentenced to 700 lashes for being absent without leave for five months, but cut his throat with a razor in front of his assembled regiment. In 1795 a member of the 107th at Cirencester tried to dull the agony by taking a mixture of laudanum, gin and gunpowder before the punishment, but took too large a dose and it killed him. A member of the 5th Foot had a convulsive seizure whenever he was about to be flogged for theft; suspecting fraud, a military surgeon threatened to have him 'burned to the bone' with red-hot irons if he had another fit, and remarked subsequently that even if genuine, the fits had been cured by the threat of an even more dreadful ordeal.

If the flogging were not bad enough, a punished man had a shilling (in some regiments sixpence) deducted from his pay to cover the expense of the 'cat'.

One soldier complained that floggings were carried out 'under the eyes of people professing Christianity and civilization; who were yearly inundating Parliament with petitions against flogging negroes with a cart-whip . . . while the blood of their countrymen was sprinkling a barrack-square, and their cries were ringing in their ears!'[14]; but actually objections to corporal punishment were not limited to Parliament. William Cobbett, himself an ex-NCO, commented on the fact that there was no flogging in Napoleon's army: 'Buonaparte's soldiers have never yet with tingling ears listened to the piercing screams of a human creature so tortured: they have never seen the blood oozing from his rent flesh . . . . In short, Buonaparte's soldiers cannot form any notion of that most heartrending of all exhibitions on this side of hell, an English Military Flogging.'[15] (For his protests, Cobbett himself suffered: in 1810 he was fined and sentenced to two years' imprisonment for seditious libel after publishing criticism of the flogging of members of the Cambridgeshire Local Militia who 'mutinied' in protest against having pay stopped to pay for their knapsacks.) Evidence of more widespread public revulsion would seem to be indicated by an incident at Chesterfield in July 1805, when a drummer of the 2/59th was ordered to be flogged for striking a sergeant. Such was the anger of the local people at a public flogging that a mob virtually besieged the officers in their lodging, booing, hissing and pelting the soldiers with missiles. The regiment had to assemble under arms at the request of the magistrates before the unrest was suppressed.

Curiously, a number of soldiers who had witnessed or even suffered floggings were convinced of its necessity. John Cooper of the 7th wrote that 'It has frequently been stated that the Duke of Wellington was severe. In answer to this I would say, he could not be otherwise. His army was composed of the lowest orders. Many, if not most of them, were ignorant, idle, and drunken . . . . By the discipline [Wellington] enforced, the British army became more than a match, even at great odds, for the best of Napoleon's boasted legions.'[16] Benjamin Harris stated that he hated the sight of the lash, but was convinced the army could not do without it, while William Lawrence left a rare account of the experience of being flogged.

Sentenced to 400 lashes for being absent without leave for twenty-four hours, his first offence, Lawrence 'felt ten times worse on hearing this sentence than I ever did on entering any battle-field; in fact, if I had been sentenced to be shot, I could not have been more in despair, for my life at that time seemed of very little consequence to me.' He was 'lashed to the halberds, and the colonel gave the order for the drummers to commence, each one having to give me twenty-five lashes in turn. I bore it very well until I had received a hundred and seventy-five, when I became so enraged with the pain that I pushed the halberds, which did not stand at all firm, on account of their being planted on stones, right across the square, amid the laughter of the regiment. The colonel, I suppose, thinking then that I had had sufficient, ordered, in the very words, "take the sulky rascal down," and perhaps a more true word could not have been spoken, as indeed I was sulky, for I did not give vent to a single sound the whole time, though the blood ran down my trousers from top to bottom.'

Lawrence added, 'Perhaps it was good a thing for me as could then have occurred, as it prevented me from committing any greater crimes which might have gained me other severer punishments and at last brought me to my ruin; but for all that it was a great trial for me, and I think that a good deal of that kind of punishment might have been abandoned with great credit to those who ruled our army.'[17] This opinion was echoed by an officer who had risen from the ranks, Captain T. Moyle of the 67th: 'I was never worth a damn till I got 300 lashes!'[18]

Some could have argued against Cobbett's comments on the absence of flogging in Napoleon's army by stating that they made much greater use of executions, which were rare in British service. Relatively few crimes could not be dealt with at regimental level but instead warranted a general court martial, and capital convictions were even rarer. Indeed, it was stated that during the whole of the Peninsular War there were only about 500 courts martial above the level of the regiment.

Examples of serious crime can be shown in sentences passed in the Peninsula in 1809. Death could be imposed for desertion and murder; this sentence was passed on Doderick Gerlock of the 5/60th for deserting and entering French service ('to be hanged or shot to death'[19]) and on the deserters Privates John Campbell and George Lee of the 2/24th and Thomas Jones of the 3rd (shot), while Francis Johnstone of the 88th was sentenced to be hanged. Other deserters were sentenced to be flogged, but both William Harnyman and Frederick Knaupft, awarded 800 lashes, were pardoned by Wellington on account of previous good conduct. Private John Dely of the 87th was sentenced to be hanged for the murder of Private Owen Lahy of the same regiment; Private Patrick Mater of the 97th got 800 for stealing a bundle of cartridges, nine men of various regiments were sentenced to 500 lashes for stealing shoes from a convoy they were escorting (two pardoned for previous good conduct), and three men of the 53rd received either 500 or 700 lashes for plundering beehives. Private John Biggs of the 40th got 1,000 for striking Ensign Pepper of the 87th. Private Charles Rankin of the 23rd Light Dragoons was clearly a practised thief who stole silver items from Marshal Beresford, no doubt using his position as servant to Beresford's ADC William Warre, a noted Peninsular memorialist. In his possession Rankin had a valuable snuff box and other trinkets, and £49 2s 8½d; Warre was asked to try to trace the owners of the items, and the money was donated to the fund for widows and orphans of soldiers, as it was impossible to determine where Rankin had obtained it. He had no further need of it: he was sentenced to be hanged.

As in some of the cases quoted above, even sentences passed by a general court martial were not necessarily approved. This was also demonstrated in a case of August 1809, when Private John Henry of the 28th was arraigned for the murder of a Portuguese civilian who had objected to having two mules impressed for military service. He was found not guilty by virtue of acting under orders from Sergeants John Dale and William Wright of the same regiment, who had ordered him to shoot. They were convicted of 'unsoldierlike conduct' for attempting to seize the mules illegally and for giving Henry the order, and were sentenced to be reduced to the ranks and to receive 800 lashes; but Wellington quashed the sentence and ordered them to return to duty as sergeants when the full facts were revealed, which involved an urgent need to find means for transporting the sick.

Given that in civil law the death penalty was possible for any theft of more than forty shillings' value (even if such sentences were often commuted), capital punishment in the army was rare. Excluding any summary justice on those caught in the act by a provost marshal, in the entire Peninsular War apparently only some seventy-eight men were shot (almost all for deserting to the enemy) and about forty hanged, generally for murder, the most serious thefts, the maltreatment of civilians, and apparently one for sodomy.

Like floggings, military executions were turned into an awesome spectacle as a warning to the watching troops. A noted case occurred in 1795 after members of the Oxfordshire Militia were implicated in a two-day riot at Seaford and Newhaven, which began as a protest against high food prices. The ringleaders were court martialled, six sentenced to be flogged and Edward Cook, John Haddock and Henry Parish received the death sentence. One capital conviction was commuted to ten years in New South Wales, but the other punishments were carried out at Brighton on 14 June in the presence of the regiment, cavalry and artillery (with guns loaded to discourage further trouble). The ceremony was fairly standard for such occasions: 'all the troops . . . were drawn up in two lines, and after three out of the six who had been sentenced to be flogged received their punishment in a very exemplary manner, the three others were pardoned. The men capitally convicted were then marched up between the two lines of the army, accompanied by a clergyman, they were shot by a party of the Oxfordshire Militia, who had been very active in the late riots, but had been pardoned . . . . One of them knelt down upon one coffin, and one upon the other, and they both instantly fell dead; though, lest there might be any remains of life, a firelock was let off close to the head of each immediately after . . . . The men appeared very composed and resigned, and the party who shot them were very much affected after. Indeed, several of the men seemed greatly agitated and concerned. The awful ceremony concluded by the marching of all the regiments round the bodies of the unhappy soldiers as they lay on the ground.'[20] As a final lesson on the perils of misbehaviour, an account of the court martial was read on parade to every regiment in Britain.

Benjamin Harris, when a member of the 66th, formed part of a firing squad for a private of the 70th who, it was said, had deserted sixteen times. Harris dreaded the duty, 'and when I looked into the faces of my companions, I saw, by the pallor and anxiety depicted in each countenance, the reflection of my own feelings.' The culprit was blindfolded and made to kneel before a coffin, and the drum major in charge of the execution 'gave the signal, previously agreed on (a flourish of his cane), and we levelled and fired . . . the poor fellow, pierced by several balls, fell heavily upon his back; and as he lay, with his arms pionioned to his sides, I observed that his hands waved for a few moments, like the fins of a fish in the agonies of death. The Drum Major also observed the movement, and making another signal, four of our party immediately stept [sic] up to the prostrate body, and placing the muzzles of their pieces to his head, fired, and put him out of his misery. The different regiments then fell back by companies, and the word being given to march past in slow time, when each company came in line with the body, the word was given to "mark time", and then "eyes left", in order that we might all observe the terrible example.'[21]

On campaign the task of policing the army was allocated to provost marshals, NCOs appointed on a temporary basis and who wielded enormous power. The regulations stated that the provost marshal and his deputy were to make frequent tours of any camp to arrest any disorderly person, to patrol nearby villages and seize anyone there without a pass and apprehend plunderers. The provost marshal had the authority to execute any prescribed punishment on the spot, without recourse to higher authority, if a perpetrator were caught in the act, even execution: 'If any Soldier is base enough to attempt to desert to the Enemy, on being apprehended he will suffer immediate Death'[22]; and all punishments were also applicable to camp followers.

Such was the importance of the provost marshal that appointments were announced in General Orders, like those in June 1809 in the Peninsular army, of Webster Boyle of the 7th Fuzileers and the wonderfully-named Xenophon Mosscroft of the 48th. Not unnaturally, they were highly unpopular; Thomas Morris remarked that they were regarded by the army in the same way as the hangman Jack Ketch.

Joseph Donaldson recalled how in the Pyrenees a soldier from his division was hanged for stealing from an officer's portmanteau, and another shot for pointing an unloaded musket at a sergeant of the Cavalry Staff Corps, a unit whose duties included assisting the provost marshal. 'Every one thought he would be pardoned, or at least his sentence commuted, as it was said there was some unnecessary provocation given by the sergeant; but mercy was not extended to him. We were often inclined to think that the provost marshals were possessed of more power than they ought to have had, particularly as they were generally men of a description who abused it, and were guided more by caprice and personal pique than any regard to justice. In fact, they seemed to be above all control, doing what they pleased, without being brought to any account, and were often greater robbers than the men they punished.'[23]

Such was the dislike of provost marshals that when they returned to ordinary duty they usually transferred to another regiment, where their previous provost duties might not be known.

Desertion remained a constant problem. Its scale was considerable: there were some 53,759 instances in the period between 1803 and 1812 inclusive,[24] the highest number being 7,081 in 1805. These statistics should be considered in terms of the size of the army during these years: for the second half of 1805, for example, for troops in Britain and Ireland, there was one desertion for every 157 men, whereas for 1806-07 there was one in 263, the fall partly explained, it was believed, by the introduction of 'limited service' enlistment. Most desertions occurred when the men were under the supervision of recruiting districts rather than when they had been inducted into their regiments.

A small number of deserters were professional fraudsters, who enlisted simply to get the bounty money and then absconded. It was sufficiently common for there to be a slang expression for the fraud, 'pear-making', but few can have been as adept as Thomas Hodgson, alias 'Tom the Devil', who was executed for robbery in 1787 at age twenty-six, who admitted enlisting under various names some forty-nine times and always deserting after a few days, in the process raking in the sum of 397 guineas.

In many cases desertion seems to have been caused simply by a dissatisfaction with the military life, or even on a whim, so the crime was treated sympathetically by understanding officers. The efficacy of alternatives to corporal punishment was shown by a story recounted by Thomas Morris, concerning a soldier apprehended after having deserted. 'The colonel sent for him to his own room, spoke kindly to him, pointed out the consequences of his conduct, and promised to relieve him of his confinement, if he would solemnly promise to behave well for the future. The stubborn will of the man was subdued by kindness. He would have taken his punishment without flinching; but he now cried like a child; he knelt before his officer, and swore atonement: and he kept his oath inviolate.' He rose to the rank of sergeant major but, said Morris, 'one touch of the "cat" would have made him a vagabond.'[25]

A similar story was told of Thomas Garner, a native of Leek, a reliable NCO until a bout of carousing led to his being absent without leave. Fearing humiliation he deserted and returned to his old trade of silk weaving, but after encountering one of his old officers in the street he feared arrest, so escaped and re-enlisted in another regiment. His conscience was so troubled that he wrote to the Duke of York, explaining his actions, and when the Duke next reviewed his regiment fell on his knees to beg forgiveness. Characteristically, the Duke pardoned him and he served out his enlistment before returning to his weaving.

There was a reward payable for the apprehension of a deserter, rising from

£1 to £3 in July 1812, but as mentioned before, there was generally public sympathy for deserters. The consequences of desertion, however, could be immediate and fatal. For example, in May 1800 William Jackson, a deserter from the Cornish Fencibles, was being escorted under arrest by a party of Foot Guards at Covent Garden when he slipped his handcuffs; he had run no more than 6 yards when one of the guardsmen, Charles Bexton, shot him dead on the spot through the back of the neck. This was no isolated example, and indeed some deserters on the loose were a menace to society, like Samuel Leeson, who in 1809 was arrested for attempted murder and for threatening and robbing an old, infirm but apparently wealthy farmer at Wheddon, Buckinghamshire, in the course of which crime Leeson had helped himself to three quarts of strong ale, fired a pistol up the chimney, and 'attempted the chastity'[26] of the farmer's maidservant. It was revealed in court that his real name was Walker and that he was a deserter from the 14th Foot.

Some desertions occurred on active service, though opportunities to live outside the military environment were more restricted. Desertion to the enemy, however, was a very different matter and usually regarded with revulsion by the soldiers, and often attracting the severest punishment. When Ciudad Rodrigo was captured in 1812 some twenty British deserters were found there, and Lieutenant Robert Knowles of the 7th Fuzileers reported how the whole of his division was assembled 'to see the sentence of a General Court Martial put in force on two deserters, who were taken in Ciudad Rodrigo. They were sentenced to be shot; it was the most awful sight I ever beheld.'[27] Indeed, an obvious turncoat would be lucky to be taken prisoner, but instead receive summary justice at the hands of his ex-comrades if they realized that he had gone over to the enemy.

There were other modes of punishment as well as execution and the lash, but they were not common. The Mutiny Act of 1811 suggested that court martials might imprison malefactors instead of flogging them, and although the ability to imprison had always existed – usually in a cell known colloquially as a 'black hole', but this was the first official exhortation for an alternative to corporal punishment. In the 1st Foot Guards, for example, the first instances of confinement occured when the regiment was in Sicily in 1807, but the first example at home was at Knightsbridge Barracks in December 1814. When he gave evidence before a Royal Commission on Military Punishments in 1836, Wellington dismissed the concept of imprisonment as a replacement for flogging, stating that it would be impossible on campaign and unfair on others: of a hundred men in a company, he stated, 'there will be eighty of them who never incur a fault of any description . . . but there are twenty . . . constantly disturbing the peace and the comfort of the eighty.'

Were they imprisoned, 'those eighty are obliged to do their duty for them; so that . . . you are doing the greatest injustice to those who do obey your orders.'[28]

Other punishments were less authorised. One officer recalled how in Spain an artillery officer he knew would punish a miscreant by tying him to a gun wheel for some hours, and how the sergeant major of the 4th Foot would carry a couple of canes to chastise any offender on the spot; but unlike the practice of some European armies, there was little physical violence against recalcitrant other ranks. (One officer was dismissed for unauthorised use of the lash – Major Richard Archdall of the 40th, in the Peninsula in 1813 – and a salutory lesson must have been learned from the execution in January 1802 of Joseph Wall, governor of Goree, after a trial at the Old Bailey, for having a sergeant flogged until he died.)

A more inventive punishment was the temporary attachment of a ball-and-chain to a malefactor's ankle. When this had no effect upon Tom Crawley of the 95th, his humane commanding officer, Sidney Beckwith, made him wear instead a smock with a green cross painted back and front. Instead of this acting as a mark of shame, Crawley elicited sympathy from local civilians by claiming it was the new regulation to identify Roman Catholics within the army!

Minor punishments could be inflicted by a miscreant's comrades, including 'cobbing' (beating the man on the backside with a stick or cross-belt), and 'booting', a cavalry practice in which the soles of the feet were hit with a belt. Even slighter punishments included 'cold burning' or 'bottling', in which cold water was poured into an upheld sleeve. Such forms of 'soldiers' justice' could have consequences for officers who permitted them: in 1828 a dragoon was punished at Sheffield by his comrades after being suspected of stealing a watch, and sued his officers for not protecting him. He won £500 damages, and Wellington reprimanded the officers for neglect of their duty of care.

At home, soldiers were also subject the the ordinary civil law, as one J. Greenhough, a guardsman, discovered in November 1806. For 'attempts to commit unnatural offences', in November 1806 he was made to stand in the pillory at Charing Cross, to be pelted with mud and eggs by women 'highly exasperated at the enormity of the offence.' After the pelting he and another man were sent to serve twelve months' imprisonment at Tothill Fields Bridewell.[29]

The most serious military crime was mutiny, but this was a rare occurrence, generally motivated less from inherent malevolence than from anger at a perceived injustice. Perhaps the best-known incident was the mutiny of the Strathspey Fencibles in 1794 over fears that they were to be forced to serve outside their terms of enlistment, and a worse case in the following year at Dumfries when a gang of soldiers attempted to rescue one of their comrades who was under guard for insubordination. Three officers were jostled and though the trouble died down quickly, five men were court martialled, four capitally convicted and two actually shot. Other disturbances in the same unfortunate year involved the Londonderry Regiment at Exeter, its men unhappy at being drafted into the 43rd, unrest only quelled by the arrival of a troop of the 25th Light Dragoons. Another fairly serious incident occurred at Gibraltar over Christmas 1802, caused by strictures imposed by the Duke of Kent, a martinet of the worst kind who as governor punished men for the most trivial reasons. On Christmas Eve the 2/1st Royals (of which Kent was himself colonel) broke out in mutiny, intent on murdering him, and, though that was suppressed, two days later the 25th Foot erupted in rebellion. Benjamin Miller of the Royal Artillery, ordered to point his cannon towards the mutineers, admitted that he was more afraid of them than when fighting the French, it being infinitely 'more dangerous to fight against exasperated British soldiers standing out for their rights.'[30] When the trouble was quelled, three men were shot and eleven transported.

Transportation to inhospitable colonies was used to dispose of civilian criminals, and a military version also existed, in sending rogues to serve in penal corps in disease-ridden climates. Civilians could also be sent there, as reported in 1795: 'Yesterday 44 prisoners under sentence of transportation at Newgate, who received His Majesty's pardon on condition of their inlisting [sic] in the 60th regiment of foot in the West Indies, were removed to Southampton, in order for their embarkation.'[31] David Stewart of Garth, an experienced officer, commented on the different mode of discipline required by the two types of men he had commanded: honest, steady Highlanders and the complete contrast in the criminals who comprised the Royal West India Rangers, 'men of reprobate habits . . . whom it was impossible to reclaim . . . men debased and devoid of principle,'[32] but who could nevertheless be made into effective soldiers. Such men were intended to remain abroad even if their original regiment returned home, but in 1803 it was decreed that after seven years' satisfactory service they too could be allowed home.

7

'At the Head of His Company':
Promotion, NCOs and Officers

At the head of his company he boldly does stand,
In defence of the King and the laws of the land

A New Song in praise of the Warrington
Volunteers, by 'J.B.', c.1803

No part of a regiment was more valuable than its noncommissioned officers, the connector between the officers and 'other ranks'. Their importance can hardly be overstated; as Rees Gronow remarked when he joined the 1st Foot Guards in 1813, officers like him had received so little education that only the excellence of the NCOs prevented them from meeting disaster when they encountered the enemy.

These were the very men who received some lukewarm praise from Wellington, who observed that NCOs of the Guards 'regularly get drunk once a day – by eight in the evening – and go to bed soon after, but then they always take care to do first whatever they were bid.'[1]

John Williamson, author of *The Elements of Military Arrangement* (1791) described the sergeants as 'the nerves and sinew of the corps' who, with the corporals, were responsible for 'the discipline of the company, and consequently that of the corps . . . . For it is more immediately their business, than that of the commission-officers, to instruct and form the soldiers; and from their continual intercourse with them they have it in their power to attend to matters which cannot so well come under the notice of the others'; although, to preserve discipline, he exhorted the sergeants not to mix off duty with lower ranks. Sergeants, he stated, should be literate and numerate, with 'some knowledge of mankind', and should be able not only to command but to obey, with 'that respectful and submissive deference to his superior officers, let their characters be what they may, which it requires length of time for an

96

The soldier: Sergeant Hooper of the Royal South Gloucestershire Militia demonstrating the drill position 'charge bayonets'. The fur cap was a distinctive feature of grenadiers, and the shoulder wings of both flank companies.

Englishman to attain in perfection.'[2] In camp, he explained, sergeants had a tent to themselves, but lived with the lower ranks in barracks, where they kept discipline, cleanliness and smartness. When drilling, the sergeant acted as instructor; in the field, he kept a close watch on his particular men. Williamson stated that there should be one sergeant to every twelve or eighteen other ranks, a ratio that seems to have been common: on the day of Waterloo, for example, in the infantry there was on average one sergeant to every fifteen and a half rank and file.

Corporals, thought Williamson, should be young men, for if older and more experienced soldiers were promoted, they might be unfit for active service by the time they became candidates for sergeant's rank. Corporals, he explained, were there to superintend the conduct of their particular section, to instruct the young soldiers how to clean their accoutrements and musket, to allocate men for duty and to post and relieve sentries; but when in the ranks to give no orders but to obey their superiors just like the privates.

An experienced officer (Lieutenant Colonel Wilkie) implied that bravery was not necessarily the best criterion for promotion to NCO, given that 'many of our soldiers, who are the most troublesome to manage in "peaceable times", are the most forward dashing fellows in contact with the enemy . . . . It is of no use to make a pickle a non-commissioned officer . . . .'[3] Indeed, the appointment to sergeant was generally the highest aspiration of the ordinary soldier, and given the low educational standard of most recruits, a smart man who could read and who kept away from trouble might receive fairly rapid promotion. Wellington, however, sounded a note of caution about NCOs: 'notwithstanding the encouragement which I have given to this class, they are still as little to be depended upon as the private soldiers themselves; and they are just as ready to commit irregularities and outrages,'[4] a comment that would seem to be unduly harsh. Wellington believed that the difference in pay between NCOs and privates was insufficient as an incentive for self-improvement, and certainly there were innumerable cases of NCOs being 'broken' (reduced to the ranks) more than once, for disciplinary reasons. For example, during the pernicious reign of George Quentin as colonel of the 10th Hussars, referred to before, a sixth of the men punished were NCOs, usually for crimes involving drink, but a good man who was broken was not infrequently promoted again fairly rapidly, like Quentin's sergeant, William Hodges, punished for having a disorderly woman in barracks. Eighteen months later he was fighting at Waterloo, a sergeant again.

The importance of the NCOs in a leadership role was demonstrated in extreme circumstances. With most infantry companies having no more than about three officers, casualties in a hot action might leave it under the command of a sergeant, or even under one of lower rank: at Albuera, for example, Corporal Thomas Robinson of the 23rd was commanding his company at the end. Even the lowest ranks could provide leadership, as recounted in a story concerning the assault on Bunker's Hill in the American War, when all the officers and NCOs were disabled. Someone said, 'Fall back, there is no one to command'; whereupon an old private stepped forward and declared, 'Never retreat, boys, for want of a leader, while I have a musket to point the way to go.'[5]

Other appointments included the sergeant major, the most senior NCO who acted as a conduit between the sergeants and the adjutant, and who was expected to have so intimate a knowledge of administrative affairs that he could perform the duties of adjutant and quartermaster. The quartermaster sergeant, said Williamson, 'should have a perfect knowledge of accounts, and should be endowed with activity, exertion, and an indefatigable attention to business . . . a man of sobriety and integrity, one in whom confidence can be reposed.'[6] In some regiments the drum major ranked as a sergeant; his duties included instruction of the drummers and supervision of corporal punishment. The pay he received to reflect his responsibilities varied, Williamson noting that it was common for the drum major to receive six guineas per annum from the regimental band fund, to which the colonel and officers subscribed, and he also acted as the regimental postmaster, receiving a penny for every letter he delivered.

In July 1813 the rank of colour sergeant was instituted, as a reward of merit for one sergeant per company; it was distinguished by an elaborate badge on the right sleeve. This rank did not necessarily imply service in the battalion's colour escort, though this was a duty undertaken by sergeants. The battalion colours comprised a regimental colour of the regimental facing-colour, with a small Union flag in the upper canton nearest the pole, and the King's Colour, a large Union, both emblazoned with regimental devices; they were the symbols of the regiment's very being, its connection with the monarch in whose name they fought. Used as a rallying point in the confusion of battle, their preservation from the hands of the enemy was paramount, and countless heroic deeds were performed in their defence. For all the honour attached to their protection, it was not a task universally relished, for a colour party was inevitably among the centres of the enemy's attention. William Lawrence of the 40th recalled how at Waterloo, in mid-afternoon 'I was ordered to the colours. This, although I was as used to warfare as any, was a job I did not like at all . . . there had been before me that day fourteen sergeants already killed and wounded while in charge of those colours, with officers in proportion, and the staff and colours were almost cut to pieces.'[7] He had a right to be apprehensive; just after his arrival at the colours a roundshot decapitated Captain William Fisher, standing next to him, and struck down more than twenty-five other men.

Similar dangers were demonstrated with the 61st at Salamanca, in an incident that exemplified the esprit de corps of the ordinary rank and file. So heavy were the casualties that no officers or NCOs were left to carry the colours, so they were picked up by Privates William Crauford and Nicholas Coulson, who bore them to the end of the action. Crauford was immediately promoted to sergeant, but Coulson declined promotion, saying that his comrades' thanks and cheers were reward enough.

A coveted position: an officer's servant. In this campaign scene the soldier-servant has temporarily laid aside his musket to prepare his master's – and his own – breakfast. (Print after Thomas Rowlandson)

Although not holding rank, another prized appointment was that of officer's servant. One 'other rank' was assigned to each officer to look after his kit and prepare his meals, a position that generally excused the soldier from attending drill and paid an extra shilling per week. Considerable latitude had been allowed to such 'soldier-servants', but regulations were tightened so that they could only be drawn from an officer's own company and that they were fully trained: 'No Soldier is to be employed as an Officer's Servant, who is not perfect in the Drill, and who has not acquired a complete knowledge of his Duty as a Soldier . . . . They are to mount Guard with the Officers they are allowed . . . . They are to fall in with their respective Companies at all Reviews, Field Days, Inspections, and Marches.'[8] Although serving in the role of valet-cum-butler, most were still essentially soldiers, like Patrick Kelly, servant to Surgeon Walter Henry of the 66th, 'five feet nothing in his stockings, full of good humour and good nature,' but still formidable, 'a very valiant little chap, and a good shot, and had brought down many a bigger man in the Peninsula.'[9] David Roberts of the 51st described in verse the ideal attributes:

'A D----'d good Fellow, but I rather think,
He now, and then, will take a drop of drink;
But otherwise, good-humour'd, sharp, and civil,
John Bull with drink, but fight like any Devil.'[10]

William Grattan of the 88th wrote warmly of his servant, Dan Carsons, who was accompanied in the Peninsula by his formidable wife, Nelly. When Grattan was shot at Badajoz in 1812 he was helped back to camp by two of his men, one being wounded as he tried to shield his officer from enemy fire. They took Grattan to his tent, to find his straw matress occupied by Nelly, too drunk to be roused; so they laid him alongside her so she could keep him 'nate and warm'. Subsequently Dan appeared with a huge pigskin of wine to act as a pillow, placing the spigot so that Grattan could suck a drink whenever he wished, while Nelly prepared tea and hot chocolate as a restorative. They superintended Grattan's recovery, even to the extent of intimidating the doctor into doing his utmost.

The extraordinary loyalty that could exist on the part of an officer's servant was described by one officer who took his leave when going on half pay. The servant, Thomas Douglass, and his wife were in tears at the parting, and ventured to say that the officer would find things financially difficult when living on half pay. Fumbling in his pocket, Douglass pulled out their life savings, fifteen pounds, 'which we don't want at this present,' and asked the officer to 'take charge of 'em for us.' Immensely touched, the officer assured them that he would have enough money to live, but 'I was sorry to see how much pain my refusal to profit by this offer gave these worthy souls.' Douglass, worried about who would polish the officer's boots in future, proposed to apply for regular leave so that he could travel to London, and ' "Ye'll let me clean yer boots, any way, sir?" bawled Douglass, as I hurried out of the the the barracks.'[11]

Although the rank and file might express dislike or even hatred towards an officer who was adjudged unduly harsh or too great a martinet, the fires of battle could forge a bond of cameraderie between the ranks that transcended the usual separation of the social classes. Relations could be much freer than would become possible at a later date, while always maintaining a respectful attitude towards an officer. Perhaps a vestige of the old feudal system, in which the ordinary soldiers followed their overlord into battle, there was an undoubted attitude among the rank and file that they expected their leaders to be above them in the social heirarchy. Benjamin Harris remarked that the ordinary soldier responded best to an officer who had 'authority in his face', was proud of officers who were brave and considerate, and added that an act of kindness was often the cause of an officer's life being saved on the battle-field. One officer recalled his sergeant lamenting his departure: 'I said, "You have got a smart officer, Mr B------, to look after you all." "Yes, Sir," he replied, "but he is not a gentleman."'[12] This attitude also seems to have worked in the reverse, perhaps exemplified by the case of Lieutenant General

John Whitelock, who was dismissed for his catastophic mishandling of the expedition to South America, who was described as having the 'military knowledge of a drill-sergeant, the manners of a turnkey, and the language of the stews.'[13] He attempted to ingratiate himself with the rank and file by deliberate use of coarse language, but apparently this only led to them despising him for not acting like a gentleman.

Extraordinary loyalty and devotion was often displayed towards an officer. Deep affection for a commanding officer was exemplified by the case of Charles Donellan of the 48th, an eccentric who dressed in an archaic manner including powdered hair long after it had been abandoned by others. When Wellington inspected the army before Talavera, Donellan rode with him, and the ceremony was interrupted by noise and movement from the 2/48th, who called out, 'There goes Old Charley . . . God bless the old boy.' Wellington's annoyance evaporated when he learned the reason for the commotion, and Donellan himself, to the delight of the regiment, 'uncovered, and shook the powder from his cocked hat in waving a cordial salute to his worthy soldiers.' In the ensuing battle Donellan was mortally wounded; beckoning his second-in-command, he 'took off his hat and resigned the command just as if he had been on the parade of a barrack-yard. His enraged men went on like lions, taking ample revenge upon their enemies – and that too with the cold iron.'[14] Perhaps the fact that Donellan ran his regiment without resorting to flogging helped increase their devotion.

A similar attitude was displayed by the 42nd towards their commanding officer, Sir Robert Macara, who at Quatre Bras was being carried to the rear, gravely wounded, when he was callously murdered by French cavalry. In return, it was reported, when French troops called for quarter they were answered by the 42nd 'by the appalling cry of "no quarter!" [and] "where's Macara?" . . . until it was necessary for our officers, from a sense of humanity, to intervene in favour of the French, and they did all that was possible to restrain the fury of their men, often at the imminent peril of their own lives. An officer of the Highlanders . . . in relating to me these particulars, declared that he never saw our men so savage, and that for awhile it was impossible by any means to curb their fury.'[15]

Some recorded examples of devotion to an officer are quite remarkable, like that concerning Sergeant Robert McQuade, an Ulsterman in the 43rd, during that regiment's attack at the Coa in 1810. Heading for a gap in a bank behind his 19-year-old lieutenant, McQuade saw two French soldiers with loaded muskets covering the gap; he pulled back the officer, calmly saying that he was too young to be killed, charged on alone and was fatally shot by both Frenchmen. This act of self-sacrifice, which in later ages would surely have merited a major decoration for gallantry, saved the life of the young officer, who was to become General Sir George Brown, one of the most important generals of the Victorian era, and who led the Light Division in the Crimea.

This was no isolated incident, for such conduct was evidently not uncommon. When the 92nd was under heavy fire at Maya, Sergeant William Cattanach, whose position was behind his officer, tapped him on the shoulder. When the officer turned Cattanach said, 'Oh, sir, this is terrible work, let me change places with you for a few minutes.'[16] The officer thanked him but declined his offer of protection, and when he tried again a few moments later was told not to mention it again. Looking disappointed, Cattanach returned to his post, but was killed shortly after.

Another example of risking life to save his officer concerned Charles Filer of the 40th. When Lieutenant John Ayling was incapacitated by a ball in the thigh at the storm of Badajoz, at his pleading Filer hoisted him onto his shoulders and struggled with his burden for more than half a mile, under constant exposure to enemy fire. Unfortunately, during his ordeal a cannon ball had struck off Ayling's head, unbeknown to the exhausted Filer, who remarked to the doctor to whom he carried the lieutenant that he still had his head on when he hoisted him up! With typical black humour, Filer was subsequently teased by his comrades with calls of 'Who carried a headless man to the doctor?'[17]

George Napier of the 52nd wrote movingly of a visit he received from an Irish drunkard in his company, John Dunn, after Napier had been severely wounded by a ball that had shattered his wrist. Dunn had walked 7 miles to find his officer to see how he was: 'Didn't I see you knocked over by the bloody Frenchman's shot? . . . . I pursued the inimy as long as I was able, and sure I couldn't do more; and now I'm come to see your honour, long life to you.' Napier saw that Dunn also was wounded, but didn't realise the extent of it – perhaps Dunn had his greatcoat over his shoulder – 'Why sure it's nothing, only me *arrum* was cut off a few hours ago below the elbow joint, and I couldn't come till the anguish was over a bit, for it's mighty cruel work; by Jasus, I'd rather be shot twenty times.' Napier then asked for news of Dunn's brother, another member of his company; Dunn hesitated, sobbed and said, 'I seed him shot through the heart alongside wid me just as I got shot myself, and he looked up piteously in my face and said, "Oh, John dear, my poor mother!" And sure I couldn't look at him again for the life of me, my heart was broke, and I came away to the rare. But, captain, he died like a soldier, as your honour would wish him to die, and sure that's enough. He had your favour whilst he lived, God be with him, he's gone now.'

Napier was so touched that he wrote: 'After this anecdote who will dare to say private soldiers have no feelings? By Heavens! it makes my anger rise and my blood boil to hear people talk of soldiers as if they were a different race of being from themselves. Here was a poor fellow, an Irishman and a Catholic, who, out of pure affection for his officer, having seen his brother killed by his side in action, and suffered the amputation of his own arm, walks near seven miles, without meat or drink, to see his captain, who he knew was severely wounded! Could a brother have done more?'[18] (After his discharge, Dunn received financial help from Napier, who believed it his 'bounden duty to see and relieve those who, although from circumstances in a lower grade than myself, fought as bravely and bled as freely as I ever did for that country which is the common parent of all Britons!')[19]

The concept of an officer having a faithful NCO, as notably portrayed in

The faithful NCO: Sergeant James Livsey of the Royal Horse Artillery in later life, wearing his Waterloo and Military General Service medals. It was this stalwart old soldier, rather than a fellow officer, who was entrusted with conveying the body of the famed Norman Ramsay from Waterloo to his ancestral home.

fiction, was no literary device. An example was provided by Sergeant Robert Fairfoot of the 95th, who had served alongside Lieutenant George Simmons through the long years of the Peninsular War, and even though himself severely wounded at Waterloo, supervised Simmons' evacuation from the field when the officer was grievously hit, having supported him during the operation to remove a musket ball. Simmons wrote that 'all the officers know how much Sergeant Fairfoot merits my praise. If I can do him a service he may always command me; his character as a brave soldier stands with the first in the regiment.'[20] When Fairfoot died as quartermaster in 1838 the regiment's officers erected a memorial tablet in Galway Cathedral in recognition of 'his good and gallant services'.

Another example of the mutual comradeship, transcending the barrier of class, is provided by the case of Captain Norman Ramsay, perhaps the most renowned officer of the Royal Horse Artillery of the period, celebrated for saving his guns at Fuentes de Onoro. An NCO who accompanied him in that action was James Livsey, a weaver from Bury who had enlisted at age fifteen, who served through the Peninsular War as a sergeant with Ramsay. After Ramsay was killed at Waterloo it was the faithful sergeant, not a fellow officer, who arranged for the body to be returned to Britain. Seamen were too superstitious to allow a corpse aboard ship, so Livsey had it packed into a box labelled soap, and managed to take it to Ramsay's family home at Inveresk. So obvious was the affection for his officer that Livsey named his son born in 1819 as Norman, and this name has been carried by each succeeding generation down to the present day.'[21]

Aside from promotion, there were few methods available to reward the rank and file for distinguished service. The only medals available were those awarded by regiments, though this was very much a minority practice. A noted example was an engraved silver medal awarded to Private John Skinner of the 1st Foot Guards for unspiking a cannon at Walcheren, under heavy fire, for which he was also promoted to sergeant. Financial rewards were few, but William Penteney of the 31st, who removed a smouldering match left in the magazine at St. Helier in 1804, received not only a silver medal but two pensions amounting to £32 per annum, and was authorised to wear a ring of silver lace on his sleeve, a singular distinction. A few regiments had good conduct medals, notably the 5th Foot, established in 1767, in three tiers, for seven, fourteen and twenty-one years' good conduct, which was said to stimulate good behaviour and to produce a body of NCOs among the best in any regiment. Allowed to lapse, probably in 1797, it was revived in 1805 and continued to be awarded even after the institution of the official army Long Service and Good Conduct Medal in 1830. It was emulated by other

A small number of soldiers received medals from their regiments for some outstanding deed, but few such awards were available more widely. The Order of Merit of the 5th Foot was one, which was instituted in 1767 but lapsed after about thirty years, to be revived in 1805. This later example was the un-named silver version awarded for fourteen years' service. The ribbon was in the distinctive regimental facing colour, gosling green.

regiments, such as the 88th's Order of Merit, established in 1818 with different grades according to the number of actions in which the recipient had been present, and those of the 42nd and 48th, both instituted in 1819.

Despite the social division between ranks, it was possible for a 'ranker' to be commissioned as an officer, and indeed the practice was much more common than is the usual perception of the officer class. The easiest route was for a capable sergeant to be appointed as adjutant or quartermaster, duties involving administrative functions that might not appeal to the conventional 'officer class'. In the period of the Peninsular War, no less than 803 NCOs were commissioned, of whom 392 were line officers (ensigns or cornets), 139 to serve as adjutant, and 271 quartermasters. Although many of these might not progress much further, at a dinner of the King in 1835 to officers of the Royal Horse Guards, Coldstream Guards and 8th Hussars, among the most socially exclusive regiments in the army, there were present eight officers who had risen from the ranks.

Arguably the most meritorious route to a commission was the performance of some great deed in action, as was the case of the 79th Highlanders at Fuentes de Onoro. Enraged by the mortal wounding of their commanding officer, Lieutenant Colonel Philips Cameron (which provoked a furious cry *'Thuit an Camshronach'*, 'Cameron has fallen') the regiment fought so fiercely that three days later Wellington ordered his military secretary to write to the

Hand-to-hand combat between infantry was rare, but it was in such an action at Barrosa that Sergeant Patrick Masterson of the 87th captured the 'Eagle' of the French 8me Ligne. He was rewarded with a commission in the 87th, which was authorised in April 1811 to use the French Eagle as a regimental badge, which it retained until the end of its independent existence as the Royal Irish Fusiliers in 1968. (Print by Clark & Dubourg)

officer who had succeeded to command that he 'will have great pleasure in submitting to the Commander-in-Chief, for a commission, the name of any non-commissioned officer of the 79th Regiment whom you may recommend, as his lordship is anxious to mark his sense of the conduct of the 79th during the late engagement.'[22] The man chosen was the 25-year-old Sergeant Donald Macintosh from Inverness-shire; he was commissioned ensign in the 88th Foot and served throughout the war, being wounded by an exploding shell at Orthez. Put on half pay at its conclusion, he joined the 94th as lieutenant and adjutant in 1824. His case was not unusual for a promoted 'other rank': those without sufficient wealth to purchase a 'step' in rank might remain at the lowest level.

Similarly, a worthy NCO might be appointed to a commission in a regiment not popular with the conventional 'officer class', notably those stationed in unhealthy climates. This was the case of one of the most celebrated NCOs, William Newman of the 43rd, who rallied stragglers on the retreat to Corunna and beat off the French vanguard; his reward was an ensigncy in the 1st West India Regiment. Others, however, were commissioned into their original regiment, like Patrick Masterson of the 87th, who captured an 'Eagle' from the

French 8th *Ligne* at Barrosa. Another was John Winterbottom, a weaver from Saddleworth who joined the 52nd at age eighteen. He was clearly a remarkable individual; sergeant major from 1805, he was commissioned in the same regiment in 1808, serving as adjutant from 1810 in such a way that his commanding officer, Sir John Colborne, stated that incidents of his distinction were too many to record. He was never absent from his enlistment until his death from yellow fever in Barbados in 1838, save for the time recuperating from four wounds. He accepted the post of 52nd's paymaster in 1821, on account of seeing no prospect of promotion; but on his death 130 officers who had served with him subscribed for a monument in the parish church of his native town, recording 'his extraordinary talents as an officer, and his acknowledged worth as a man'. It still exists, and includes the symbols of commissioned rank, shako, sash, sword and belt, doubtless something that could never have been envisaged by the young weaver when he first enlisted to seek his fortune in the army.

The circumstances of another 'battlefield commission' involved a remarkable example of unwillingness to profit from the discomfiture of fellow soldiers. After the Battle of Albuera, commanding officers were requested to recommend a sergeant for promotion to ensign. The choice of the l/7th Royal Fuzileers fell upon Sergeant William Gough, who had recovered the regimental colour of the 3rd Foot, lost when Colborne's Brigade had been overrun, and the 7th also re-possessed some guns abandoned in the same incident. The battalion commander stated that it was the wish of the regiment that they should not profit from their heroism if the reporting of their deeds caused their fellow soldiers embarassment in having lost the guns and colour, and would 'willingly forgo any credit to be acquired at the expense of brave soldiers who discharged their duty to the utmost.'[23] Despite such noble sentiments Gough was commissioned in the 2nd West India Regiment and rose to the rank of lieutenant in August 1813.

Among the most distinguished of those elevated to an administrative position was Matthew Stevens of the 69th, appointed quartermaster of his regiment in December 1810. Serving aboard the fleet at the Battle of Cape St. Vincent, he was the man who had beaten in the stern gallery windows of the Spanish ship *San Nicolas* to permit Horatio Nelson to execute his famous boarding action. (Stevens demonstrated a remarkable sense of humour at Waterloo; when a man beside him was killed, he remarked, 'Aweel, it is time for a respectable non-combatant to gang awa'!')[24] He died, still the 69th's quartermaster, in India in 1821.

Reliable NCOs were also involved in administrative tasks, like Sergeant John Weir of the Scots Greys, a native of Mauchline, who was responsible for his troop's pay. It was said that he could have avoided action at Waterloo as part of the regiment's administrative staff, but he insisted on standing by his comrades, and was killed. When his body was found it was seen that he had written his name on his forehead with his own blood, it was supposed so that he could be identified with the dead and not suspected of having absconded with the money in his charge.

Perhaps the most unusual twist in examples of officers having risen from the ranks concerns Samuel South, who spent his career in the 20th Foot. From sergeant major he was commissioned, was a captain by 1805 and lieutenant colonel in 1818, and commanded the regiment when it first provided Napoleon's guard at St. Helena. For a private soldier to end his military career as an officer having authority over an emperor represented a remarkable journey.

Despite the experiences of those like Winterbottom, some commissioned 'rankers' must have encountered difficulties, even prejudice, from those officially their equals in terms of holding the King's commission, but originally of a higher standing in society. Wellington articulated a view that was probably widespread but inaccurate: that 'I have never known officers raised from the ranks to turn out well, nor the system answer; they cannot stand drink.'[25] Lieutenant Nathaniel Hood of the 40th, author of *Elements of War: or Rules and Regulations of the Army*, was even more extreme in stating that soldiers should never be commissioned, for 'Soldiers are but soldiers, and officers are soldiers and gentlemen. Under this consideration the line of distinction is preserved, the profession, through all its tracts of honour, guarded.' General Hon. Henry Murray, who led the 18th Hussars at Waterloo, stated that 'for officers raised by their merit from the ranks, I have always entertained respect and regard,' but regretted that promotion often caused them difficulties 'which in their previous more lowly and safe rank they might have escaped.' He believed that such promotions should be rare events, 'else it would virtually annul that principle which has hitherto so much conduced to exalt the character of British officers'; namely, 'he who holds His Majesty's commission shall not only discharge his duties as an officer, but observe the behaviour and conduct of a gentleman. To this a liberal education and some acquaintance with the habits of polished life are almost indispensible.'[26]

This was a common view: 'the condition of a British soldier whose education and views have been bounded by the plough-tail and the musket, is not improved by transferring him from the canteen to the mess-table . . . into a sphere where he becomes comparatively inefficient, if not worse, and wholly out of his element.'[27] Another writer drew a comparison between the officer class of the British and French armies; Waterloo, he wrote, 'was gained by an army officered by gentlemen over an army officered from the ranks, and was in that light almost the triumph of mind over matter . . . . Let us copy the French institutions when the French beat us.'[28]

A few accounts suggest the nature of the problems encountered by commissioned 'rankers'. One story told of a sergeant who was commissioned but asked to revert to his previous rank, for none of his fellow officers would associate with him, as a person of inferior social position. In a typical gesture, the Duke of York resolved the problem by deliberately walking arm-in-arm with the ex-sergeant to demonstrate to the other officers that he was just as good as them, after which the officers deliberately cultivated his friendship as one apparently so close to the army's commander-in-chief! Lord Hill recounted another story of a worthy sergeant who was rewarded for his merits with a commission. Hill encountered this officer, who in the story is called Macbride – not his real name, to shield him from embarrassment – and asked him, 'How do you feel in your new character? You are a *gentleman* now, you know.' 'Thank you, my Lord', was the reply; 'for myself I feels perfectly comfortable, but I trembles for Mrs Macbride.'[29]

Even for 'rankers' commissioned for the most meritorious of reasons, their subsequent careers did not always run smoothly, as demonstrated by the case of John English. Probably born in Ireland in 1762, he enlisted in the 11th Foot in 1783, rose to the rank of sergeant major and after service in the Mediterranean was captured in the disastrous expedition to Ostend in 1798. Apparently he made great efforts to maintain morale among the prisoners and after return home, following a glowing reference from his commanding officer, Rufane Donkin, he was appointed regimental adjutant shortly before he was commissioned as ensign. His career as an officer was not without incident; shortly after he was commissioned he was held under arrest on charges by a fellow officer that proved false, possibly malicious, and was released by the personal order of the Duke of York. Perhaps a poisonous atmosphere in the regiment, and his humble background, was the reason he left it in 1801, transferring several times before he joined the 66th as a captain in 1805. Having contracted a bigamous marriage (his original wife went to live in Nottingham) he joined his regiment in Ceylon, taking with him a daughter whose school fees he left unpaid. His troubles continued in Ceylon when he was court martialled for using abusive and insulting language, and for conduct unbecoming an officer and gentleman, in a dispute with the Customs Master at Trincomalee over the duty to be paid upon a lady's bonnet. English clearly thought himself ill-used, conceivably because of reactions to his origin – his commanding officer suggested that he had a 'disgraceful' character and had two, perhaps three, wives – and during the trial English accused the said commanding officer of having broken his word of honour. This charge was thought so serious that the court was cleared and English put under close arrest until the verdict, which suspended him for six months. He died of illness some eighteen months later.[30]

Those commissioned from the ranks were not all the recipients of criticism that was unjustified. One such seems to have been William Carr Royall, who having been a sergeant major became adjutant of the 58th in 1792. It took him twenty years to attain the rank of lieutenant colonel – not unusually slow progress for one unable or unwilling to purchase a 'step' in rank – and in the Peninsular War he was nominally in command of the 61st, though it was stated that on the prospect of action he always went to the rear, supposedly with an indisposition. He appears to have carried his sergeant-majorly habits into his career as an officer, and was known as a martinet if not a tyrant, and was so unpopular that one of his men remarked that if ever he had gone into action, he would not have come out alive. (He was perhaps especially disliked for replacing a commanding officer who was universally beloved by his men, John Stratford Saunders, an officer of more than thirty years' service, who had to leave after Talavera when his rheumatism became too severe to permit him to ride.) Royall's brutality was such that impelled a worthy sergeant, Andrew Pearson, to desert while the regiment was in the Peninsula; he walked its entire length until he reached Oporto, from where he took a ship for home. Pearson's own account condemned Royall's conduct, and he stated that finally Royall was forced from his command under a cloud.[31]

A further route to a commission was open to young men of good family but without funds to purchase a commission. With the permission of a unit's commander, they could serve as a 'volunteer': carrying a musket and bayonet and serving in the ranks alongside the ordinary soldiers, but generally living with the officers, until a vacancy occurred for an ensign, to which they could be appointed. An outstanding member of this type of semi rank and file was Christopher Clarke, who greatly distinguished himself in hand-to-hand fighting at Waterloo while serving as a volunteer with the 69th; he killed three cuirassiers while sustaining twenty-two sabre wounds. Upon his recovery he was rewarded with a commission in the 42nd.

In rare cases the process of promotion from the ranks operated in reverse: officers who had resigned their commissions sometimes enlisted as private soldiers. Perhaps the best-known was John Shipp, an orphan from Saxmundham who joined the army as a boy to escape the poorhouse, on merit rose to the rank of lieutenant, relinquished his commission when he ran into debt, re-enlisted as a private and for the second time earned a commission. Perhaps unduly touchy over his origins, Shipp became involved in a row with a superior officer over the purchase of horses, was court-martialled for ungentlemanly conduct and, probably unfairly, was dismissed the service. It was a sad end to a military career of thirty years; his young wife had died in childbirth and he had to leave his two little children in India, unable to afford their passage home. Subsequently a superintendent of the Liverpool Police, he ended his life as it had begun, in a poorhouse, though in this case as governor of Liverpool Workhouse; but was still in debt when he died.

Ex-officers rarely seem to have prospered. William Surtees of the 95th, who himself rose from the ranks to be commissioned as quartermaster, recalled four such individuals in the 95th. One was a steady man who enlisted while still drawing the half pay of a lieutenant – presumably insufficient to support himself and perhaps his family – and whose abilities led to his appointment as the commanding officer's secretary, until he reverted to full pay when appointed to his old rank. The other three were sadder cases: one became a corporal but was 'excessively wild' and rose no further, and another became a pay sergeant, but his dissipated habits led to embezzlement and suicide. The third had been a light company officer of the 35th, had twice relinquished a commission, also had bad habits and to escape the regiment's strict discipline deserted and tried to sail to France; he was apprehended and transported for life. Surtees reflected on his fate: once 'a gay and handsome young officer, moving in the circle of men of gallantry and honour; and now behold him a wretched culprit, stretched on the wooden guard-bed, manacled like a felon. In contrasting his miserable situation with my own so much happier lot, what ample cause had I for gratitude to that kind and indulgent Providence, which had preserved me from those excesses, which entailed so much misery on others.'[32]

8

'She Trudged with Her Babes in a Wallet Behind': The Army's Women

O! what in this world, can deter a true Lover?
. . . As she trudged with her babes in a wallet behind

Mary Marton: A Ballad [on the plight
of a soldier's wife], by John Mayne[1]

Soldiers' wives, both legal and unofficial, formed part of every regiment, even on campaign. Despite whatever useful function they fulfilled they were not always welcomed by those in authority, to the extent that there was an official instruction that marriage should be actively discouraged by officers, by emphasizing the miseries to which soldiers' wives were susceptible on campaign. Soldiers required the permission of their commanding officer to marry, and it was recommended that this indulgence be used sparingly: 'The single man is certainly better calculated for a soldier than the married, and could it possibly be so managed, there never ought to be above three or four women in a company, that number is necessary to keep the linen, &c. in order, but more become a burthen.'[2] Doing soldiers' laundry, for a fee, helped in the upkeep of a soldier's family, although it was calculated that food for a wife and three children should cost barely more than that for the husband himself.

Despite their performance of useful chores, some found women in barracks a great annoyance. Major General Arthur Hill Trevor, who served with the 33rd at Waterloo, articulated the most extreme view: 'the evil begins . . . where the wretched creatures are allowed to crowd into Barracks, with their starving children . . . taking up the room, bedding, tables, fires of the men – destroying their comfort, and all attempts at cleanliness – making the Soldiers discontented & driving them to the Canteen or Beer Shop and frequently to Desertion. Soldiers' wives, are generally the greatest nuisances – and I have had more trouble to control their conduct & behaviour than I can

113

describe – altogether the system of admitting them into the men's rooms is revolting to decency.'[3] Occasionally soldiers' wives might lodge outside barracks, but otherwise they lived in the barrack rooms with no more than a blanket partition to preserve their modesty. The possible consequences are obvious, as in the case of Eliza Goodlad, wife of a private of the 36th; in 1814 three members of the Royal Sappers and Miners were committed for trial 'for dreadful personal insult and cruelty' against her while stationed at Fort Cumberland, near Portsmouth.[4]

A number of wives were permitted to accompany their husbands on campaign, as explained by the regulations: 'the lawful Wives of Soldiers are permitted to embark in the proportion of Six to One Hundred Men, including Non-Commissioned Officers.'[5] The unfortunates who were not allowed to embark with their husbands were given an allowance, not exceeding 2d per mile, to take them to their homes or intended place of resi-dence, in the form of a certificate to be presented to the Overseers of the Poor in the towns through which they passed, who would provide the necessary funds. No further allowances were granted once the wife had reached her destination.

Varied methods were used to select those who would sail with their husbands when their regiment was sent overseas. One such was described by a naval officer who saw on the shorline at Northfleet that 'the soldiers had formed into a circle, in the centre of which stood their officers round a drum, whilst outside the circle, at a short distance, a number of women were assem-bled in distinct groups, and all seemed eagerly watching the proceedings . . . the women kept approaching stealthily towards the circle, and endeavouring to get a glimpse of what was passing within its bounds . . . . The circle continued unbroken, except by the soldiers, who in turns quitted the ranks to advance to the centre; and I was surprised to hear the rattling of dice which were thrown on the drum-head, and the throws were frequently followed by a long drawing of the breath as if it had been held for several minutes, and sometimes by an hysterical laugh of joyous certainty . . . . They had been casting lots to ascertain who were to go, and who to stay behind. By some it was treated as a matter of indifference, but those were generally the successful parties; but to others it seemed the issue between life and death . . . the day was delightfully lovely, and all inanimate nature was redolent of beauty; yet within this small space on which the sun was pouring out his golden radience, oh how many were the aching hearts and wounded spirits!'[6]

On campaign, soldiers' wives followed their husbands every step of their way, in all conditions and all weathers. One officer endeavoured to correct a common perception of the army's women:

Rated as incumbrances, sneered at as objects of pity, stigmatized as idlers and slatterns, vicious and unprincipled, soldiers' wives have perhaps evinced a more heroic self-devotion, a more tender love of offspring, and more touching conjugal affection, than any wives and mothers on record . . . . The sight of a soldier's wife on the march may in some create pity, whilst with others it may afford subject for ridicule; but those who have watched her patient and cheerful endurance on such an occasion can scarcely fail to honour her. See her toiling along the road with a couple of children running at her side, trudging in the rear of the column, ready always during the halt to minister to her husband's wants, and encourage him by conversation; or, seated on the baggage-cart, with an infant in her arms, keeping a watchful eye on the little box which contains all her store of barrack-room comforts. Behold her at the end of the march; her weariness is forgotten to attend to her husband's necessities, to prepare his meal, or his clothes for next day . . . nimbly she runs to provide refreshment for him and her children, and to establish in the billet a sort of temporary home.[7]

A soldier's family on the march, led by the pipe-smoking wife carrying the family belongings, one son a drummer, the other wearing a cut-down uniform, the husband at the rear wearing the fur cap and apron of a pioneer, and carrying his axe.

Others presented a somewhat less idealized picture of the army wife on campaign. George Bell of the 34th wrote how they 'stuck to the army like bricks.' Unwilling to accept military discipline, they went their own way, frequently impeding the march of the army by preceding the troops rather than trailing in the rear. This was explained by the wife of Dan Skiddy of the 34th, Bridget or Biddy Skiddy, a celebrated character styled by Bell as 'Brigadier General of the Amazons' who led the way on her donkey, 'Queen of Spain': the wives' duty, said Biddy, was to set up the night's camp before the men arrived, 'to have the fire an' a dhrop of tay ready for the poor crathers after their load an' their labour.'[8] She also accounted for her presence by saying if Dan were to fall, who else would bury him?

Not all soldiers were receptive to the concept of having a wife on campaign with them; William Wheeler of the 51st conceded that there were 'sweets' involved in having a pretty young woman as a companion, but recognized the 'bitters' as well, and declared that a soldier should have no ties but be as free as air.

There were, certainly, many bitters when the army was in difficult circumstances. Robert Ker Porter was shocked at the tribulations of the army's women on the retreat to Corunna: 'Were I to enumerate every afflicting object which met my view during this dreadful mountain march, I should fill a volume instead of a sheet; I should unman your heart, and send my reader weeping from the tale . . . we saw the body of a woman lying in a situation, that for misery, while she was sensible to its horrors, must have been unequalled. She was dead; and two little babes, to which she had just given birth, lay struggling in the snow. The scene was too agonizing to bear a second glance. A blanket thrown over her soon hid her from our sight; and we had the satisfaction of seeing the poor infants given in charge of a woman who came up in one of the bullock carts.' Such sights convinced him that women should not be permitted to accompany the army: 'Indeed it is truly pitiable so see the trains of women burthened with poor helpless infants, either tied on their backs, or stuffed into the panniers of asses, trudging along, exposed to cold and wet, and all the terrible accidents attending their unassisted situation . . . they only fill the men with anxieties respecting their safeties and accomodation; and in many cases occupy the conveyances intended for the sick and weary; and consume half the provisions which is necessary for the support of the army.'[9]

The husbands' anxieties mentioned by Ker Porter could be well-founded when the army was retreating, for women trailing in the rear could be overtaken by the enemy vanguard. This did occur on the retreat to Corunna, when soldiers' wives were apprehended by the French, who ill-used them and then sent them on their way. George Landmann came across a group who had been caught washing in a river by a party of French dragoons, who had 'taken the biggest liberties with us' and then stolen their shoes, 'a dirty, unmanly, mean, vile, cowardly, blackguard, ungentlemanly trick, to pass off on us poor creatures, who had never once given dem an ugly word.' Landmann expressed his horror at the assault, but it was not that that seemed to bother the woman: 'Ough de dirty villains! to take away our shoes was worse nor anything!'[10]

Wives whose husbands were killed usually remarried, sometimes within hours. George Gleig of the 85th commented on this apparent callousness: 'I have always been struck with the great coolness of the women; indeed they become as indifferent to danger as their husbands . . . the sort of life which they lead, after they have for any length of time followed an army in the field, sadly unsexes them . . . I recollect but one instance in which any symptoms of real sorrow were shown even by those whom the fate of a battle had rendered widows . . . they are, of course, perfectly sure of getting as many husbands as they may choose; and hence few widows of soldiers continue in a state of widowhood for any unreasonable length of time.'[11] James Anton had rather more sympathy, remarking that re-marriage on campaign, 'although slightingly spoken of . . . is perhaps the only alternative to save a lone woman's reputation [and] the peculiar situation in which she is placed renders it necessary, without consulting false feelings, or regarding the idle remarks that may be made, to feel grateful for a protector.'[12] (This somewhat cavalier attitude could pertain on both sides: in 1805 the 4th Foot's mulatto big drummer bought the wife of a man who worked in the Shorncliffe Canal for 6d, and in 1818 a Waterloo veteran, William Sobey, recently discharged from the 28th, paid the same price for a wife put on sale in Bodmin market.)

In addition to formal wives, many soldiers acquired Spanish or Portuguese partners during the Peninsular War, who displayed as much fortitude and loyalty as those whose relationship was more formalized. Some married foreign wives on campaign, like Drum Major Thorp of the 88th, the son of a prosperous Lancashire family that supplemented his pay with regular remittances from home. Perhaps because Thorp was that unusual creature, a respectable 'gentleman ranker', he attracted the amorous attention of Jacintha Cherito, daughter of the mayor of Campo Mayor. As her father would not condone her marriage to an ordinary soldier, they decided to elope. Finding her gone, the father insisted on searching the regiment as it marched away, but found no trace of the girl, not realizing that she was hidden in the band, in uniform and with a blackened face, masquerading as an African cymbal player. They were married next day, and Thorp's career prospered, his bravery earning promotion to sergeant major. He was determined to win a commission and at Toulouse he stood undaunted under heavy fire as the battalion took cover, exclaiming 'they can't hit *me* I think,' when he was immediately cut in two by a roundshot. On the day after his death news was received that he had been commissioned as an ensign. It may have been some small consolation to his widow that the fact that he *had* become an officer led to a reconciliation with her father.[13]

Those not formally wed were not permitted to accompany their menfolk back to Britain at the conclusion of the Peninsular War, though Wellington did note in a General Order that a few who had proved 'useful and regular' might be allowed to continue with their regiments if they were ultimately to be married. The remainder were the object of desperate and heart-rending scenes as their men were forced to leave them; Joseph Donaldson remarked that 'the generality of them were not married, but the steady affection and patient endurance of hardship which they exhibited, would have done credit to a more legal tie . . . although they were willing to have sacrificed country and relations to follow us, the sacrifice could not be accepted.'[14] They were indeed hard done by.

Many soldiers' wives experienced the same dangers of combat as their husbands, and there were casualties among them. Their plight had a profound effect upon those of a reflective disposition, like the officer who on the retreat from Burgos saw a woman hit by a roundshot: 'she was borne off by her distracted husband to a neighbouring house, where she died in about half an hour, after suffering great agony; and her screams as they bore her off even now ring in mine ear. The scene was truly distressing; a death so unnatural and horrible for a woman, clinging with devoted affection, in life or death, in weal or woe, and braving even the battle-field to follow her husband, in whose arms the poor creature expired. These are the real horrors, the true miseries of war; it is not the thousands of soldiers that fall nobly and bravely in battle – it may be called their natural death, and is often an enviable and glorious one . . . but when helpless women and children fall the victims of war . . . then, indeed, comes the iron scourge.'[15]

Many soldiers' wives did not actually accompany their husbands right into the firing line, but remained in the rear, anxiously awaiting news. Charlotte Eaton watched the army march out of Brussels on the eve of Waterloo and saw the soldiers 'taking leave of their wives and children, perhaps for the last time, and many a veteran's rough cheek was wet with the tears of sorrow. One poor fellow, immediately under our windows, turned back again and again, to bid his wife farewell, and take his baby once more in his arms; and I saw him

'The Heroine of Matagorda': Agnes Reston draws water for the beleaguered garrison under heavy fire.

hastily brush away a tear with the sleeve of his coat, as he gave her back the child for the last time, wrung her hand, and ran off to join his company.'[16]

On occasion the conduct of army wives was nothing less than heroic. A notable example was Agnes Reston, wife of a sergeant of the 94th, who was present, with her 4-year-old son, at the siege of Matagorda fort near Cadiz in 1810. Under heavy bombardment, she helped the surgeon attend the wounded, tearing up her own linen for bandages, carried sandbags to repair the defences as they were shot away, and most notably drew water from the fort's well under heavy fire, and distributed it to the wounded and to the men manning the guns. Other women were evacuated from the fort, some in hysterics, but she refused to leave until the place became untenable, when she crossed the shell-swept ground three times to bring off her goods and finally her little son, bending over to shield him with her own body. She received no reward for her heroism, even though recommended by the commander-in-chief; the secretary at war replied that no funds were available for such a purpose. Her husband's pension ended with his death and she had to seek refuge in the Glasgow workhouse, but when the plight of the 'heroine of

Matagorda' was brought to public attention a fund was raised to purchase an adequate annuity for her final years.

Another was Mary Anne Hewitt, nèe Wellington, the daughter of a soldier, born at Gibraltar and married at age sixteen to Thomas Hewitt of the 48th. She followed him through the Peninsular War and was herself most distinguished, 'a heroine in every sense of the word. Firm, undaunted, ever confiding in God, she moved an angel of mercy and goodness amongst the sick, the wounded, and the dying, through all the horrors of the Peninsular War.' Left destitute by the death of her husband, she received help from none other than Queen Victoria, Queen Adelaide and the Duke of Wellington; and a review of her biography noted that 'we are acquainted with no case possessing stronger claims to general kind and benevolent consideration.'[17]

There are recorded cases of a wife actually rescuing her husband from the battlefield and saving his life, but not all were such angels of mercy. George Landmann recounted a horrific incident at Rolica when he interrupted a woman about to use a rock to beat in the brains of a wounded British soldier in order to plunder his body. Landmann had half drawn his sword when a German rifleman of the 60th ran up, 'his rifle half up to his shoulder, and without any parley or ceremony, merely muttering as he sprang upon her, "You be no fouman, py Got! you be de tifle!" he put his rifle close to her head, and before I had time to form any clear conjecture as to his views, the upper half of her head vanished, and was dispersed into atoms amongst the bushes.'[18] Landmann shouted 'Bravo!' and as he went to aid the wounded man, the German removed the woman's apron, which was full of watches, rings and similar loot, and made off with it; Landmann thought it best not to stop him lest he turned the rifle on him.

In addition to the devoted women who followed their husbands on service, those compelled to remain at home should not be forgotten, having neither financial support nor news of their spouse, usually for years. Long absences on active service might end with the idealized reunion of Burns's *The Soldier's Return*, in which a veteran returns home to find his faithful sweetheart still waiting, but an alternative was exemplified by the case in 1803 of Sergeant James Hoskinson, a light dragoon, who on his return from ten years abroad married a young woman in Croydon, overlooking the fact that he already had a wife awaiting his return in Newcastle. He was sentenced to seven years' transportation for bigamy.

The significance of soldiers' families on campaign is often overlooked, but they were not entirely forgotten. The Royal Welch Fusiliers had a regimental tune, *Jenny Jones*, played at their annual St. David's Day dinner, named after the wife of a soldier of the 23rd. She died in her 95th year, and her gravestone, at Tal-y-llyn, Merionethshire, records how she accompanied her husband at Waterloo and was on the field of battle for three days. The scriptural quotation upon it, from Hebrews 13, 5, would have been appropriate for the countless wives and companions who loyally followed their men on campaign: 'I will never leave thee nor forsake thee.'

9

'To A Far Bloody Shore': On Campaign

Borne on rough seas to a far bloody shore,
Maybe to return to Lochaber no more

Lochaber No More

It was on campaign that the merits of the soldier could be best evaluated. Throughout the Napoleonic Wars there were examples of British units behaving badly, of troops giving way under pressure, but these were relatively few. Never was there a general *sauve qui peut* as affected many European armies; indeed, as Wellington remarked, he had no real objection to troops running away, providing they came back again; and, no doubt, that they kept hold of their muskets. More common were occasions when individuals or units performed feats of exceptional stoicism or bravery.

There was no single motivation that impelled soldiers to remain in their ranks on the battlefield, but a subtle combination of factors. It was certainly not the fear of the lash. Discipline and training were vital elements, and self-preservation in the knowledge that was safer to stand shoulder-to-shoulder with comrades, no matter how heavy the fire, than to break and run when the individual became helpless prey to an advancing enemy. For all a possibly wretched existence in civilian life, simple patriotism must have been a factor to some degree, though it is not easy to evaluate its effect. Despite economic hardships and some political agitation, the army throughout remained solidly loyal to its king and country, and there were instances of ordinary soldiers acting on their own initiative against perceived threats. The rank and file of a number of regiments acted spontaneously against the circulators of seditious literature, subscribing for rewards to discover the perpetrators. When hand-bills were distributed among marines at Chatham, they issued a reply signed by their NCOs on behalf of all: 'You ask, Are we not men? We are men, we know it, and should the enemies of our King, our Country and our Constitution ever oppose us, we will prove ourselves. You ask, Are we anywhere respected as Men? Yes, we are not only respected as men, but by many good men regarded as Protectors of our country.'[1] When the Nore mutineers invited the 23rd Fuzileers to join them, the rank and file submitted a loyal address to the King, which, it was said, led to the regiment being excused drinking the loyal toast, as the King had no doubt of their loyalty. A more robust reaction was that of the 6th Dragoons when quartered at Norwich, when it was said that an agitator was due to make some inflamma-tory speeches: parties of soldiers ransacked some public houses in search of him, until their officers persuaded them to desist.

It is difficult to ascertain exactly how spontaneous were such incidents, or whether they were encouraged by their officers; but one case demonstrates how such things could occur without any official sanction. While the Reay Fencibles were quartered at Belfast in 1797, a rumour arose that some of the Monaghan Militia were planning to liberate four of their number who had been capitally convicted of mutiny. Entirely without the knowledge of their officers, the Reays sent a strong contingent to reinforce the official guard party and the whole of the rest of the regiment sat up all night in their quarters, fully dressed and armed, in case the threatened insurrection occurred. 'All this was done without any order or hint from their officers, and with such prudent caution, that the circumstance was not known to the other corps, and no ill will or jealousy existed, in consequence, between the soldiers of either regiment.'[2]

The belief in the existence of national 'character' was exemplified by Samuel Johnson's *The Bravery of the English Common Soldiers*, which was reprinted during the French wars[3] and clearly must have been regarded as having some validity. Johnson questioned the maxim that French officers would lead if their soldiers would follow, but that British soldiers would follow if their officers led: instead, he thought that in British service there was 'a kind of epidemic bravery, diffused equally through all its ranks. We can shew a peasantry of heroes, and fill our armies with clowns, whose courage may vie with that of their general.' Discipline and regulation were not the most crucial factors, nor reverence to leaders from a superior strata of society, for the Englishman was 'born without a master'; instead, Johnson claimed, the most significant factor was personal independence and the knowledge that a man was 'no less necessary to his employer than his employer is to him.' This absence of inherent subordination, thought Johnson, meant that 'some inconveniences may from time to time proceed . . . but . . . they who complain, in peace, of the insolence of the populace, must remember, that their insolence in peace, is bravery in war.'

A reviewer of William Napier's history of the Peninsular War remarked of the ordinary soldier that as he could not expect riches or advancement, 'how great must be his spirit, how quick of impulse to good, how patient, how forbearing! Let no gross natures measure his worth by their own. To those who fancy that plunder and pay are his coveted reward, his daring must appear madness, his patience folly; but there are noble natures among the poor who fight for a glory not given in a Gazette; and love their country's honour, even though that country be ungrateful.' Henry Marshall would have agreed: 'Nowhere have I met with more honourable and more excellent men, that I have found in all ranks of the Army.'[4]

One NCO remarked on the sense of pride and duty he identified in most soldiers: those 'who have any character to uphold, consider disgrace worse than death; and if they had witnessed, as I have done, the reluctance with which soldiers in general left their regiment, when sick, even on the eve of battle, and what anxiety they evinced to join, when restored to health, they would think differently' (from the common perception of soldiers).[5] (Perhaps in confirmation, it is worth observing that among the troops assembled along the ridge of Mont St. Jean at the commencement of the Battle of Waterloo, no fewer than 933 were 'present sick', i.e. wounded or infirm men who were still with their regiments, many no doubt having been wounded at Quatre Bras two days earlier, but evidently unwilling to leave for treatment; though it is likely that some of the most lightly wounded would have been refused permission to go.)

For whatever its motivation, the sense of duty was often far in excess of what might have been expected. David Roberts of the 51st told how men of his regiment were swept off their feet crossing the fast-flowing river Esla in Spain in May 1813, and recalled the unwillingness of one man to part with his musket, which, perhaps, he recognised as King George's property entrusted to his care: 'he was seen by an Officer, who rode to the brink of the Rock; as the man floated down the stream, supported as he lay on his back, by his Knapsack, the Officer said, "Can you swim?" "No your honour." "Then throw away your Firelock." "No, your honour; I'll bring she to the shore with me – I won't part with She." Fortunately the current bore Him so near to the Rock, the Officer could reach his Bayonet, and the Man was saved.'[6]

Campaigns always began with a sea voyage, following the troops' departure from their barracks. This could be emotional, as when the 42nd left

Regimental baggage on the march: a wagon loaded with kit, women and children. (Print after W.H. Pyne, 1802)

Edinburgh in 1815, their band playing 'Dinna think, bonnie lassie, I'm gaun to leave ye', and accompanied by a vast throng, 'a great proportion being females . . . wives or sweethearts, mothers or sisters; and these clung as closely to the dear objects of their affection as the movements and discipline of a body of troops would permit, that not a moment which could be spent in their society might be lost . . . too many on that occasion felt that they were gazing in all probability for the last time on each other.'[7]

A more dispiriting departure was recorded at a somewhat later date. The troops cheered as they left; '"Ah!" remarked an old soldier, as we passed through the gate, "You shouldn't cheer till ye were comin' back: there won't be so many of you, I warrant, and you'll not be in a cheering humour."'[8]

The sea voyage could be a great trial, with troops 'packed like a parcel of pigs in an Irish boat,'[9] in the same confined and unpleasant conditions as customarily experienced by seamen. Disasters sometimes overtook the transport ships, one of the worst incidents occurring when the 2/59th, many of its members veterans of the Peninsular and Waterloo campaigns, was sailing from Dover to Ireland in January 1816. Their transport *Seahorse* was driven ashore in Tramore Bay, Waterford; of sixteen officers, 300 other ranks, thirty-one women and forty-two children, only four officers and twenty-two other ranks reached safety. Especially poignant was an event in 1809 when the 7th

A halt on the march: troops stowing baggage under cover at an inn. (Print by J. Hill after J.A. Atkinson, 1807)

Hussars, having survived the Corunna campaign, returned to Britain, 'each form of danger past/Strain their glad eyes to view her hills at last'[10] as stated on their monument at the parish church of St. Keberne's, some 7 miles from the Lizard. Their transport *Dispatch* was wrecked on the Manacle Rocks near Helson; of three officers, seventy-two other ranks, five women and thirty-six horses, only seven other ranks and four horses survived. A curious local legend held that on the night of the disaster every year a ghostly roll of the 7th could be heard being called along the shoreline.

One tragedy had a profound effect upon a particular small area. In 1795 the 63rd had a fruitful recruiting expedition at Waterside, a district of Colne, Lancashire, thanks to the local connections of one of their officers, Captain Ambrose Barcroft. With 'tears shed by wives and sweethearts left behind . . . these Colne lads, wearing rosettes in their caps, and accompanied by relatives and friends as far as Whitewalls, marched away never to return.' On 15 November 1795 their transport was wrecked on Portland beach, and 'no celebrated field of carnage ever presented, in proportion to its size, a more awful sight than that exhibited by the Chisell Bank. For more than two miles it was literally strewed with the dead bodies of men and animals.' A memorial tablet stated the loss to have been eleven officers and 215 other ranks, the

officers identified by their hands not showing evidence of manual labour, and
Barcroft by wound scars. 'When the sad news reached Colne, there was
general lamentation, for hardly a home in Waterside but mourned the loss of
some dead one.'[11]

Having reached their destination, the troops were decanted from their
transports into small boats to convey them to land, as described by a naval
officer: 'The first division of troops in flat boats assembled alongside our ship.
I recollect seeing many of the Guards in them, very sea-sick, and relieving
their minds over the boats' sides. Nothing looks more picturesque than to see
a parcel of men with powdered heads and cocked hats puking.'[12]

Having arrived on a foreign shore, many troops will have gained their very
first experience of foreigners, which in general seems to have confirmed a
belief of the inherent superiority of Britain in general. This had existed for
countless years, reinforced from the beginning of the French wars, and
especially after the rise of Napoleon, by a relentless tide of propaganda, often
in the form of poems and songs, that poured scorn upon the enemy, and
especially on Napoleon, who 'From a Corsican dunghill this fungus did
spring' (and this was written by a distinguished clergyman, headmaster of
Clitheroe Grammar School!).[13] This disdain extended beyond the ranks of the
enemy: 'In my dear country, Women are delightful/None here I've seen as
yet, but what are frightful.[14]

The British soldier seems to have maintained a healthy disregard for the
troops of other nations, whether allied or foe (though the Portuguese army,
reconstructed under British supervision and with many British officers, was an
honourable exception). In the same way that most British soldiers believed their
own regiment superior to others, so their opinion of foreign soldiery: as William
Surtees of the 95th described his Spanish allies, 'nothing better than mere
rabble – no organization, no subordination . . . . In their best days . . . more like
an armed mob than regularly organized soldiers.[15] The view of the British by,
and their interaction with, their allies is demonstrated by the Spanish popular
song that included the lines 'Long live the English who say, "God damn you."'
However right or wrong, this belief in the innate superiority of the British Army
must have had an effect in terms of morale on the battlefield.

No matter how strange foreign customs may have appeared, the soldier
quickly adjusted to his new environment, picking up essential foreign words
even if the pronunciation was shaky, just as 'plonk' and 'san fairy ann' became
common in the First World War.[16] For example, the term 'pong' was used in
the Peninsula for bread ('yellow pong' bread made from Indian corn), from
the Portuguese word for the same, '*pão*'. Perhaps the longest-lived term is
'padre', a chaplain, also Portuguese, and although its first English usage was

recorded in India in the sixteenth century its use must have been reinforced by service in the Peninsula. Increasing fluency in the language also helped in liasons with the locals.

There were difficulties of acclimatization; many soldiers, for example, remarked on the unhygienic practices encountered in some parts of the Peninsula, as William Grattan observed: 'The Portuguese are a filthy race, no doubt, but they have one merit . . . they feel and seem to know themselves to be a dirty race, and do not pretend to what their neighbours do, by any affectation of false pride in a matter in which both are equally involved – dirt.'[17]

In general, relations with civilians were good; as at home, there were cases of dreadful crimes perpetrated by a small minority of soldiers, but there was little overt hostility. Unlike the French army, whose entire system of operations depended upon their ability to forage for provisions without consent or recompense – in effect unbridled theft – the British Army made stringent efforts to pay for forage and foodstuffs acquired from the civilian population, leading to a markedly different attitude on their part towards the British, rather than the hatred directed towards the French.

Life in winter quarters overseas was not radically different from service at home, once the strangeness of foreign customs had been overcome, but

A fieldpiece being manhandled into position, a task that required much physical exertion: here infantrymen are assisting the gunners. The handspike inserted into the trail of the gun carriage was the means by which the gun was traversed. (Print after W.H. Pyne)

campaigning was very different, and almost always involved arduous and fatiguing marching. With the need for artillery and baggage to keep up, 15 miles per day was a good pace, but forced marches, undertaken in emergencies, were very different. The best known was the march of Craufurd's Light Brigade to join the army at Talavera, traditionally 62 miles in twenty-six hours, but this was evidently a miscalculation based on the measures of different Spanish 'leagues'; the actual distance was apparently 42 miles in twenty-six hours, with an additional 4 or 5 miles then undertaken to forward positions beyond Talavera, in the height of summer, over bad roads, with few men falling out.

Even ordinary marches, carrying heavy equipment and especially in hot weather, were a severe trial, so that some men would fall by the way and have to catch up to the night's camping ground at their own pace. Even excluding retreats like those to Corunna and from Burgos, when many died from exhaustion, hard marches could prove fatal: as to Sergeant William Cheetham of the Coldstream Guards, a young man from Leicester, highly regarded in his regiment, who died at Badajoz in October 1809 from 'excessive marching and uncommon fatigue.'[18]

As much as in action, high morale was necessary during fatiguing marching, and it was in these circumstances that a relentless good humour is mentioned by many writers. Some claimed that the Irish were the most prone to jokes and witticisms, but laughter and banter was widespread even under – perhaps because of – the most trying circumstances. This might not have been a particularly British trait, but one officer able to compare nationalities recorded that while Germans bore hard marching with less complaint, before the enemy they became silent and mechanical, while the English 'were all sarcasm, laughter and indifference.'[19] Spirits could be lifted during an arduous march by music or even by a beautiful view, as that in the Ebro Valley: 'The influence of such a scene on the mind can scarcely be believed. Five minutes before we were all as *lively* as stones. In a moment we were all fruits and flowers; and many a pair of legs that one would have thought had not a kick left in them, were, in five minutes after, seen dancing across the bridge, to the tune of *The Downfall of Paris*, which struck up from the bands of the different regiments. It was in such circumstances that the value of a regimental band was most marked: not merely a ceremonial adjunct but a way of helping to maintain morale, even in action. Bandsmen were often tasked with helping the wounded in battle, but there were incidents of encouraging music being played while the fight was raging. Even when the band was not playing on the march, troops often made their own music; it was remarked that British troops either whistled or hummed popular airs, but the German Legion created the greatest impression by their musical ability, three or four voices beginning and the whole unit joining in a harmonoius chorus, enchanting all who heard them.

One form of music, however, sometimes had to be kept in check, for the moral power of the Scottish bagpipes was well known. At a most desperate moment at Maya, Pipe Major Cameron of the 92nd struck up *The Gathering of the Camerons* for his weary colleagues, and 'the effect was instantaneous – every Highlander was on his legs in a moment, and, with their eyes sparking fire, only waited for the order to advance.' Realizing that a charge at that moment could be disastrous, their divisional commander, Sir William Stewart, ordered Cameron to stop playing, and when after a pause he began again he was forbidden to play again at the hazard of his life. Observing the enemy numbers increasing he muttered, in Gaelic, 'If he'll not let me play, every man in the land of France will be here.'[21] As British reinforcements appeared, Cameron piped up the charging tune *Haughs of Cromdale*, where-upon 'the Highlanders rose, and, without waiting for orders, rushed on their

A hero: Piper George Clarke of the 71st who at Vimeiro, despite severe wounds, continued to play his pipes to hearten his comrades with Up and Waur Them A', Wullie, *reputedly declaring, 'Diel ha my saul, if ye sal want music.' He survived and for his bravery was presented with a set of silver-mounted pipes by the Highland Society of London.*
(Print by Clark & Dubourg after Manskirch)

numerous foes with the utmost undaunted courage, who, panic-struck by their audacity, wheeled about, and ran, pursued by the whole corps.'[22]

When executing marches on campaign, a daily routine might include commencing an hour or two before daylight in hot weather, as in the Peninsula. Long before that the quartermasters and 'camp colour men' (those equipped with small flags to stake out each unit's ground) would depart early, to establish the next night's camping ground. Drums would beat the 'general' call, when guard parties and sentries would rejoin their units and baggage be packed. An hour later the 'assembly' would beat, when any tents not sent ahead would be stowed on the wagons, and twenty minutes later the march would commence, with a halt of twenty minutes every 3 or 4 miles, to give the men a break, obey calls of nature and permit the rear of a column to catch up. Measures were taken to prevent gratuitous straggling – men stealing away in search of plunder – but generally only the exhausted fell out, usually to be rounded up by parties detached for the purpose. One soldier who had fallen out from fatigue described the relief in rejoining his regiment as 'like getting to my father's door.'[23]

Upon reaching the night's camping ground, where some men and soldiers' wives would already have begun to make camp, the first task was to establish security by posting sentries and establishing a patrol. Though unpopular, sentry duty was the most responsible position held by any soldier and one in which he could exercise authority, for not even an officer could pass without identifying himself, usually by means of a password, a challenge given by the sentry – usually a name or 'parole' - and an answer, or countersign. It was advised that these words be easily understandable; it was recounted that a 'place-name' countersign used in the American War of Independence was 'Ile aux Noix', but when this was spoken in its correct French pronunciation the sentry refused to accept it. The officer wishing to pass thought for a moment and said 'Ile ox nox', presuming this to be the version given the sentry by his sergeant; 'Pass, friend', said the sentry!

Not even the highest ranks could pass a sentry without challenge: on the night of Salamanca the commander of Wellington's cavalry, Stapleton Cotton, was shot and wounded by a sentry whose challenge he had failed to answer. Sentry duty was especially difficult after a hard day's march, and punishment severe, even capital, for those who fell asleep, so one member of the 42nd stated that a sentry should always be moving, and recommended his own habit of pricking himself with a pin and rubbing urine in his eyes to stay awake. George Gleig of the 85th identified another factor when posting sentries on an old battlefield: they should always be in pairs to prevent a single man from being unnerved by superstitition; as one said, indicating a dead body, 'I don't care for living men, but for Godsake, sir, don't keep me beside *him*.'[24] Gleig recalled one of his sentries who suffered a complete mental collapse at the sound of wild dogs feeding off nearby corpses.

The soldiers' rations were supposed to be the same on campaign as at home, but even when the commissariat personnel were conscientious – far from universally true – they were dependent upon an inadequate transport system. The military transport service was absurdly small, so the army depended upon hired wagons and carters; some Portuguese muleteers were efficient, but the majority had a poor reputation. In 1812 Wellington complained that 'we must expect disappointments when we have to deal with Portuguese and Spanish carters and muleteers . . . . What do you think of empty carts taking two days to go ten miles on a good road? After all, I am obliged to appear satisfied, or they would all desert!'[25] John Cooper had his own method of enforcing co-operation: when a driver refused to take six sick men onto his cart, 'I drew my bayonet, took it by the small end, and swinging round, gave him such a blow on the mouth with the heavy end as stunned him. Then I got them into the car, and he drove on, holding his mouth as if he had got the *tic*.'[26]

The difficulties of supply, especially if the army were advancing or retreating, meant that very often soldiers were left without rations and had to resort to extreme measures. There are accounts of men eating acorns or even leaves, and in a case described by Cooper just before Vittoria, food intended for French cavalry horses: unsifted barley that he made into dumplings that appeared 'like little frightened hedgehogs. To get a mouthful, I had to pick lots of prickles out of the mass.' Small wonder that he remarked that once a man had enlisted 'he should have parted with half his stomach . . . . Sometimes we were reduced to half rations, and once, for a whole week, we had nothing but one pound of bad beef daily. When bread could not be obtained, we got a pint of unground wheat, or a sheaf of wheat out of the fields, or else two pounds of potatoes.'[27]

On campaign soldiers might encounter food of which they had no experience, including the coffee first encountered by a Highlander in the Peninsula. Observing how the cook skimmed the liquid from the top of a kettle, he presumed it was a ploy to save the grounds for himself, so demanded 'some o' the sik and well as the sin' (thick as well as thin). He began to eat the grounds with his spoon from his mess tin, 'but after taking two or three spoonfuls, grinding the coffee grounds between his teeth, and making wry faces, he threw the tin, contents and all, out of the tent door, exclaiming, "Tarn their coffee! you might as weel chow heather, and drink pog water as that teevil's stuff. Gi'e Donal a cog o'brochan before ony o'your tea or coffee either.'[28] In extreme cases, comestibles purchased from local merchants might not be entirely nutritious, such as the pork slices sold to the army by Spanish and Portuguese hawkers, which were actually, it was said, cut from dead men. Harry Ross-Lewin became violently ill after eating something he suspected came from such a source, and two officers of the 28th were prostrated by it, and 'for two years after the bare mention of pork was sufficient to make them shudder.'[29]

Under such circumstances it is not surprising that troops plundered food from the local population. Knowing it was vital to retain the trust and co-operation of the local people, Wellington raged against such practices: 'The Officers with the army do not appear to be aware how much they suffer in the disgraceful and unmilitary practices of the soldiers, in marauding and plundering every thing they lay their hands upon. The consequence is, the people of the country fly their habitations, no market is opened, and the Officers, as well as the soldiers, suffer in the privation of every comfort and every necessary.'[30] The theft of beehives was a constant worry and the source of a number of General Orders in the Peninsula, and a story was told of how Wellington himself met a Connaught Ranger running off with a beehive on his head. The Duke challenged him and asked where he got it; his head wrapped in a great-coat for protection, the soldier must not have recognized the source of the question, for he pointed where the hives were and added, 'if ye don't make haste they'll all be gone.'

A bivouac on campaign: a camp fire shared by both officers and soldiers. (Engraving after William Heath)

Plundering of this nature was largely responsible for what little hostility there was towards the British in the Peninsula, a point Wellington made in reaction to the deaths of a Corporal Booth and Privates Gilbert Wyatt and Richard Jew of the 53rd at the hands of local peasants, 'one of the consequences of the irregularities of which the soldiers have been guilty, which have had the effect of turning into enemies a people who were grateful for the benefits which they had received from the British nation, and manifested their gratitude by affording to the soldiers every comfort and assistance which was in their power.'[31]

Nonetheless, plundering was sometimes given tacit approval. A story concerned Sir Denis Pack, commanding the 71st in the Peninsula, who ordered his quartermaster to organize a party to find vegetables, to prevent the men roaming unsupervised. The quartermaster instructed a sergeant 'to parade three men a company to steal vegetables'; Pack overheard and said, 'I did not say, sir, to steal vegetables, but to procure pompions' (pumpkins),[32] but as there was no intention of paying for them the difference was theoretical. Another commanding officer who took a pragmatic view was Major David Roberts of the 51st, who ordered his men to fill their haversacks with whatever they could forage, for the commissariat had nothing for them, and once prevented a provost marshal from flogging a man for stealing potatoes. He impounded the evidence and lectured the culprit for being so stupid as to be caught, then returned the stolen potatoes to the man, minus a few kept for his own dinner. He would have agreed with the member of the 42nd who excused his plundering, at a time of starvation, by writing that 'those who won't fight for their victuals won't fight for their king.'[33]

The usual problems of intoxication were always evident on campaign. Roberts stated that 'For the purpose of getting Liquor, the invincible British soldier will commit every species of depredation: he will rob a House, plunder a Church, steal from his Comrade, and strip his own [wounded] Officer in the midst of death and slaughter.' He said that the desire for drink led to the cavalry neglecting its horses, contrasting with the care exhibited by the troopers of the King's German Legion: 'A German Soldier will sell his Bread to feed his Horse – a British Soldier will sell the Corn to purchase Drink.'[34]

It is easy to overstate the prevalence of drunkenness affecting duty, but there were some glaring incidents. Charles Palmer, ex-10th Hussars, spoke in Parliament of how a party of his own regiment was sent to reconnoitre a town in Spain, an officer being sent after them when they failed to return: 'on his arrival he found them all beastly drunk, and their horses tied up in different parts of the town in the most disgraceful situation.' Such incidents convinced him that it was impossible, on service, to keep up discipline without flogging, even though he knew of men who had received 400 lashes and then 'in two hours afterwards been found drunk in the streets.'[35]

The situation was worst when discipline had broken down completely, as in the retreats to Corunna and from Burgos. One of the worst examples occurred in the former, at Bembibre, described by Robert Blakeney:

> . . . the scandal here presented by the British troops, or the degrading scenes exhibited through their debauchery. Bembibre exhibited all the appearance of a place lately stormed and pillaged. Every door and window was broken, every lock and fastening forced. Rivers of wine ran through the houses and into the streets, where lay fantastic groups of soldiers (many of them with their firelocks broken), women, children, runaway Spaniards and muleteers all apparently inanimate, except where here and there a leg or arm was seen to move, while the wine oozing from their lips and nostrils seemed the effect of gunshot wounds . . . some lay senseless, others staggered . . . obscenity was public sport.[36]

In the camping ground the experienced soldiers quickly made themselves comfortable, where possible constructing rude shelters from branches and blankets if no tents were available; a rough shelter known as a 'Portuguese tent' was common, consisting of two gable ends made from muskets, connected by a central pole, with blankets draped over to form the roof. James Anton

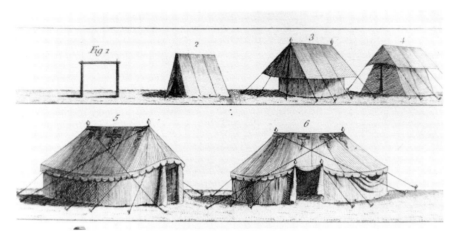

Military tents: top, those used by the ordinary soldiers, including (left) the simple internal supports, and at right, 'fly' tents with awnings. Below, larger tents used by officers. (Engraving by N.C. Goodnight)

A British camp in the Bois de Boulogne, 1815. The shelters are conical bell tents in which soldiers would sleep like the spokes of a wheel, the feet next to the central tent pole. At left is a civilian booth selling comestibles to the soldiers, one of whom, wearing a forage cap, appears more interested in the vendor than in her wares. (Print by Dubourg after Manskirch)

described how the usual arrangement of twelve soldiers in a tent, lying like the spokes of a wheel with their feet towards the centre, was not something that his young wife could share with decency, so whenever they camped he would build a tiny hut for the two of them, improving it with a chimney and fireplace if they remained in that location long enough. This became commonplace in the Peninsula, with camping sites comprised of many little huts, some so snug that it was with reluctance that the troops abandoned them when the march continued. When action was imminent, however, shelter and rations were often unattainable. Never was this better demonstrated than on the night before Waterloo, when the rain fell in diluvian proportions. Thomas Morris recorded how the ground was so muddy that they could not lie down, so his comrades spent the night sitting on their knapsacks with blankets over their heads, trying to keep out the rain. Their only cheer was the thought that in the Peninsula a pouring wet night was always an omen of victory.

Another trial to be overcome was the deterioration of uniforms and equipment, which were often poorly made even before the rigours of active service. Shortage of shoes was the worst aspect; it was remarked that some men, notably from Ireland, had never worn shoes until they enlisted, and they managed quite well barefoot, but others often had to leave the route of march to find softer ground to walk on, trying to ignore their cut and bruised feet.

One soldier remarked that lucky was the man who possessed *one* shoe, so he could change feet when one became sore. Many expedients were employed to try to keep the army shod, not always successfully: 'We were served out with a kind of shoe made in the country [Portugal]. They were very clumsy, and of a dirty buff colour; and as many amongst us were without stockings, their rough seams made their wearers hobble like so many cripples.'[37] Another method was derived from the ration beef that accompanied the army on the hoof: pieces of raw hide could be strapped around the foot to form a shoe, though when a dry day followed a wet one the hide became so hard that the men could not walk until it had been softened with water.

Having become used to the realities of life on campaign, the soldier had to confront that to which his entire training had been directed: encountering the enemy. Despite the aforementioned propaganda concerning the French and the 'Corsican ogre' who led them, there was little real animosity towards the enemy. Because of the horrors perpetrated by the invaders upon the civilian populations of the Peninsula, Spanish and Portuguese entertained a deadly enmity towards the French, and responded to brutalities in kind; but between British and French, when not actually in battle, there was little bitterness, even fraternization. The absence of malice was perhaps best articulated by George Napier, recalling how the commander of an opposing French outpost had been entertained to supper by the British: 'There is never any personal animosity between soldiers opposed to each other [which] I hope always will be the case. I should hate to fight out of personal malice or revenge, but have no objection to fight for "fun and glory"'[8]; evidence, wrote Charles Parker Ellis of the 1st Foot Guards, 'that feelings of respect and courtesy may exist between two gallant and and chivalrous nations, although opposed to each other in a stern and bloody warfare.'[39]

The contemporary belief that it was immoral to sacrifice lives to no purpose might have been expected from officers of liberal education and relative refinement, but there is wide evidence that it was also prevalent among the rank and file. Moyle Sherer overheard two soldiers discussing the death of a bold French officer in the Pyrenees. '"I was sorry to see him drop, poor fellow," said one. "Ah!" said another, "he came so close there was no missing him; I did for him!" "Did you!" rejoined the first speaker; "By God, I could not have pulled a trigger at him. No; damn me, I like fair fighting and hot fighting; but I could not single out such a man in cold blood."'[40]

Such attitudes seem to have been commonplace. Many seem to have made a distinction between impersonal volley firing at a mass of foemen and the deliberate act of aiming at an individual, and although the latter was the essence of a rifleman's duties, even with them it was sometimes regarded

Light Dragoons skirmishing, wearing the classic 'Tarleton' helmet. The front-rank men discharge their pistols at the enemy, while the corporal at the rear has his carbine at the ready. (Engraving by Sadler after Thomas Rowlandson)

as distasteful. One rifleman recalled how at Vera he shot a French voltigeur, and when he ran up to plunder the body – a universal practice – he found the dying man kissing a small silk packet suspended around his neck. After he died he prised open the Frenchman's hand and found the packet contained a lover's knot of dark and blonde hair. Ever after he kept it in his pocket book and admitted that it half spoiled him as a sharpshooter, as every time he pulled the trigger he thought of the young Frenchman and his raven-haired sweetheart. Another rifleman, Edward Costello, admitted that he deliberately shot a French sharpshooter because his blood was up, and felt unbearably guilty, almost like a criminal, when he saw him fall, even more so when a wounded Frenchman lying nearby reproached him with '*vous avez tué mon pauvre frère*' ('you've killed my poor brother').

The morality of engaging the enemy came into even sharper focus in the hand-to-hand combat in which the cavalry engaged. Despite the excitement of the moment, examples of humanity were common. Sergeant Matthew Colgan of the 18th Hussars recalled overrunning French artillery carriages at Waterloo: 'I galloped to the outrider or driver on the foremost horse, and he was only a "boy" . . . I knock'd him off the horse with the flat of my sword (the poor young fellow looked so sheepish . . . here I confess I regret him tumbling under the leader's feet . . .).' Subsequently he engaged some more French troops, including one man who refused to surrender: 'I showed him mercy as long as I considered my life safe, and when not, I gave him the fatal blow . . . [I was] obliged to take the life of a fellow creature, but He, whose judgment I have yet to meet, and who knows the circumstances, seen [sic] I endeavoured to be merciful. I requested him to give up before I gave the fatal blow, but of no use.'[41]

The advance of the 52nd at about the same time provided further examples. Private Samuel Whittam encountered an unhorsed French cuirassier who slashed at him; Whittam could easily have killed him, but he was a Rochdale man perhaps familiar with the old Lancashire 'sport' of 'posing' or shin-kicking, so felled the Frenchman with a violent kick to the leg and took him prisoner, saying, 'Tha'll not cut at me again, will ta?' One of his comrades was less forgiving: as the regiment overran a French battery, a bold veteran wearing the Legion of Honour stood firm. The 52nd man 'threw him on the ground, and keeping him down with his foot, reversed his musket to bayonet him. The repugnance to the shedding of human blood unnecessarily . . . burst forth in a groan of displeasure from his comrades. It came too late; the fatal thrust had passed.' Sergeant Major Edward Cotton of the 7th Hussars, himself a Waterloo veteran, wrote that the boos and jeers of the rest of the 52nd demonstrated that 'in the bosom of the truly brave a spark of humanity is always smouldering.'[42]

Nonetheless, baser instincts could negate finer feelings. George Landmann recalled an incident at Vimeiro, when he saw a French voltigeur taking aim at him. He turned to a nearby German rifleman of the 60th and asked him to shoot at the voltigeur. He got a dusty reply: 'he pettishly and half turning round, said, "Silence! ton't tisturp me; I want de officeer." "Why do you want to kill the officer?" cried I, with as much vexation as he had manifested. "Pecause ter pe more plunder," muttered the wretch, keeping his eyes fixed on the object of his ambition.'[43]

The general absence of animosity between British and French was exemplified by what might be termed a 'live-and-let-live' system that operated between opposing outposts. These were clearly in sight of each other on many occasions, but hardly ever were hostilities begun, and on rare occasions when one sentry took a shot at another, apologies were usually transmitted on the following day. Once in the Peninsula a rifleman named Humphrey Allen of the 95th deliberately shot a French sentry, leading to a general fusillade. When this had died down, Allen was hauled before his colonel, the inspirational Sidney Beckwith, and asked to explain his unwarranted act. Allen said he hadn't eaten for two days and thought he might find something in the Frenchman's knapsack; he escaped with a reprimand.

Far more usual was fraternization between foes away from the battlefield, including the barter of food, alcohol and tobacco between outposts, and sometimes even entertaining each other to supper. William Grattan described a typical example in July 1812, when the contending armies were encamped on either side of a small river:

> . . . although both armies kept their guards on their respective sides of the water, and that the movements of each were cautiously watched, not one life was lost, nor one shot fired by either army . . . the French and British lived upon the most amicable terms. If we wanted wood for the construction of huts, our men were allowed to pass without molestation to the French side of the river to cut it. Each day the soldiers of both armies used to bathe together in the same stream, and an exchange of rations, such as biscuit and rum, between the French and our men, was by no means uncommon.[44]

A common habit was for British troops to buy liquor from the French, placing money and a canteen between the opposing picquets; the French would take the money and fill the canteen with brandy. The following happened on more than one occasion, though this incident involved a soldier named Patten. The French failed to supply the brandy, so Patten grabbed the opposing sentry and stole his accoutrements, which he held as security for the completion of the deal. A French officer then appeared under a flag of truce and pleaded for the return of the equipment, as its loss could cost the sentry his life; so they were returned, and Patten sentenced to be flogged. Lord Hill attended the punishment parade, spoke on the inadvisability of such conduct, and then, characteristically, remitted the sentence.

A further misunderstanding was reported by George Landmann, who observed British and French sentries on either side of a stream. Though neither understood the other's language, the Englishman struck up a conversation: 'I say, mounseer, how do you do? parle vou france? I say, how is master Nap?' After some by-play the Frenchman tossed a large lump of bread across the stream to 'Monsieur John Bull'. In return, John Bull waved his canteen and said, 'I say, come here, you're a good fellow; come down here, and take a drop of rum to old Georgy's health.' The Frenchman crossed over, touched his cap and took a long swig, and, 'smacking his lips, and unable to mark his gratitude in any other way, threw both his arms round John Bull's neck, and began kissing him with all the affection he would have shown to his own father. John, at this, started back, tearing himself from the Frenchman's embrace; and, full of rage, he exclaimed, "Do you take me for a girl, or what sort of pranks would you be after?" and . . . fetched him a dry wipe across the face with the back of his hand, which well nigh floored him.' The Frenchman drew his sabre but Landmann intervened and explained each other's customs before the affair turned any nastier.[45]

A similar distinction between British and French was believed to exist when battle began. Unlike the French, some thought the British soldier too dull to be animated, and indeed his stolid and phlegmatic conduct was one of the army's great strengths. William Napier fulminated against the suggestion that the firmness of the British soldier was 'the result of a phlegmatic constitution uninspired by moral feelings. Never was a more stupid calumny uttered. Napoleon's troops fought in bright fields, where every helmet caught some beams of glory; [but for the British soldier] no honours awaited his daring, no dispatch gave his name to the applause of his countrymen; his life of danger was uncheered by hope, his death unnoticed. Did his heart sink within him, therefore? Did he not endure with surprising fortitude the sorest of ills, sustain the terrible results in battle unmoved, and, with incredible energy, overthrow every opponent, at all times proving that, while no physical quali-fication was wanting, the fount of honour was always full and fresh within him?'[46]

A marked difference between British and French was that the Briton was singularly unimpressed by heroic harangues from his officers; what animated Napoleon's troops had no effect on the redcoat. The contrast was marked by Harvey Jones of the Royal Engineers who was asked by a French officer how British soldiers motivated when required to advance; Jones replied that they just said 'Forward!' The Frenchman replied, 'Ah! that way will not work with us; we are obliged to excite our men with spirits, or work upon their feelings by some animating address.'[47] Another officer stated that during his captivity on St. Helena, Napoleon asked one of his British guards whether Wellington had much talent for haranguing his troops; and was surprised to be told that not only had the Duke never attempted it, but that he would have been laughed at if he had. Thomas Brotherton of the 14th Light Dragoons concurred, comparing Wellington's silence with Napoleon's theatrical decla-mations such as 'From these pyramids twenty centuries look down on you!'; had this been addressed to British soldiers, he asserted, they would have called out 'Fudge!'. The less said to British troops the better, he believed, and that nothing more than a call of 'Steady!' was required.'[48]

Realizing this, British officers who did address their men before battle generally kept their remarks short and laconic – 'short and sweet, like the gallop of a jackass' as one put it.[49] Typical was the address of Lieutenant Colonel Robert Barclay of the 52nd at Busaco, a man known for his dry wit: '"Do you see those rascals coming up the hill?" he said, turning to the men. Some of the soldiers began to laugh, for they knew that something rich was coming. "What the devil are you grinning there for, you set of fools, when in five minutes more some of us will be laughing on the wrong side of our faces? Fix your bayonets, and come along. Knock them heels over tip, and give them a taste of the Barclay touch!"'[50] Equally unadorned was the speech of Major Peter O'Hare of the 95th, to recruits in their first action: 'Look at those fellows, they are the French, and your enemy: if you don't shoot them, they will shoot you.'[51] Alexander Wallace of the 88th was another; his address at Busaco was:

> When I bring you face to face with those French rascals, drive them down the hill – don't give them the false touch, but push home to the muzzle! I have nothing more to say, and if I had it would be of no use, for in a *minit* or two there'll be such an infernal noise about your ears that you won't be able to hear yourselves.[52]

10

'March, Brave Boys, There's No Retreating':
Battle

Colours flying, drums are bayting,
March, brave boys, there's no retrayting!

War Song of the Gallant Eighty-Eighth,
or *Love, Farewell!*[1]

No matter how heartening were the homely exhortations of the officers, the experience of combat must still have been profound. The moments before an engagement were often solemn, as George Gleig of the 85th recalled:

> . . . time appears to move on leaden wings; every minute seems an hour, and every hour a day. Then there is a strange commingling of levity and seriousness within [the soldier] – a levity which prompts him to laugh he scarce knows why, and a seriousness which urges him from time to time to lift up a mental prayer to the Throne of Grace. On such occasions privates generally lean upon their firelocks, the officers upon their swords; and few words, except monosyllables, at least in answers to questions put, are wasted. On these occasions, too, the faces of the bravest often change colour, and the limbs of the most resolute tremble, not with fear, but with anxiety . . . it is a situation of higher excitement, and darker and deeper feeling, than any other in human life; nor can it be said to have felt all which man is capable of feeling who has not gone through it.'[2]

Few ordinary soldiers wrote at length of their emotions on entering battle, but the thoughts of Thomas Morris were probably common:

> I have often been questioned as to the state of my mind on going
> into battle; but I must confess my utter inability to define correctly,
> what were my feelings at such a moment. A man must have a very
> good heart, or a very bad one, who can enter on such scenes
> without fear. I have heard some men boast, that they had no more
> fear on going into a battlefield, than on entering a cricket ground.
> But I did not believe them; and I have known some of those
> boasters, when tested, prove the rankest curs imaginable. I always
> felt myself somewhat of a coward on going on; but, when once
> fairly engaged, those fears would subside, and a sort of reckless
> enthusiasm succeeds which puts humanity to flight, and makes
> man, for a time, a devil.[3]

No amount of training could prepare completely for the reality of combat, when those who lacked experience could be undone, as recounted by Major J. Patterson of the 50th, describing how at Vimeiro inexperienced troops fell victim to experienced French sharpshooters: 'Getting bewildered among the corn-fields and olives, the young hands scarce knew which way to turn . . . they were literally mowed down, falling like ninepins amid the standing corn.' He then wrote of the 2/43rd, just arrived from England, 'A finer, more robust, and healthy-looking body of soldiers it would be difficult to find, but, poor fellows! "the pipe-clay was soon shook out of their jackets," for getting somehow exposed to a galling range of fire, they were most severely handled . . . . With scarcely anything beyond a smattering of Dundass [sic], with sundry evolutions at the double-quick, their military education was supposed to be complete, but the men knew nothing of the business.'[4] Such events explain why experienced men were so valuable, and why Wellington was so desperate to hang onto his veteran units in the Peninsula, even though their numbers had been drastically reduced by years of campaigning.

As the enemy approaches, it is necessary to consider what impelled soldiers to stand their ground. Discipline, regimental pride, duty, and fear of punishment or ostracization by their comrades must all have been factors, but traditionally it has been said that a prime motivation has been to support one's comrades, or, in modern idiom, 'mates'. This was articulated by Private Shadrach Byfield of the 41st; sent away from the firing line with another soldier, when their task was completed, 'my comrade said to me, we could stop where we were, we had no need to go back to the fight; but I replied to him, "What! see your comrades fighting and not go back to help them: if you don't go back I'll shoot you."'[5] James Hope of the 92nd recorded three similar cases in his company on one day, in the Pyrenees on 30 July 1813. John Brooks had been hit in the neck, his stock turning the ball but leaving him so bruised as to deprive him of speech; he refused to go to the rear when ordered and was killed by a shot in the very same place. William Dougald could hardly walk but when told to fall back replied, 'No, I will rather die than leave my comrades!'; he too was killed. Hope's servant, Hugh Johnstone, was ordered to look after the baggage train but sneaked back to stand with his comrades, and was mortally wounded, proving him to be 'as good a man, and brave soldier, as ever graced the ranks of the British army.'[6]

The call of duty on the part of an 'other rank' could even put officers to shame. At Quatre Bras the 33rd was hit by artillery fire giving the effect of the scythe of a mower as one of them described, and they gave way in the face of onrushing French cavalry. Corporal William Holdsworth and a young officer hid in some standing corn when, according to Holdsworth, they saw 'a cuirassier with one of our colours, which he was bringing off, shouting. I said . . . "We are disgraced for ever, for there is our colour; but if you will allow me, I'll fire at that man." The officer replied, "It is as much as our lives are worth if you do, but I won't say you shall not."' After this lukewarm reaction, Holdsworth shot the Frenchman and reclaimed the colour, covering the officer as he took it back to the battalion. Wounded at Waterloo, Holdsworth was congratulated for saving the colour when the prudent course would have been to remain hidden, and by his own account received an extra 4d per day pension in recognition.[7]

In all his career in the 95th, Benjamin Harris claimed that only once did he encounter a soldier so jittery as to be on the point of flight, in his first action in Denmark: 'We now received orders ourselves to commence firing, and the rattling of the guns I shall not easily forget. I felt so much exhilarated that I could hardly keep back, and was checked by the Commander of the company (Capt. Leech), who called to me by name to keep my place.' But a man in front, Jack Johnson, tried to hang back, whereupon Harris 'swore by God that if he did not keep his ground, I would shoot him dead on the spot; so that he found it would be quite as dangerous for him to return as to go on. I feel sorry to record the want of courage of this man, but I do so with the less pain as it gives me the opportunity of saying that during many years' arduous service, it is the only instance I remember of a British soldier endeavouring to hold back when his comrades were going forward.'[8] Harris's threat was overheard and ever after Johnson was held in contempt by his comrades.

Nonetheless, in every action there were men who absented themselves from the firing line, sometimes on the excuse of helping a wounded comrade to the rear. Soldiers were generally unforgiving of perceived backsliders, as in a case recounted by William Lawrence. At Waterloo, clearly terror-stricken, a grenadier named Bartram asked to be excused; Lawrence pushed him back into the ranks, whereupon Bartram collapsed and refused to move. Lost to sight in the smoke of battle, he was not seen again for six months, and when he did reappear was flogged for desertion, and subsequently three times more for selling his equipment. The drummers who administered the flogging went to with a will, 'for there is no one [soldiers] feel more strongly against than a coward.' Shunned by his fellows, after the fourth flogging Bartram was turned out of the regiment: 'the colonel ordered his coat to be turned, and a large sheet of paper pinned on it with the words "This is a coward, a very bad soldier, and one who has been whipped four times"; and he was then drummed out of the barracks.'[9]

A similar case with a different outcome concerned Richard McLaughlan of the 73rd, nicknamed 'The Lady McLaughlan' from his effeminate manners. He fainted at the sight of the first casualties at Waterloo, was not seen again on the day of battle and his Waterloo Medal seems to have been withheld. Yet three years later in Ceylon he behaved with such extraordinary heroism in saving a small party that had been cut off that the commanding general stated his conduct had been without parallel and in reward he was awarded both the 1818 Ceylon Medal and a gold medal from his regiment. He died of fever before he received them.

Although in action the individuality of the rank and file soldier was usually merged into the mass of his battalion or regiment, the anonymous individual could still exert a profound influence. John Kincaid of the 95th stated that in battle, soldiers 'are apt to have a feeling that they are insignificant characters – only a humble individual out of many thousands, and that his conduct, be it good or bad, can have little influence over the fate of the day. This is a monstrous mistake . . . for in battle, as elsewhere, no man is insignificant unless he chooses to make himself so.' He divided soldiers into three: a small number who thought themselves insignificant, a large number who just did their duty, and a large number who did all they could, 'many of whom are great men without knowing it.' He recalled an incident when the 95th was pinned down by heavy fire, sheltering behind trees and humps in the ground. 'When it appeared to me certain death to quit the cover, a young scampish fellow of the name of Priestly, at the adjoining tree, started out from behind it, saying, "Well! I'll be hanged if I'll be bothered any longer behind a tree, so here's at you," and with that he banged off his rifle in the face of his foes, reloading very deliberately, while every one right and left followed his example, and the enemy, panic struck, took to their heels . . . the individual did not seem aware that he had any merit in what he did, but it is nevertheless a valuable example for those who are disposed to study the causes and effects in the art of war.'[10]

(If this were the Rifleman Joseph Priestly wounded serving with the 95th at Waterloo, it is satisfying to record that he survived to claim his Military General Service Medal with clasps for Pyrenees, Orthes and Toulouse.)

A similar circumstance was described by John Cooper at Orthes. His company began firing from behind a large farm building, 'bo–peep fashion' (darting out from cover to shoot, then dodging back again), and, having found a wine store, 'the game was "Drink and Fire, Fire and Drink".' This form of warfare was evidently not to the liking of Sergeant Tom Simpson, who shouted, 'Come, let us charge these fellows!'; the company burst from cover and routed the enemy but Simpson was shot dead in the charge.

One of the most famous incidents of an 'other rank' exerting a profound influence was that involving Sergeant William Newman of the 43rd, as already mentioned. With no officers present, near Betanzos on the retreat to Corunna, he rallied a number of sick and wounded men to repel French cavalry, and by sheer force of personality held them together, standing off repeated attacks as he slowly withdrew for a distance of about 4 miles, until relieved by British cavalry. His conduct was reported as 'seldom exceeded by one in that rank'; he was commissioned and received a grant of £50 from the Patriotic Fund to defray the costs of equipping himself as an officer.[11]

The classic image of the British Army of the Napoleonic Wars is that of a 'thin red line' standing firm against the attack of French columns, the formation that had brought victory to French arms on countless fields. Firepower was a factor in the British defeat of this formation, for in a two–deep line all muskets could be brought to bear, whereas with a column only the first few ranks could reply, but the tactic of the line was much more than just a firing device, but one that brought the bayonet into play. In its classic form, the British line would be hidden from view behind the crest of a ridge, so that only skirmishers thrown forward would be visible to the advancing enemy. As the column approached the crest the line would advance, appear to the French and mow down the head of the column by overwhelming musketry. As the column reeled the British would charge, but bayonets were rarely crossed, for the column would break at the sight, and as they fled the British would rally, retire to their original position and await the next onslaught.

There was also a psychological dimension in the conduct of the British. The French would advance with beating drums, cheering and shouting, their officers waving and encouraging at the front, but the British were contemptuous of such theatricality, one witness comparing the French to 'going to scare crows from a corn-field,' with officers 'swaggering like showmen at a fair.'[12] By contrast, the utter silence and stillness of the waiting British had a powerful effect in unnerving the advancing French. Recollecting Talavera,

A two-deep line of infantry prepares to engage an onrushing French column. The front rank is about to fire while the rear rank is at the 'make ready' position that was adopted before aiming. The uniform is that worn from 1812; at the left is a colour sergeant, identified by his elaborate sleeve badge, and armed with a spontoon. (Print after Richard Simkin)

the Marquis de Chambray described how it appeared to the attackers: 'The French charged . . . being arrived at a short distance and the English line remaining immobile, the soldiers hesitated to advance. The officers and non-commissioned officers cried to the soldiers: "Forward – march – do not fire!" – some of them even exclaimed "They surrender!" They then continued their forward movement, and were very near the English line, when it opened a fire of two ranks, which carried destruction into the French line, stopped its progress, and produced some disorder . . . [then] the English, leaving off fire, charged with the bayonet. Every circumstance was favourable to them – good order – the impulse given – the determination to fight with the bayonet: among the French, on the contrary, no longer an impulse . . . they had no alternative but flight.'[13]

A further psychological factor was the British cheer as they charged. French cheers were 'one of their discordant yells – a sort of shout, in which every man halloos for himself, without regard for the tone or time of those about him,'[14] but the British cheer was co-ordinated and infinitely more intimidating.

The classic British infantry tactic demonstrated at Busaco: French attacking columns receive a volley of musketry and then a British bayonet charge. (Print by C. Turner after Thomas St Clair)

William Grattan described its effect at Salamanca: as they neared the enemy, they 'for the first time *cheered!* The effect was electric; [the French] were seized with a panic . . . . Their mustachioed faces, one and all, presented the same ghastly hue, a horrid familial likeness throughout . . . they reeled to and fro like men intoxicated [and] the mighty phalanx, which but a moment before was so formidable, loosened and fell in pieces'[15] before the British bayonets.

The ability to stand unwavering as the enemy approached was equally valuable. Officers took great pains to have their men hold their fire until the optimum moment, even if using the minimum of oration, like Captain William Alexander Gordon of the 50th near Bayonne. Sensing that his men were over-eager to begin shooting, though he 'himself could scarcely withstand his natural tendency in this way . . . he raised his voice to the highest pitch . . . "Dinna fire, men, till ye see the *wheights* of their *eyes.*"'[16] It was, though, impossible to preserve fire discipline in a protracted musketry duel when file-firing was employed instead of volley. John Mitchell described how 'one man is priming; another is coming to the present, a third is taking . . . aim; a fourth is ramming down his cartridge. After the first few shots the entire body are closely enveloped in smoke, so that the enemy is totally invisible; some of the soldiers step out a pace or two, in order to get a better shot; others

*The rear of an infantry line in action, its appearance very different from the precise forma-
tion practised on the parade ground. The position of the sergeants is marked by their
spontoons.* (Print by Bowyer)

kneel down; and some have no objection to retreat a step or two. The doomed
begin to fall – and even bold men shrink from the sight; others are wounded,
and assisted to the rear by their comrades; so that the whole becomes a line of
utter confusion.'[17]

Another battlefield hazard was compounded by soldiers' attempts to reduce
the hurtful recoil of the musket by emptying powder from their cartridges
onto the ground. Powder underfoot could be ignited by sparks, burning the
undergrowth, a terrible prospect in dry weather, as at Talavera: 'Lines of
running fire half a mile in length were frequent & fatal to many a Soldier, some
by their pouches blowing up in passing the fire, other Wounded unable to
reach their respective Armies lying weltering in their gore with the devouring
element approaching & death most horrid staring them in the face.'[18] George
Wood of the 82nd said that the bodies looked like roasted pigs, and that the
French could only be distinguished from the British by their earrings.

All the senses were assailed in battle, increasing a sense of disorientation:
eyes stinging from powder smoke that obliterated almost everything from
view, and when it cleared revealed appalling sights; the taste of powder and
the raging thirst that came from biting cartridges; the reek of burned powder;

hands blistering from touching searingly hot musket barrels; and ears filled with the roar of conflict and the cries of the wounded. Perhaps the most unnerving was the sound of incoming musket balls, which young soldiers might mistake for the buzz of bees or the drone of beetles. Experienced men could distinguish between balls fired at close range or 'spent balls' at the extremity of their flight that no longer possessed the impetus to pierce the body, but only bruise; these latter gave out 'a long melancholy whistle . . . but as we approached nearer the enemy, they flew past in full force, with a noise resembling the chirping of birds.'[19]

Ingrained discipline and a strong mental constitution was also required when standing immobile under artillery fire. Roundshot – solid iron balls that made up the greater proportion of artillery projectiles – could sometimes be seen approaching, when there was a natural reaction to duck. This was regarded as unmanly, and John Colborne, commanding the 52nd at Waterloo, stopped his men from ducking by calling 'For shame! for shame! That must be the 2nd Battalion, I am sure,'[20] whereupon every man straightened, not wanting to be compared to recruits. Under the same bombardment, Sergeant Major William Ballam of the 73rd saw Private William Dent duck as a shot

Hand-to-hand fighting normally occurred only when one side was already broken, or a position or trophy was disputed. This is an imaginary episode at Waterloo but conveys an impression of the smoke and confusion of battle. (Engraving by Freeman after W.H. Brooke)

The decisive manoeuvre: at Maida, British infantry charge a French formation already shaken by musketry.

whirled past; 'Damn you, Sir!' cried Ballam, 'what do you stoop for? You should not stoop if your head was off!' At that moment a ball hit Ballam in the face and killed him on the spot. Dent exclaimed to the corpse, 'Damn it Sir! what do you lie there for?'[21] even though *his* head was off. Even when round-shot landed they were a danger, for they bounced up – Frederick Pattison of the 33rd compared Waterloo to a giant cricket match, tempting a man to step out and drive at the roundshot as with a bat – and even when rolling on the ground had enough impetus to strike off a foot. When at Waterloo this happened to a young soldier of the 73rd, he advanced on his stump to fire a last shot at the enemy.

Equally disturbing were artillery shells, which might splutter on the ground before exploding. Accounts exist of troops advancing deviating from their course to avoid the explosion, but troops in static formations had no such option; though when one landed amid the 23rd at Waterloo the 17-year-old Private James Farrer (or Farrow) grabbed it and hurled it away like a cricket ball. (No reward existed for such acts of heroism, but forty years later the very first Victoria Cross was awarded for just such a deed.)

Discipline and resolution were also required in the execution of a charge, though usually one or other side turned away before bayonets were engaged.

The bayonet was the supreme psychological weapon; William Napier explained that soldiers knew a bayonet 'will prick their flesh and let out life, and therefore they eschew it. Many persons will stand fire who will not stand a charge, and for this plain psychological reason – that there is great hope of escape in the first case, very little in the second, and hope is the great sustainer of courage.'[22] Bayonet fights were so rare that they were usually remarked upon when they occurred, like the officer who at Vimeiro asked a soldier of the 50th why he was wiping his bayonet: 'By Jasus, your Honour, I skiver'd three of 'em.'[23] There are few first-hand accounts, but Robert Eadie wrote of one in an alarmingly matter-of-fact way, recalling Fuentes de Onoro: 'the person with whom I had to encounter in this trying and dreadful moment, exhibited rather an athletic appearance. With infuriated looks he assailed me, and thrust the point of his bayonet into my chin; but by a sudden retrogression, I got rid of it. Without losing one moment's opportunity, I rushed on him, and putting by his musket, which he still presented in as elevated a position as formerly, I buried my bayonet in his breast. I speedily extracted my steel; he fell, and was numbered among the slain.'[24]

Similarly unemotional was the description of the brutality of cavalry combat, in Charles Ewart's account of how he captured the 'Eagle' of the

The vulnerability of infantry to cavalry is exemplified in this scene from the Peninsular War, in which a British hussar compels two French officers to surrender.
(Print by M. Dubourg after William Heath)

The cavalry trumpeter performed a vital function in transmitting orders on the battlefield, notably, as in this Waterloo scene, sounding the rally after a charge (not always obeyed by British troopers due to the excess of ardour). (Print by R. Havell after I.M. Wright)

One of the most celebrated of the army's 'other ranks' was Corporal of Horse John Shaw of the 2nd Life Guards, by virtue of his status as a bare-knuckle prizefighter. A Nottinghamshire man, he was mortally wounded at Waterloo, having slain several French cuirassiers. (Print published by Kelly)

Private Samuel Godley of the 2nd Life Guards – nicknamed 'The Marquess of Granby' on account of his bald head – distinguished himself at Waterloo when, having lost his own horse, he killed a French cuirassier and appropriated his mount. (Print published by Kelly)

French 45th Ligne at Waterloo: 'The Enemy . . . and I had a contest for it; he thrust at my groin – I parried it, and cut him through the head; after which I was attacked by one of their lancers, who threw his lance at me, but missed the mark, by my throwing it off with my sword by my right side; then I cut him from the chin upwards, which cut went through his teeth; next I was attacked by a foot soldier, who, after firing at me, charged me with his bayonet – but he very soon lost the combat, for I parried it and cut him down through the head; so that finished the contest for the Eagle.'[25] (Ewart was rewarded with a commission, but never rose beyond the rank of ensign; he died at Salford in 1846, aged seventy-seven, but more than ninety years later was re-interred on the esplanade of Edinburgh Castle. A more prominent memorial was the adoption of the French Eagle as the badge of his regiment, still worn by its successor, the Royal Scots Dragoon Guards.)

The description of an encounter in the Peninsula also emphasises the appalling nature of cavalry fights, concerning Harry Wilson of the llth Light Dragoons, an even-tempered, sober man and a brave and proficient swordsman: 'I saw him engaged hand to hand with a French dragoon: I saw him . . . give and receive more than one pass, with equal skill and courage. Just then, a French officer . . . delivered a thrust at poor Harry Wilson's body; and delivered it effectually. I firmly believe that Wilson died on the instant: yet, though he felt the sword in its progress, he, with characteristic self-command, kept his eye still on the enemy in his front; and, raising himself in his stirrups, let fall upon the Frenchman's helmet such a blow, that brass and skull parted before it, and the man's head was cloven asunder to the chin. It was the most tremendous blow I ever beheld struck; and both he who gave, and his opponent who received it, dropped dead together. The brass helmet was afterwards examined . . . and the cut was found to be as clean as if the sword had gone through a turnip, not so much as a dint being left on either side of it.' The writer then expressed an accurate appraisal of the difference between the British cut and the French thrust: that wounds caused by a sabre cut 'were all very hideous . . . as far as appearances can be said to operate in rendering men more timid, or the reverse, the wounded among the French were thus far more revolting than the wounded among ourselves.'[26]

The besieging of an enemy fortification was an aspect of campaign service unlike any other. The army's engineers were not only ill-equipped but hardly existed, at least until the formation of a new corps of Royal Sappers and Miners in 1812 began to improve the situation. Otherwise, all manual work had to be performed by infantrymen, some of whom would have possessed useful skills from their civilian employment. When a fortification was besieged, large numbers of troops were required to dig the trenches that edged ever closer to the enemy's walls, to construct batteries to bombard the place, and to guard the trenches from enemy raids. It was calculated that to besiege a fortress with a garrison of 5,000 men, 8,000 were required to labour in the trenches, in four shifts; 11,250 to guard the trenches, in three shifts, and 7,700 in support, not including replacements for casualties.[27] John Kincaid, whose men sharpshooted at the enemy, described the combination of manual labour and fighting as an apprenticeship to the dual calling of gravedigger and gamekeeper.

Much worse was the prospect of storming a fortification, when artillery had broken a breach in the wall. At this point, by the etiquette of the time, the garrison could surrender honourably; but if they compelled the besiegers to carry the place at bayonet point, it was accepted that the attackers had the right to sack the fortification. This was to give them some recompense for what was almost a suicide mission; yet no prospect of plunder can explain the

The storm of a breach: 'As respectable representation of hell itself as fire, and sword, and human sacrifice could make it,' as John Kincaid described Badajoz.

competition to lead the attack, the nature of which can be gauged from the name of the leading part, 'forlorn hope', deriving from the Dutch *verloren hoop*, 'lost party'.

When volunteers were called for this duty there was always intense rivalry among the rank and file; Kincaid, selecting men in his role as adjutant, said that there was as much competition as if he had been distributing sinecures, not death warrants. When William Green was chosen as one of the buglers to join the 'forlorn' at Badajoz a comrade, Bugler West, bribed the bugle major to go in Green's place; outraged, Green reported the incident to Kincaid and was restored to his place. (It was his last service: he was shot through the thigh and had his left wrist so shattered that he had to be discharged. Even as he lay wounded amid the carnage, he continued to blow his bugle, until an officer told him to stop as he was drawing fire.) Another method of selecting volunteers from all those who wished to go was to draw lots, to prevent accusations of favouritism, and in the case of the 51st at Badajoz in 1811, the adjutant played a deadly form of blind man's buff, passing along the ranks of volunteers blindfold, touching men at random. One of the 'lucky' men at San Sebastian was an old corporal of the 7th, John Styles; when he discovered he had won his place he tossed a coin to see whether he was destined for Heaven or Hell, and thus expected to survive. Survive he did, with a musket ball through the knee; he was told that the limb must be amputated but when the surgeons came he was drunk and refused to be parted from it. The injury healed but left him crippled, but he limped back to his regiment and fought to the end of the war. He had often been flogged for drunkenness, but in this case being drunk had saved his leg.

Why membership of so desperate enterprise should be so prized is hard to fathom. There was equal competition among the officers, but at least those who survived were often rewarded by promotion, but no such prospect was held out for the ordinary soldiers. Kincaid thought it simply was the serving in a 'post of honour'; and once a unit had been allocated a role in the storming, it probably made little odds whether an individual went first or in a succeeding wave.

In the hours before the appointed time for a storming, participants recalled a 'desperate calm'. William Grattan of the 88th, writing of Badajoz, described it as consisting of expectation, hope and suspense, intensified by homely music played by regimental bands to while away the last hours. This was especially true of the 88th (Connaught Rangers), whose band played Irish airs that could inspire melancholy at the best of times. Grattan left a memorable snapshot of his men as they formed their column for advance, which could surely represent any battle-hardened British battalion from the period:

> . . . the men were ordered to stand to their arms. Little, if any directions were given; indeed, they were unnecessary, because the men, from long service, were so conversant with the duty they had to perform, that it would have been a waste of words . . . unencumbered with their knapsacks – their stocks off – their shirt-collars unbuttoned – their trousers tucked up to the knee – their tattered jackets . . . their huge whiskers and bronzed faces . . . but, above all, their self-confidence, devoid of boast or bravado, gave them the appearance of what they in reality were – an invincible host.[28]

Nothing was so terrible as the storm of a heavily-defended breach. The physical task was bad enough – clambering into the ditch surrounding the wall, encumbered with ladders for the purpose, sometimes with huge sacks of grass used to break their fall when leaping into the ditch, and then attempting to stuggle over the debris of the breach – but all the while assailed by a storm of cannon shot, musketry and incendiary balls. Storming was usually carried out at night, so that the only light was from the flames of the enemy's munitions. Two of the greats assaults of the Peninsular War – Ciudad Rodrigo and San Sebastian – were bad enough, but Badjoz was never surpassed as a scene of the most intense horror. More than one witness compared it to the infernal regions 'as a respectable a representation of hell itself as fire, and sword, and human sacrifices could make it,'[29] while William Napier thought that the breaches 'seemed like the mouth of some huge dragon belching forth smoke and flame.'[30]

It was the truth: the breaches at Badajoz could not be forced, and the place was taken instead by a successful escalade on another part of the defences; but the troops who did assault the breaches tried again and again, despite unimaginable slaughter. Several survivors mentioned men standing in the ditches, waiting to be struck, knowing that advance was impossible, but hardly any mention is made of troops attempting to extricate themselves from the carnage. It was after the fall of Badajoz, however, that even greater horror unfolded.

Looting the bodies of the dead was so commonplace as to be routine, even at the height of battle. The prospect of rich pickings often led soldiers temporarily to neglect their duty, as William Wheeler described at Waterloo. He and two comrades were behind a rock in the skirmish line on the right flank of Wellington's position when a French cavalry officer rode up to reconnoitre. Wheeler asked his pal Private James Chipping if he could hit him. Chipping was a crack shot and declared that the Frenchman's death warrant was as good as signed, and after he dropped the officer the three light infantrymen dragged his body behind the rock, found forty gold pieces, and even stripped the bullion lace off his uniform, for even that had a value.

Scavenging on the battlefield, however, was very different from what occured at Badajoz. It was there that the full implication of the unwritten 'law of war' that permitted a stormed city to be plundered became evident. After the indescribable horrors of the assault, perhaps the soldiers were temporarily unhinged by the trauma, conduct exascerbated by the alcohol that was sought, perhaps to dull the senses after the ordeal; but no excuse could be made for what occurred, which filled every right-thinking witness with utter horror. The sack of the city was one of the most disgraceful episodes in the annals of the British Army, as troops ran wild amid scenes of unbridled excess, looting, rapine and destruction as houses were plundered, innocent civilians abused and even murdered by units transformed into a drunken, vicious mob. This account by an officer is typical:

> The town had now become a scene of plunder and devastation; our soldiers and our women, in a state of intoxication, had lost all control over themselves . . . In addition to the incessant firing through the keyholes of the front doors of houses as the readiest

way of forcing the locks, a desultory and wanton discharge of musketry was kept up in the streets . . . many of our own people were thus killed and wounded . . . I was glad to escape from this scene of infuriated licentiousness, in which all the worst passions of human nature seemed to be in unrestrained operation. An attempt was in vain made on the day following to collect our soldiers; the troops sent into the town for the purpose, however, joined in the work of plunder.

He returned to Badajoz after a night and a day to find:

The scene which presented itself on my arrival would require the pencil of a Hogarth to describe. Hundreds of both sexes were lying in the streets in a state of helpless intoxication, habited in various costumes. Among them were those who had fallen by the hands of their comrades. Nor was it easy to discriminate between the drunken and the dead; both were often equally pale and motion-less . . . . The old and the young were equally victims of the most savage brutality, less the natural disposition of the men than the result of maddening intoxication; and subsequent enquiry left no doubt but that every woman who had not concealed herself incurred outrage . . . . The city still continued, on the third day after the assault, in the exclusive possession of a disorganised and tumultuous soldiery; acknowledging no law, considering every thing within their grasp their own, and allowing no impediment to interpose themselves between desire and gratification.[31]

Finally, Wellington ordered the erection of gallows to represent the ultimate sanction, and the outrages ceased; or perhaps the perpetrators were simply sated. Such was the lust for unbridled vice that it was only with great difficulty that a few men – mostly drunk – were assembled to help the countless wounded who still lay among the heaps of dead in the ditches.

Otherwise, only rarely did the soldiers' desire for loot materially affect the operational competence of the army, but the aftermath of the victory of Vittoria was notorious in this regard. The whole of the French baggage train fell into the hands of Wellington's army, much of which temporarily dissolved as it was ransacked. Describing 'our vagabond soldiers' Wellington stated:

We started with the army in the highest order, and up to the day of the battle nothing could get on better; but the event has, as usual, totally annihilated all order and discipline. The soldiers of the army have got among them about a million sterling in money . . . . The night of the battle, instead of being passed in getting rest and food to prepare them for the pursuit of the following day, was passed by the soldiers in looking for plunder. The consequence was, that they were totally knocked up . . . we now have out of the ranks double the amount of our loss in the battle.[32]

Amid such a total breakdown in discipline, staggering amounts of wealth could be acquired. Joseph Brown of the 45th 'liberated' a French strongbox containing coin to the value of £549. He recalled that he would have been overjoyed to have found a few dollars, but a sum of this magnitude caused him endless worry; yet felt only resentment, not relief, when the army authorities took it off him.

It was not exclusively the rank and file who indulged in such practices; it was at Vittoria that the 14th Light Dragoons captured Joseph Bonaparte's silver chamber pot, which has been used by the regiment ever since as a punchbowl. Probably the most famous piece of loot in the entire period was the baton of the French Marshal Jean-Baptiste Jourdan, which was found in the French baggage, which Wellington sent to the Prince Regent as a trophy, and received in return the baton of a field marshal of Great Britain, the origin of this symbol of rank in British service. It was said to have been captured by the 87th Foot, but in the following year a story surfaced that it was actually captured by Corporal James Fox of the 18th Hussars. He must have been a canny individual for he unscrewed the gold ends from the baton, believing them valuable, and put them in his pocket; and in the night the remainder of the baton was stolen from him by a member of the 87th. Subsequently, his conscience must have troubled him, for he surrendered the gold ends to his commanding officer, Major James Hughes, who sent them to Wellington and thus they were reunited with the rest of the baton.

If discipline could break down in the aftermath of victory, it was much worse in retreat. In the retreat to Corunna the army's rearguard performed prodigies, and (as usual) the Foot Guards remained stalwart, but otherwise straggling, drunkenness and plundering was so rife as almost to destroy the army, causing its commander, Sir John Moore, to issue a notably caustic order on the subject. (He declared that rather than survive such disgrace he would rather be killed by an enemy cannon ball; which he was, in the battle at the end of the retreat.)

One officer, who recalled how on the retreat from Burgos in 1812 he had found soldiers literally drowned in wine after the wine store at Duenas had been broken open, sought to explain why order collapsed under such circumstances: 'An English force is ever a difficult one to manage on a retreat – the soldier's spirit flags, he becomes sulky, growls, and grumbles, because he is not allowed to turn and fight . . . he cannot be made to understand why he is to retire, and be harassed by forced marches, to get away from a foe he had so often drubbed.'[33]

This reason for the collapse of good order would seem to be confirmed by Basil Hall of the Royal Navy, who witnessed the exhausted, tattered rabble that had finally reached Corunna. They appeared so disheartened that he asked an army officer if anything could rouse them: 'You'll see, by-and-by, sir, if the French there choose to come over.' Just then the French artillery opened fire, but its announcement of the prospect of imminent, violent death, far from destroying what heart was left, restored morale in an instant:

> At the first discharge from the French battery, the whole of the British troops, from one end of the position to the other, started on their feet, snatched up their arms, and formed in line with as much regularity and apparent coolness as if they had been exercising on the parade in Hyde Park . . . . I had already noticed the silence which reigned over the field; now, however, there could be heard a loud hum, and occasionally a jolly shout, and many a peal of laughter . . . . All had become animation and cheerfulness in minds from which, but a short time before, it seemed as if every particle of spirit had fled.'[34]

If fears of death or mutilation could be overcome by the factors that led to such morale, the realities were clear to any soldier. The army's medical service was small and unable to cope rapidly with the number of casualties that might arise from a battle. A small number of staff surgeons could be deployed at headquarters level, but most of the work fell upon the battalion or regimental surgeon with one or two assistants. There were no medical orderlies or 'other rank' staff outside hospitals, so having established the unit's aid post a short distance behind the firing line, a regimental surgeon could be overwhelmed with work in a very few moments. In the British Army at Waterloo, for example, there were apparently only forty-seven regimental surgeons and ninety-four assistants, and thirty-eight staff surgeons, approximately one medical officer for every forty-five casualties in the campaign, and they also had to treat countless enemy wounded left on the field after the French retreat.

Given that the medical facilities were so few, and that techniques of surgery, no matter how complex, were performed in the most insanitary conditions, it is astonishing how many soldiers survived severe and even multiple injuries, like Richard Whitehead of the Royal Horse Guards who survived sixteen sabre and lance wounds at Waterloo. Others were wounded time and again, and still returned to their duty.

During an action, the only soldiers officially permitted to remove casualties from the firing line were the regimental drummers or musicians; otherwise the wounded lay where they fell or made their own way to the rear, which accounts for the snakes of limping, hobbling men sometimes remarked upon by those approaching the front line. Those unable to move might lie un-attended on the battlefield for many hours, even days, the delay in treatment leading to the death of multitudes who might otherwise have survived. At the conclusion of an action parties would normally be sent out to find and succour the wounded – the enemy's casualties usually had to wait – but probably more soldiers scoured the field for profit rather than assisting their fellows.

Indeed, plunder was regarded as the right of those who had survived a vic-torious action, as exemplified by the account of an officer who, wounded at Waterloo, lay helpless on the field all through the night. As dawn was breaking two British grenadiers approached, a middle-aged sergeant and a much younger private. The officer called to them and pointed out a Prussian scavenger who had just murdered a wounded man to plunder his body; without compunction the sergeant killed the Prussian on the spot. Having revived the officer with copious drafts of brandy and water, the two made to leave, but not before presenting him with a loaded musket: 'we must not leave him without the means of keeping stragglers at a distance,' as the sergeant told his companion. The officer asked their names, that he might commend them; the sergeant explained that the best service would be his silence, as they should have been with their regiment instead of 'collecting lost property': 'Well, we fought hard enough yesterday to allow us a right to share what no one claims, before the Flemish clowns come here by cock-crow.' The officer then proffered some guineas as a reward, but these were declined: 'We have made a good night's work, and your money, young Sir, we neither want, nor take. If we have rendered you a service, it was for the sake of the old country.'[3]

Abandoning wounded if the army had to withdraw was a painful experi-ence. In the Pyrenees John Bainbrigge of the 20th recalled that 'The wounded who were too much hurt to be capable of being removed from the ground were collected and placed near the fires; small cards were then pinned to their jackets, having a few words written on each in French, consigning them to the mercy of our gallant enemy. This appeal was strictly adhered to.'[36] Wounded left behind did not always fare so well: there was universal outrage when

British casualties were deserted by the Spanish army after Talavera, when it had been expected that they would be cared for.

Some soldiers wrote accounts of how they had to shift for themselves to reach medical attention, as recorded by Shadrach Byfield of the 41st in 1813:

> I . . . said to my comrade, 'There is a man, and I'll have a shot at him'; just as I had said these words, and pulled my trigger, I received a shot under my left ear and fell immediately, and in falling, cut my comrade's leg with my bayonet; he exclaimed, 'Byfield is dead,' to which I replied, 'I believe I be.' As soon as I had sufficiently recovered so as to raise my head from the ground, I crept away on my hands and knees, and as I was creeping I saw a serjeant in the rear, who said, 'Byfield, shall I take you to the Doctor?' I answered, 'Never mind me, go and help the men.' I at length arrived where the Doctor was, who . . . put a sticking plaister to my neck, and ordered me to go to a barn which was appointed for the sick; as I was going, the blood flowed so freely from my wound as to force off the plaister . . . . I saw a man [who] told me he was wounded in the leg; I observed to him, that if I had not been worse wounded than he was I should be back helping the men; I then asked him to give me a pocket handkerchief to tie round my neck to stop the blood; he told me he had not got one; I observed, that if I did not get something I should bleed to death, when he took and tore off the tail of his shirt and tied it round my neck. I then went to the barn and lay down with my fellow sufferers.'[37] [Byfield recovered from his wound, only to lose his left arm in the following year.]

Having reached the aid post, the wounded soldier would have to endure brutal procedures without anaesthetic, with amputation the universal treatment for a mangled limb. The scenes were horrific: an operating table made from something like an old door, sluiced down with water between operations if any were available, all amid piles of severed limbs. The stoicism of many soldiers was beyond belief. George Landmann walked into a makeshift operating theatre in the Peninsula and recoiled at the sight of a soldier's leg being taken off: 'the patient was seated on a table, holding up with both his hands the stump of his leg under operation, which was below the knee, and singing "God save the King" with the utmost strength of his voice; but on my begging pardon and turning away, he suspended his song, and exclaimed with a strong Irish accent, "Walk in, Sir, no offence at all, Sir."'[38] Sergeant Thomas Jackson of the Coldstream Guards described in horrific detail how his right leg was amputated at Bergen op Zoom (he declined a blindfold and watched the operation intently). The procedure, conducted with him seated on a table, took half an hour because the surgeon's saw was blunt, and it was only with difficulty that the shattered limb could be hacked off. Edward Costello of the 95th observed what he considered the difference between British and French patients: after Waterloo he saw a weather-beaten Royal Dragoon calmly chewing tobacco while his arm was taken off below the elbow, showing no emotion, while next to him was a Frenchman making a fearful noise as a surgeon probed for a ball in his shoulder. When the dragoon's arm was off, he struck the Frenchman across the face with the severed part, exclaiming, 'Take it, and make soup with it, and stop your damned bellowing!'[39]

After recovering the wounded, a task in the immediate aftermath of battle was to dispose of the dead, if only for reasons of hygiene, which was urgent if the army remained in the vicinity of the field of battle: shortly after Vimeiro Wellington noted that the army must move on, or 'we shall be poisoned here by the stench of the dead and wounded,'[40] which gives some idea of the ghastly nature of a recent action. Local civilians could be recruited to help, and after Waterloo some of them sought a different kind of plunder: 'some Russian Jews

The aftermath of battle: bodies are stripped of their clothing and equipment and tumbled unceremoniously into mass graves. This scene is just south of La Haye Sainte, a day or two after the Battle of Waterloo. (Print by J. Rouse)

were assisting in the spoilation of the dead by chiselling out their teeth, an operation they performed with the most brutal indifference. The clinking hammers of these wretches jarred horribly on my ears . . .'[41]; the purpose being to sell the teeth for the manufacture of dentures.

Burials were often perfunctory, with bodies tossed without ceremony into communal pits and sometimes covered so negligently that limbs might protrude, or the remains easily scratched up by scavenging animals. Sometimes a regiment might bury its own dead, as must have occurred in Holland in 1799 when Robert Hullock of the 31st, shot through the jaw, was buried in a shallow grave by his comrade John Cames; but Hullock was not dead, recovered his senses, dug himself out of the hole and rejoined his comrades. Seven years later he was observed digging a grave almost ten feet deep; when questioned he remarked that it was for Cames, and if he got him in so deep 'it will puzzle him to creep out as I did.'

Those who survived the first shock of injury, and the ministrations of the over-worked and under-resourced surgeons in the field, were usually transported, often at slow pace over many miles, to a hospital, frequently without much medical attention. Their plight was described by a light dragoon who met a convoy of 700 casualties from Albuera, riding in carts:

Casualty evacuation: wounded are conveyed in impressed carts, passing La Haye Sainte, while local civilians loot the dead in the process of burying them, immediately after the Battle of Waterloo. (Print by J. Rouse)

No doubt they had received, when first taken in hand by the surgeons, all the care which the nature of the position would allow. But they had performed since that period a long journey, through a barren country, and under a broiling sun – and their wounds remaining undressed all this while, were now in such a state as to defy description . . . . [We] gave ourselves up to the business of cleansing their hurts – the smell proceeding from which was fearful. Over and over again we were forced to quit the miserable patients in a hurry, and run out into the open air, in order to save ourselves from fainting . . . weeks passed away ere I was able utterly to overcome the effect which the distressing occupation had upon me. I could neither eat nor sleep, for everything seemed to be tainted with effluvia from these cankered wounds, and my dreams were all such as to make sleep a burden.[42]

Arrival at hospital (usually buildings appropriated temporarily, with no medical facilities) frequently brought no relief. Some were run admirably – soldiers billeted on private citizens in Brussels after Waterloo, for example, reported in some cases exemplary care – but many were beyond description. John Cooper visited a number of hospitals in the Peninsula, large and small, and left a horrifying catalogue of their situation, like that at Elvas, which had between 1,000 and 1,500 men just laid on the floor, or Villa Viciosa, 'a convent; about 150 patients in the four corridors; next to no ventilation; small windows; great barrels or tubs for all purposes; the stench horrible; logs of fir burning at the four corners of the building, to drive away the infection; smoke blinding.'[43]

Improvements in medical administration did have an effect, such as the prefabricated, portable hospitals established by the humanitarian James McGrigor in the Peninsula, which by accompanying the army saved count-less wounded the long and often fatal trips in unsuitable vehicles from the battlefield to a place of convalescence. Despite the terrible conditions in some hospitals, the recovery rate for even the grievously wounded is surprising, and belies some contemporary comments about the ineptitude of medical officers, though unquestionably many deserved criticism. For example, statistics published by the Adjutant General in April 1816 stated that in the British Army in the Waterloo campaign, some 1,715 had been killed and 7,687 wounded, of whom some 66 per cent had by that time returned to their regi-ments, and just over a further 2 per cent had been passed fit for limited service in Garrison or Veteran Battalions. Only 11.1 per cent of those who had reached a hospital had died, and about the same proportion still remained under treatment some ten months after they had been wounded.

In addition to physical injury, psychological consequences must have existed to some degree, although not fully recognized at the time. Lord Moran's theory held that courage resembled a bank balance,[44] reduced by each 'withdrawal' or period of combat; in which case the time of acute physical danger could be relatively short, which perhaps tended to reduce the potential for psychological trauma. Two soldiers qualified for fifteen clasps for the Military General Service Medal, each clasp representing a battle in the Peninsular War, the maximum awarded to any individual: Daniel Loochstadt and James Talbot. The latter, of the 45th Foot, in the fifteen battles in which he served, was probably under fire and in mortal danger for no more than a total of twenty-four hours, spread over eight years, during which time his regiment suffered 123 men killed in action (plus, without doubt, many returned as 'wounded' whose injuries proved fatal). Without in any way minimising the nature of Talbot's service, this period could well have been exceeded by only two days' service in the front line during the First World War, when the prevalence of psychological trauma or 'shell shock' was extensive.

Nevertheless, there were recorded examples of apparent psychological damage resulting from the horrors of battle, though these were usually attributed to the effects of physical injury. William Morris of the Coldstream Guards was an example: his wounds at Waterloo were said to have affected his intellect and in July 1816, having been confined in a civil lock-up after he was found collapsed, probably through alcohol, and perhaps fearing punishment, he used his braces to hang himself from a nail in the wall. His tragic case – probably far from unique – would be recognized by those who have ministered to victims of post-traumatic stress in a later century.

Rather more prominent was James Hadfield, who was said to have become deranged after receiving eight sabre cuts to the head at Lincelles while serving with the 15th Light Dragoons: he left the army after attempting to stab one of his officers, and in May 1800 fired a shot at the King at Drury Lane Theatre. His reason was unclear, for he declared that his only wish was to have another cut at the French, and upon his apprehension, taken before the Duke of York (who recognised him, Hadfield having been his orderly in the Netherlands), he declared that the Duke was 'the soldier's friend, and I love him.'[45] He was found not guilty by reason of insanity.

Those who survived the physical and emotional stresses of campaigning became, in the Peninsula, part of what Wellington described as 'probably the most complete machine for its numbers now existing in Europe.'[46] Among many contemporary descriptions of this formidable, indeed, virtually invincible, army are some that epitomise its most basic elements. Moyle Sherer saw the 29th Foot:

Nothing could possibly be worse than their clothing; it had become necessary to patch it; and as red cloth could not be procured, grey, white, and even brown had been used: yet, under this striking disadvantage, they could not be viewed by a soldier without admiration. The perfect order and cleanliness of their arms and appointments, their steadiness on parade, their erect carriage, and their firm and free marching, exceeded any thing of the kind that I had ever seen. No corps of any army or nation, which I have since had an opportunity of seeing, has come nearer to my idea of what a regiment of infantry should be, than the old twenty-ninth.[47]

As a very young officer new to the Peninsula, George Bell provided a more concise snapshot of a regiment he watched march by, which he described as merry as larks, bronze, hard as nails and as ready for a fight as for a ration of rum. The regiment in question was the 88th Connaught Rangers, but his description could surely have applied to the entire army.

11

'His Country's Stay': Homecoming

The brave poor sodger ne'er despise,
Nor count him as a stranger;
Remember he's his country's stay,
In day and hour of danger

The Soldier's Return: Robert Burns

For many soldiers, return from service abroad was unheralded, as they almost crept home without ceremony, though the welcome they received might depend upon the success of the campaign in which they had been engaged. Those returning from the Corunna campaign, for example, presented an appearance that must have been frightening, as Harry Smith wrote: 'we were literally covered and almost eaten up with vermin, most of us suffering from ague and dysentery, every man a living still active skeleton,' and when meeting his colonel in England he was greeted with 'Who the devil's ghost are you?'[1] Those returning from a successful campaign might be accorded a better reception, as were the 42nd in Edinburgh after the Waterloo campaign, though inevitably such occasions were tinged with sadness. In this case the welcome was somewhat improvised – a notice 'Welcome, gallant heroes!' on the Canongate tolbooth was written on a pocket handkerchief hung upon a Lochaber axe belonging to the Town Guard – but a multitude had gathered, shocked at the appearance of a once-glittering regiment: '... worn-out, travel-stained men .... Their once bright scarlet uniforms exhibited all the shades of depression which that colour is capable of assuming; while very few retained any remnant even of the plume which distinguishes the Highland soldier's head-dress. Most had plain bonnets, and a great many had not even their grand national characteristic article of dress – the kilt – trousers and trews having been substituted. No one who has not actually witnessed a similar exhibition of the sad and desolating effects of war can fully conceive what our feeling were on the first appearance of our poor countrymen ... some

170

truly touching episodes took place: here and there a female might be seen rushing wildly amongst the ranks of the soldiery, and anxiously inquiring whether such a one was alive . . . when, as in too many instances, an answer in the sad negative had to be given, the agonised look and suppressed scream with which it was received was truly heartrending, and brought tears to the eyes of all who were witnesses of it'[2]; but fortunately there were also joyous reunions of parents, wives and sweethearts.

Celebrations were probably most marked if a returning regiment had a marked local identity, as in the homecoming to Preston of the 3rd Royal Lancashire Militia, described in verse by their Sergeant W. Mallett:

> 'When fathers, uncles, mothers, wives and cousins,
> Crowd the streets, acquaintances by dozens,
> The eager hand stretch forth to catch the grasp,
> While fathers now their wives and babes did clasp.'[3]

Otherwise, civilian society often looked sadly askance at the returning 'heroes' in case they brought with them the evils of campaigning such as disease, like the typhus that spread at Truro from, it was said, members of the 10th Hussars on their return from Corunna.

A common fear of bad behaviour, especially on the part of soldiers newly-discharged and who might roam the land, was expressed by the City of London's Common Serjeant, in 1802: 'He meant not to insinuate any thing to the prejudice of those brave defenders of the country; but it was a fact too notorious to escape observation, that they were too apt to indulge in excesses which required the coercive arm of the law to repress.'[4]

For the individual soldier, homecoming might actually involve the happy outcome of Burns's *The Soldier's Return*, in which the veteran finds his sweet-heart still constant; but otherwise he might discover that after an absence of perhaps decades, without any contact, all his family was gone. Campaigning could so change their appearance that returning soldiers might not even be recognised. When William Green of the 95th returned to his native Lutterworth, his uniform was recognized and several enquiries made of local men in his regiment. Among those who sought news was an old man whose son was a rifleman, with whom Green sat in an inn for some while, sharing a drink, and it was a time before the old man realized that 'You are my son!'

For discharged soldiers the future might be unemployment and poverty, and even worse for those maimed in action, dependent upon charity and a small pension; not all might be as cheerful as a cargo of invalids who landed from the Peninsula at Plymouth Dock in 1814, who astonished spectators by their levity of spirit, including a sergeant who had lost both legs and joked with those who carried him off the boat not to wet his feet.

From 1806 any soldier discharged as disabled or unfit for military duty had a right to a pension. The scales of these were announced publicly in 1814, perhaps to avoid frauds perpetrated by discharged soldiers who 'are now traversing the country in all directions.' Those blinded or who had lost a limb received for life a daily pension of 1s 6d for sergeants, 1s 2d for corporals, and 1s for drummers and privates. Out-Pensioners of Chelsea Hospital, who had been examined to determine the scale of their pension, received annually, according to their disability, £18 5s for a first-class pension, £13 13s for second-class and £7 12s for third-class. Those discharged from Veteran battalions received 9d per diem, or 1s if totally incapacitated, and all soldiers received fourteen, twenty-one or twenty-eight days' pay according to the distance they had to travel home.

At the conclusion of the Peninsular War, the total effective rank and file was in excess of 237,000 (on 25 January 1814, 237,946, some 32,000 below establishment). The total number of army pensioners at that date was 31,201, giving an annual cost to the Treasury of £511,947 16s 7½d, which indicated an average pension of approximately 11d per diem.

Some retired old soldiers had always been marked out by their less adventurous neighbours, probably most notably those in smaller communities, like William Purslow of Ludlow, a veteran of the siege of Gibraltar. Though latterly on crutches in consequence of a hard life, he always declined parish relief and existed on the charity of his neighbours who recognized him as 'a man of genuine integrity and independence of soul'.[6] Clearly an object of local fame, donations he received from passing military officers led to his often being conveyed home from the inn in a wheelbarrow, and in addition to his other accomplishments he kept two hedgehogs that accompanied him on his walks like dogs.

After the end of the Napoleonic Wars, however, discharged soldiers were no longer a rarity after the very great reduction in the strength of the army brought about by peace, and many were ignored in consequence. Thomas Jackson found no great largesse. Upon his discharge he was granted a pension of only a shilling a day; he suspected that those who judged him thought he was a young man able to earn a living without a leg (he was a buckle maker by trade). He was allowed to keep his uniform, however, and as Foot Guards sergeants wore gold lace his wife was able to remove it and sell it, together with his shako cords, for thirty shillings to give him a start in his new life. He received a crude wooden leg gratis, for which, he said, he was supposed to be grateful, but instead viewed it as a dog might regard a tin kettle tied to its tail.

Stumping around with a timber leg and a miserable pension, he wrote that he felt an outcast in his native land, degraded for having been a soldier. His peg leg made him the butt of jokes of those he described as the scum of his native Walsall, one of whom said the loss of a leg had served him right. It cut him to the quick.

The mass discharge of soldiers following the end of the Napoleonic Wars coincided with a depression in many industries, causing widespread poverty; for example, in 1814 it was reckoned that in London alone, 6,000 adults and 9,288 children subsisted entirely by begging. Those who had a trade might return to it, like Benjamin Harris, who had been a shoemaker, but skills learned in the army had little use outside it; the ability to storm a rampart at bayonet point hardly carried over into civilian life. Even Harry Rowe, who put his skill with the trumpet that he had exercised in the cavalry to use as trumpeter to the High Sheriff of Yorkshire for forty-six years (and also ran a puppet show) died in the poorhouse at York.

Robert Burns' *The Soldier's Return* stated that:

> 'For gold the merchant ploughs the main,
> The farmer ploughs the manor,
> But glory is the sodger's prize,
> The sodger's wealth is honour;'

But glory and honour could not be eaten. The officer George Bell wrote bitterly on the conclusion of the Peninsular War, concerning the paucity of pensions accorded the rank and file; that while wasting the national gold in millions, the government permitted worthy old soldiers to become paupers. The sinecures held by the aristocracy and their friends, paid for doing nothing, he declared, would have relieved the circumstances of thousands of brave men who had fought nobly for their country and their king.

Occasionally there was a reaction. In the 'Highland clearances' many Scottish families were evicted from their homesteads by their landlords to introduce the more lucrative sheep farming, including worthy old soldiers and their dependents. When at the time of the Crimean War fewer Highland volunteers came forward than expected, an article in the press recorded recalcitrant Highlanders saying to the recruiters, 'You robbed us of our country and gave it to the sheep. Therefore, since you have preferred sheep to men, let sheep defend you!'[7]

Nevertheless, many might still have echoed the sentiments of the one-armed, one-legged veteran in Burns' *The Jolly Beggars*, who recalled his service under Sir Augustus Elliot at the siege of Gibraltar, where:

'. . . there I left for witness an arm and a limb;
Yet my country need me, with Eliot to head me,
I'll clatter on my stumps at the sound of a drum.'

The events of their military service stayed with many veterans, and many clearly regarded their military experiences as the highlight of their lives, especially if they were reduced to doing menial jobs when they re-entered civilian life. The all-pervading influence of army life was manifested in myriad

The only official award available to the rank and file at this period was the Waterloo Medal. This example was awarded to John Clarke of the 1st Foot Guards, the Suffolk cordwainer mentioned in the introduction.

ways. The rifleman whose story concerning the Frenchman with the lovers' knot is quoted earlier became a rat catcher following his discharge after losing a hand; he named his dogs after prominent generals, notably Wellington, 'Boney', Picton and Craufurd. Perhaps the strangest commemoration was that experienced by James Smithies, who had fought at Waterloo with the 1st Royal Dragoons and who was awarded the Military General Service Medal with clasps for Fuentes de Onoro, Vittoria and Toulouse. A Lancastrian, he had run away from home to join the army but remained attached to it – in battle he said he always imagined he could hear the bells of his local church – and returned there on his discharge to resume his old trade of silk weaving.

Reverse of the Waterloo Medal.

He wore his medals with pride on significant anniversaries but the most peculiar resonance of his service was that he always suffered a nosebleed on the
anniversary of Waterloo. Such was his pride in having served his country that
he left instructions that his regiment and campaigns should be inscribed on
his tombstone; he was killed when run over by a colliery wagon in January
1868, in his eighty-first year.

Military pride had a worse effect upon the life of James Leigh, late of sixteen
years' service in the 25th Foot and who was in receipt of a Chelsea pension.
Convicted of the murder of a man who insulted him, he explained that 'a
soldier would not brook such treatment' as he had received. Appearing calm
throughout, when he was hanged in November 1801 opposite Newgate Prison
he declared that 'I mind this no more than I would entering a field of action,'
and to a fellow prisoner executed at the same time, who was weeping, he said,
'Be a man, and die with spirit'; and by making 'use of many other exhortations . . . so far succeeded as to make [Richard] Stark hold up his head. Before
they were turned off, Leigh looked around, bowed to the populace, smiled,
and appeared quite unconcerned.'[8]

In the immediate aftermath of the wars, discharged soldiers were often disregarded or viewed as a nuisance, but as Thomas Campbell averred that
'distance lends enchantment,' so as the years passed and the surviving
veterans declined in numbers, those remaining tended to assume the status of
local celebrities. Despite their tribulations, some of the veterans were extaor-
dinarily long-lived. The last British 'other rank' who fought at Waterloo
appears to have been Maurice Shea of the 73rd, who died in Canada in
February 1892 at the age of 97.[9] In old age, some soldiers applied for a pension,
or had an application submitted on their behalf by their minister or a relative.
The circumstances of many were extremely sad, notably those resident in a
workhouse or entirely incapacitated by injuries sustained in their youth. It was
sometimes difficult to establish the circumstances of their service, many
having suffered a decline in memory in extreme old age, or no longer had their
medal to confirm their presence at Waterloo, a number being recorded as
having sold it for food. Others were still trying to earn a living, like a 78-year-
old gunner labouring as a thatcher, William Calvert. John McKay of the 42nd,
wounded three times at Waterloo, at the age of ninety was reported as making
his living wandering the country, begging; he had been born aboard HMS
Victory, his father a marine killed at Trafalgar. He finally received a pension
of 1s 6d per diem, fifty-eight years after his discharge.[10]

In their declining years, some veterans sought the fellowship of their erst-
while comrades, perhaps as a way of reliving their youth. One notable annual
gathering to celebrate the anniversary of Waterloo was held at Rochdale,

begun by one of the veterans, Richard Bentinck of the 23rd, beating the assembly with the very drumsticks he had used to sound the same call at the battle. The last assembly, in 1866, saw only five veterans attending; their last survivor was Abraham Whitworth, late of the 51st.

As the years passed, the dwindling number of surviving veterans of the Napoleonic Wars took on an almost iconic status that in earlier years they would have found bewildering. On 10 April 1889, at Weston-super-Mare, Thomas Palmer of the 32nd passed away in his 100th year, believed to have been the last survivor of the Battle of Corunna. Invalided from his regiment at age twenty-five, he had worked as a shoemaker and lived with his widowed daughter-in-law in old age. More than 5,000 people attended his funeral, and three bands, of the 1st Gloucestershire Engineer Volunteers, the Gloucestershire Artillery Volunteers and the local battalion of the Somerset Light Infantry, an exhibition of interest and concern infinitely greater than that commonly shown for old soldiers in earlier years, when they were not such rare survivors of a bygone age.

Unlike those who died full of years at home and whose service was not infrequently recorded on their tombstone, very few ordinary soldiers had any memorial to commemorate their life and death at the time of their service; with no details of next-of-kin being recorded officially, families were not even informed of their fate. There were, however, a few exceptions, for example a monument in Barbados recording those members of the Royal York Rangers who fell in action against the French colonies in the West Indies, including Martinique and Guadeloupe in 1809-10. In addition to the details of four officers, six NCOs and forty-four other ranks were named on the tablet. It is perhaps slightly ironic that men from what was virtually a penal corps should be commemorated in stone while their less controversial colleagues who comprised the vast majority of the army were ignored.

Perhaps the best-known monument to an ordinary soldier is that from a previous generation, the tombstone at Winchester Cathedral of grenadier Thomas Thetcher of the North Hampshire Militia who died in 1764 'of a violent Fever contracted by drinking Small Beer when hot,' with the comment that 'An honest Soldier never is forgot/Whether he die by Musket or by Pot.' Clearly he was not forgotten, for his regiment renewed his headstone in 1802.

A more literary inscription, written by the officer and antiquary Francis Grose, was erected to an ordinary soldier at Barnstaple:

> 'To this strange earth with warlike rites we trust
> The shrouded relicks [sic] of a comrade's dust.
> Nor shall his ashes unregarded lie,

Without the kind remembrance of a sigh;
For him shall gush the friendly drop sincere;
A soldier's grave demands the friendly tear.'[11]

Few ordinary redcoats would have thought to compose something so poetic, and surely, while perhaps recognising the truth of its sentiments, would have been more appreciative of a much simpler inscription at Ipswich to Private William Wilkinson of the 7th Light Dragoons who died in 1807 and was described as 'a good Comrade, and a steady faithful Soldier.'[12]

Another not forgotten by his comrades was Sergeant Major Johnson of the 7th Royal Fuzileers, for whom a memorial inscription was agreed at his native Shilbottle, to be produced by the great engraver Thomas Bewick. A statement was sent to his parents by his officer, John Orr:

> ... although with you, I most sincerely lament the early fate of so good a man, with you also I rejoice in the remembrance of his having nobly done his duty, both in front of the enemy and in private life. No man could be more respected than Johnson, and, consequently, none more regretted. We naturally grieve for such a loss. The corps mourns Johnson; but why should we be sorry, 'twas to that end the Almighty made us. Your son was called on in the prime of life: he knew not long sickness, and died sensible: his worth lives on record in the books of the regiment, a consequence which soldiers aspire to, and which good alone can merit.[13]

It was, perhaps, equally suitable as an epitaph for the countless rank and file redcoats who did their duty anonymously and whose names received not a mention in the cold pages of history.

Notes

Introduction

1 *United Service Magazine* 1842, I, p. 182.
2 Creevey, T., *The Creevey Papers*, ed. J. Gore, London 1934, p. 404.
3 Wheeler, W., *The Letters of Private Wheeler 1809-1828*, ed. B.H. Liddell Hart, London 1951, p. 144.
4 *Colburn's United Service Magazine* 1845, I, pp. 1, 4, 8.
5 Sherer, M., *Recollections of the Peninsula* (published as 'by the Author of Sketches of India'), London 1823, p. 145.
6 Some explanation of the name appears in Laffin, J., *Tommy Atkins*, London 1966, pp. xi-xii, where the 1815 document is reproduced.
7 *Colburn's United Service Magazine* 1845, III, pp. 17-18.
8 'A Laurel 'Neath Proud Wellington' by W.S. Passmore, ibid. 1846, III, p. 240.

Chapter 1

1 *The Anti-Gallican; or Standard of British Loyalty, Religion and Liberty*, London 1804, I, p. 97.
2 *United Service Journal* 1839, II, p. 204.
3 Donaldson, J., *Recollections of the Eventful Life of a Soldier*, Edinburgh 1854, pp. 292-93.
4 *United Service Journal* 1840, II, p. 343.
5 General Order, Coimbra, 29 May 1809.

Chapter 2

1 Stanhope, Philip, 5th Earl, *Notes of Conversations with the Duke of Wellington, 1831-1851*, London 1888, p. 18.

2 ibid. p. 14.

3 *London Chronicle*, 23 July 1795.

4 *Gentleman's Magazine*, August 1810, p. 176.

5 ibid., October 1803, p. 971.

6 *London Chronicle*, 21 November 1795.

7 Paine, J., 'Recruiting Poster: 73rd Regiment, 1813', *Journal of the Society for Army Historical Research*, Vol. XXXI (1953), p. 184.

8 14th Light Dragoons; Leetham, Lt.Col. Sir Arthur, 'Old Recruiting Posters', ibid. Vol. I (1922), p. 119.

9 *Lincoln, Rutland and Stamford Mercury*, 25 October 1793; quoted in Wylly, Lt.Col. H.C., *The Loyal North Lancashire Regiment*, London 1934, Vol. I, p. 175.

10 Royal Marines, 1812.

11 Donaldson, pp. 87-88.

12 *Morning Chronicle*, 29 April 1794.

13 Seton, Col. Sir Bruce, Bt., 'Infantry Recruiting Instructions in England in 1767', *Journal of the Society for Army Historical Research*, Vol. IV (1925), pp. 86-87.

14 Donaldson, p. 86.

15 *Colburn's United Service Magazine* 1846, I, p. 522.

16 Clerk, Revd. A., *Memoir of Colonel John Cameron, Fassiefern, K.T.S . . .* , Glasgow 1858, p. 23.

17 ibid., p. 22.

18 *Colburn's United Service Magazine* 1845, II, pp. 443-44.

19 *United Service Journal* 1839, I, pp. 528-29.

20 Morris, T., *The Three Sergeants, or Phases of a Soldier's Life*, London 1858, p. xxxii.

21 Donaldson, pp. 35-36.

22 *London Chronicle*, 16 June 1795.

23 ibid., 22 January 1795.

24 *Exeter Flying Post*, 20 June 1779.

25 *United Service Magazine* 1842, I, p. 178.

26 There were various versions of this very popular song; 'Grinfelt' is Greenfield, near Oldham.

27 *United Service Magazine* 1842, I, p. 50.

28 Morris, pp. xxviii, xxx.

29 Leetham, p. 120.

30 *London Chronicle*, 6 January 1798.

31 *The Courier*, 9 April 1811.

32 *Colburn's United Service Magazine* 1845, III, p. 396.

33 ibid. 1846, I, p. 523.

34 Napier, Sir George, *Passages in the Early Military Life of General Sir George T. Napier, KGB*, ed. Gen. W.C.E. Napier, London 1884, pp. 21-22.

Chapter 3

1 Bell, J. (ed.), *Rhymes of the Northern Bards*, Newcastle 1812, p. 310.

2 *Colburn's United Service Magazine* 1845, II, p. 102.

3 ibid., III, p. 561.

4 *United Service Journal* 1840, II, p. 455.

5 *London Chronicle*, 6 January 1798.

6 Macintosh, H.B., *The Grant, Strathspey or First Highland Fencible Regiment 1793-1799*, Elgin 1934, pp. 96-116.

7 This and the following quotations from Macpherson, C.H., 'On the Recruiting of the Army', *Colburn's United Service Magazine* 1846, I, pp. 111-19.

8 ibid. 1847, II, p. 537.

9 ibid. 1845, III, pp. 282-84.

10 ibid. p. 110.

11 *United Service Journal* 1839, III, p. 271.

12 See Holme, N., & Kirby, E.L., *Medal Rolls, 23rd Foot. Royal Welch Fusiliers, Napoleonic Period*, Caernarfon & London 1978.

13 Blakeney, R., *A Boy in the Peninsular War*, ed. J. Sturgis, London 1899, pp. 73-74.

14 *Edinburgh Evening Courant*, 27 February 1812.

15 *Morning Chronicle*, 10 September 1810.

16 Lagden, A., & Sly, J., *The 2/73rd at Waterloo*, Brightlingsea 1988, pp. 200-01.

17 Greenhill Gardyne, C., *The Life of a Regiment: The History of the Gordon Highlanders*, London 1929, Vol. I, p. 34.

Chapter 4

1 *Gentleman's Magazine*, October 1803, p. 992.

2 Porter, R.K., *Letters from Portugal and Spain, written during the March of the British Troops under Sir John Moore*, London 1809 (published under the nom-de-plume of 'An Officer'), p. 219.

3 *Public Ledger*, 9 March 1813.

4   Sinclair, Sir John, *Hints Respecting the State of the Camp at Aberdeen, in 1795*, n.d., pp. iv-v.

5   *Historical Records of the Queen's Own Cameron Highlanders*, Edinburgh 1909, Vol. I, pp. 45-46.

6   Anton, J., *Retrospect of a Military Life*, Edinburgh 1841, p. 210.

7   *Colburn's United Service Magazine* 1843, III, p. 214.

8   Ross-Lewin, H., *With the Thirty-Second in the Peninsular and other Campaigns*, ed. J. Wardell, Dublin 1904, pp. 103-05.

9   *Colburn's United Service Magazine* 1843, II, p. 86.

10 ibid. 1843, III, p. 214.

11 *The News*, 8 August 1808.

12 For an account of this singular occurrence, see Browne, T.H., *The Napoleonic War Journal of Captain Thomas Henry Browne 1807-1816*, ed. R.N. Buckley, London 1987, pp. 113-16.

13 *United Service Journal* 1831, II, p. 204.

14 Cooper, J.S., *Rough Notes of Seven Campaigns in Portugal, Spain, France and America*, Carlisle 1869, r/p 1914, pp. 85-86.

15 Both these quotations: Surtees, W., *Twenty-Five Years in the Rifle Brigade*, London 1833, p. 22.

16 Lawrence, W., *The Autobiography of Sergeant William Lawrence*, ed. G.N. Bankes, London 1886, p. 216.

17 *Gentleman's Magazine*, December 1803, p. 1179.

18 Morley, S., *Memoirs of a Serjeant of the 5th Regt. of Foot*, Ashford 1842, p. 114.

19 Cooper, p. 28.

20 *United Service Journal* 1831, II, p. 61.

Chapter 5

1   *Edinburgh Evening Courant*, 7 May 1812.

2   *True Briton*, 25 March 1803.

3   *Colburn's United Service Magazine* 1846, II, pp. 400-01.

4   *United Service Journal* 1840, I, pp. 197-98.

5   ibid. 1834, I, p. 259.

6   ibid 1847, III, p. 503.

7   Anton, p. 29.

8   'Answers to Queries from Sir John Sinclair, respecting the Situation of a British Soldier of Infantry', in *British Military Library or Journal*, London 1800-01, Vol. I, p. 479.

9   Marshall, H., 'Contributions to Statistics of the British Army', originally in *Edinburgh Medical and Surgical Journal*, July 1835.

10 *Colburn's United Service Magazine* 1846, I, p. 525.

11 Smyth, B. *History of the XX Regiment, 1688-1888*, London & Manchester 1889, p. 139.

12 *Gentleman's Magazine,* May 1804, p. 473.

13 *United Service Journal* 1839, III, p. 546.

14 *Anti-Gallican Monitor & Anti-Corsican Chronicle,* 27 September 1812.

15 *Gentleman's Magazine,* July 1809, p. 683.

16 ibid. June 1801, p. 491.

17 See Bowyer-Bower, Maj. T.A., 'Some Early Educational Influences in the British Army', *Journal of the Society for Army Historical Research,* Vol. XXXIII (1955), pp. 5-12.

18 Lagden & Sly, p. 51.

19 Illustrated in Balmer, J.L., *British and Irish Regimental and Volunteer Medals 1745-1895*, Loughborough 1988, Vol. I, p. 128.

20 His career and samples of his handwriting are in Haythornthwaite, P.J., 'A Tale of Two Guardsmen', *Military Illustrated* No. 14, 1988.

21 *Dublin Evening Post,* 27 December 1794, quoted in McAnally, Sir Henry, *The Irish Militia 1793-1816: A Social and Military Study,* Dublin & London 1949, p. 58.

22 *The Times,* 28 February 1810.

23 Mace, J.E., *Notes on Old Tenterden and the Four Churches,* Tenterden 1902, p. 52.

24 Mackay Scobie, I.H., *An Old Highland Fencible Corps: The History of the Reay Fencible Highland Regiment of Foot, or Mackay's Highlanders 1794-1802,* Edinburgh & London 1914, p. 170.

25 Cadell, Lt.Col. C., *Narrative of the Campaigns of the 28th Regiment since their Return from Egypt in 1802,* London 1835, p. 238,

26 *John Bull,* 26 November 1821.

27 Wellington, 1st Duke, *Dispatches of Field Marshal the Duke of Wellington,* ed. J. Gurwood, London 1834-38, Vol. VII, pp. 231-32 (6 February 1811).

28 *General Regulations and Orders for the Army,* London 1811, p. 122.

29 *Gentleman's Magazine,* October 1807, p. 980.

30 ibid., April 1810, p. 377.

31 *Portsmouth Telegraph,* 17 February 1800.

32 *London Chronicle,* 11 August 1795.

33 *Rules and Regulations for the Movements of His Majesty's Infantry,* London 1792, p. 3.

34 Fuller, Maj.Gen. J.F.C., 'Sir John Moore's Light Infantry Instructions of 1798-1799', *Journal of the Society for Army Historical Research,* Vol. XXX (1952), p. 75.

35 *Colburn's United Service Magazine* 1845, II, p. 389.

36 Wellington, Vol. IX, pp. 149-50.

37 *Colburn's United Service Magazine* 1846, III, p. 161.

38 *United Service Journal* 1831, II, p. 182.

39 ibid., p. 181.

40 *Colburn's United Service Magazine* 1844, III, p. 410.

Chapter 6

1   *United Service Journal* 1834, III, p. 413.

2   Sherer, pp. 180-81.

3   ibid., p. 70.

4   *United Service Magazine* 1842, I, pp. 373-74.

5   *Colburn's United Service Magazine* 1844, I, p. 251.

6   ibid.

7   ibid., p. 256.

8   ibid., p. 251.

9   Cooper, p. 14.

10 *Naval & Military Magazine* 1827, I, pp. 499-500.

11 ibid., pp. 573-74.

12 *The Times,* 22 June 1815.

13 *Cobbett's Weekly Political Register,* 22 June 1811, columns 1554-55 (this publication was not conventionally paginated).

14 *Naval & Military Magazine* 1827, I, p. 468.

15 *Cobbett's Weekly Political Register,* 27 February 1811, columns 485-86.

16 Cooper, p. 15.

17 Lawrence, pp. 48-49.

18 *Colburn's United Service Magazine* 1843, III, p. 247.

19 General Order, Coimbra, 2 June 1809.

20 *London Chronicle,* 16 June 1795.

21 *Colburn's United Service Magazine* 1846, III, p. 560.

22 *General Regulations & Orders for the Army,* London 1811, p. 123.

23 Donaldson, pp. 221-22.

24 *United Service Magazine 1842,* I, p. 185 gives the figure as 53,764.

25 Morris, p. 8.

26 *The Times,* 3 January 1810.

27 Knowles, R., *The War in the Peninsula: Some Letters of Lieutenant Robert Knowles . . .* , ed. Sir Lees Knowles, Bt., Bolton 1913, p. 51.

28 Royal Commission on Military Punishments: reply to question 5807, p. 324.

29 *The News,* 23 November 1806.

30 Miller, B., *The Adventures of Serjeant Benjamin Miller*, intro. by M.H. Dacombe & B.J.H. Rowe, Sheffield 1928, p. 30.

31 *London Chronicle*, 29 October 1795.

32 Stewart of Garth, Col. D., *Sketches of the Character, Manners and Present State of the Highlanders of Scotland*, Edinburgh & London 1822, Vol. II, p. 346.

Chapter7

1 Stanhope, p. 18.

2 Williamson, J., *The Elements of Military Arrangement*, London 1791, Vol. I, pp. 65-67.

3 *Colburn's United Service Magazine* 1845, III, p. 396.

4 Wellington, Vol. IX, p. 228, 10 June 1812.

5 *United Service Journal* 1834, III, p. 127.

6 Williamson pp. 52-53.

7 Lawrence, p. 210.

8 *General Regulations and Orders for the Army*, London 1811, p. 96.

9 Henry, W., *Events of a Military Life*, London 1843, Vol. II, p. 3.

10 Roberts, D., *The Military Adventures of Johnny Newcome*, London 1816, pp. 22-23 (published under the nom-de-plume of 'An Officer').

11 *Colburn's United Service Magazine* 1848, III, p. 235.

12 Stuart, W.K., *Reminiscences of a Soldier*, London 1874, Vol. II, p. 276.

13 *Colburn's United Service Magazine* 1848, III, p. 4.

14 *Naval & Military Magazine* 1827, I, p. 493.

15 Daniel, J.E., *Journal of an Officer of the Commissariat Department*, London 1820, p. 425.

16 Greenhill Gardyne, Vol. I, p. 295.

17 Some accounts of this incident are a little confused; William Lawrence, who recounted the story (pp. 114-15) calls the officer 'Elland', though it is clearly Ayling that was involved: casualties are named in *London Gazette*, 24 April 1812.

18 G. Napier, pp. 191-93.

19 ibid., p. 195.

20 Simmons, G., *A British Rifle Man*, ed. W. Verner, London 1899, p. 376.

21 The author is indebted to the late Terry Livsey for family information; the obituary in the *Burnley Gazette*, 22 January 1870, uses the spelling 'Livesey', but the family spelling, and that in the Military General Service Medal roll, is correctly 'Livsey'.

22 *Historical Records of the Queen's Own Cameron Highlanders*, Edinburgh 1909, Vol. I, p. 68.

23 Knight, C.R.B., *Historical Records of the Buffs . . . 1704-1914*, London 1935, Vol. I, p. 353.

24 Dalton, C., *The Waterloo Roll Call*, London 1904, p. 178, quoting Butler, W.F.A., *Narrative of the Historical Events Connected with the Sixty-Ninth Regiment*, London 1870.

25 Stanhope, p. 18.

26 *United Service Journal* 1835, III, p. 391.

27 ibid., p. 271.

28 ibid. 1839, II, p. 203.

29 Sidney, Revd. E., *The Life of Lord Hill*, London 1845, pp. 356-57.

30 The author is indebted to Allan Wood for this account.

31 Pearson's account is in *The Soldier Who Walked Away: Autobiography of Andrew Pearson*, ed. A.H. Haley, Liverpool, nd.

32 Surtees, p. 49.

Chapter8

1 *Gentleman's Magazine*, February 1807, p. 156.

2 *British Military Library or Journal*, London 1798-1801, Vol. I, p. 479.

3 MS, author's possession.

4 *The Times*, 7 November 1814.

5 *General Regulations and Orders for the Army*, London 1811, p. 255.

6 *United Service Journal* 1834, I, pp. 487-88.

7 *Colburn's United Service Magazine* 1845, I, pp. 7-8.

8 Bell, G., *Rough Notes by an Old Soldier, during Fifty Years' Service, from Ensign to Major-General*, London 1867, Vol. I, pp. 74-75.

9 Ker Porter, p. 266.

10 Landmann, G.T., *Recollections of Military Life, 1806-08*, London 1854, Vol. II, p. 200.

11 Gleig, Revd. G.R., *The Subaltern*, Edinburgh 1872, pp. 119-20.

12 Anton, pp. 142-43.

13 *Colburn's United Service Magazine* 1845, II, pp. 526-28.

14 Donaldson, p. 232.

15 *Colburn's United Service Magazine* 1844, III, p. 55.

16 Eaton, C.A., *Waterloo Days: The Narrative of an Englishwoman Resident at Brussels in June 1815*, London 1888, p. 21.

17 *Colburn's United Service Magazine* 1846, II, p. 456.

18 Landmann, Vol. II, p. 175.

Chapter 9

1 Granville Baker, B., *Old Cavalry Stations,* London 1934, p. 57.
2 Stewart of Garth, Vol. II, p. 344.
3 For example, in *British Military Library or Journal,* London 1798-1801, Vol. II, pp. 378-79.
4 *United Service Magazine* 1842, I, pp.181-82.
5 *Naval & Military Magazine* 1827, I, p. 468.
6 Roberts, p. 201.
7 *Chambers' Edinburgh Journal,* 3 May 1851, p. 287.
8 Anon., *Camp and Barrack-Room; or, the British Army as it is . . . ,* London 1846, pp. 28-29.
9 Stuart, Vol. II, p. 185.
10 Barrett, C.R.B., *The 7th (Queen's Own) Hussars,* London 1914, Vol. I, p. 329.
11 Carr, J., *Annals and Stories of Colne and Neighbourhood,* Manchester 1878, pp. 87, 89.
12 *Colburn's United Service Magazine* 1847, II, p. 581.
13 Raines, Revd. F.R., *Miscellanies: being a Selection from the Poems and Correspondence of the Revd. Thomas Wilson . . . ,* Manchester 1857, p. 81.
14 Roberts, p. 33.
15 Surtees, pp. 77, 92.
16 'Plonk' is from *vin blanc,* 'san fairy ann' from *ça ne fait rien,* 'it doesn't matter'.
17 William Grattan: *United Service Journal* 1834, I, p. 502.
18 *Gentleman's Magazine,* December 1809, p. 1174.
19 Wheatley, E., *The Wheatley Diary,* ed. C. Hibbert, London 1964, p. 8.
20 Kincaid, Sir John, *Adventures in the Rifle Brigade,* London 1830, combined edn. with *Random Shots from a Rifleman* (1835), London 1908, p. 102.
21 Greenhill Gardyne, Vol. I, p. 296.
22 Hope, J., *Letters from Portugal, Spain and France . . . ,* Edinburgh 1819, p. 180; originally published under the name 'A British Officer'.
23 Anon., *The Personal Narrative of a Private Soldier who served in the Forty-Second Highlanders, for Twelve Years, during the late War,* 1821, p. 75.
24 Gleig, p. 107.
25 Wellington, Vol. VIII, p. 514; 7 January 1812.
26 Cooper, p. 82.
27 ibid., p. 157.
28 Donaldson, p. 83.
29 Ross-Lewin, p. 205.
30 General Order, Badajoz, 7 September 1809.

31 General Order, Abrantes, 13 June 1809.

32 Ross-Lewin, p. 114.

33 Anon., *The Personal Narrative . . .* , p. 61.

34 Roberts, p. 189.

35 *The Times,* 22 June 1815.

36 Blakeney, pp. 49-50.

37 J. Emerson of the 27th, in *Peninsular Sketches by Actors on the Scene*, ed. W.H. Maxwell, London 1845, Vol. II, p. 208.

38 G. Napier, p. 177.

39 *United Service Journal* 1840, I, p. 224.

40 Sherer, p. 349.

41 C.B. Harris, *Brief Memoir of the late Lt.Col. Sir Thomas Noel Harris, KH*, London 1893, p. 48.

42 Cotton, E., *A Voice from Waterloo*, Brussels 1900, pp. 128-29.

43 Landmann, Vol. II, p. 221.

44 *United Service Journal* 1834, I, p. 507.

45 Landmann, Vol. II, pp. 293-95.

46 *Colburn's United Service Magazine* 1846, III, p. 497.

47 *United Service Journal* 1841, I, p. 196.

48 Brotherton, Sir Thomas, *A Hawk at War: The Peninsular War Reminiscences of General Sir Thomas Brotherton, CB*, ed. B. Perrett, Chippenham 1986.

49 *United Service Journal* 1836, II, p. 494.

50 *Colburn's United Service Magazine* 1845, II, p. 533.

51 *United Service Journal* 1840, II, p. 215; a slightly longer version appears in ibid., 1839, II, p. 223.

52 Grattan, W., *Adventures with the Connaught Rangers 1809-14*, London 1847, r/p ed. Sir Charles Oman 1902, p. 33.

Chapter 10

1   These verses are from *The War-Song of the Gallant Eighty-Eighth*, or *Love, Farewell!*, which seems to have been sung by the 88th Connaught Rangers at the time of the Peninsular War, hence the Irish dialect in the verse; but it probably originated earlier than that (see Winstock, L., *Songs & Music of the Redcoats*, London 1970, pp. 116-18). The text here is a slightly different version, as given in *Bentley's Miscellany* Vol. XIV, 1843, p. 501, and repeated in *The Cavalry Journal* Vol. XXI, 1931, pp. 311-12. Its popularity was quite widespread, even among the Madras Horse Artillery in the 1820s (see *The Cavalry Journal* Vol. XX, 1930, p. 458).

2   Gleig, pp. 48-49.

3 Morris, p. 117.

4 *Colburn's United Service Magazine* 1844, III, pp. 279-80.

5 *United Service Journal* 1836, II, p. 505.

6 Hope, p. 183.

7 *Colburn's United Service Journal* 1845, II, p. 293.

8 ibid. 1846, III, p. 563.

9 Lawrence, pp. 223-24.

10 Kincaid, pp. 210-11.

11 Levinge, R.G.A., *Historical Records of the Forty-Third Regiment, Monmouthshire Light Infantry*, London 1868, pp. 112-13.

12 Anon., *Personal Narrative . . .*, pp. 245-46.

13 *United Service Journal* 1834, III, pp. 505-07.

14 Gleig, p. 100.

15 *United Service Journal* 1834, II, p. 183.

16 ibid. 1841, I, p. 472.

17 ibid. 1834, II, p. 318.

18 MS account by an unknown sergeant of the Coldstream Guards, author's possession.

19 Malcolm, J., 'Reminiscences of a Campaign in the Pyrenees and the South of France in 1814', in *Memorials of the Late War*, London 1831.

20 *United Service Journal* 1834, II, p. 463.

21 Morris, p. 116.

22 *United Service Journal* 1840, I, p. 107.

23 ibid. 1836, III, p. 555.

24 Eadie, R., *Recollections of Robert Eadie*, Kincardine 1829, pp. 98-99.

25 *The Battle of Waterloo by a Near Observer*, London 1816, pp. xxvii-xxviii.

26 United Service Journal 1840, III, pp. 369-70.

27 Jones, Lt.Col. J.T., *Journals of the Sieges undertaken by the Allies in Spain in the Years 1811 and 1812*, London 1814, pp. 336.

28 Grattan, p. 197.

29 Kincaid, p. 66.

30 Napier, Sir William, *History of the War in the Peninsula and the South of France*, London 1828-40, Vol. IV, p. 425.

31 *United Service Journal* 1834, II, pp. 52-54.

32 Wellington, Vol. X, p. 373; 29 June 1813.

33 *Colburn's United Service Magazine* 1844, III, pp. 53-54.

34 Hall, B., *Voyages and Travels of Captain Basil Hall R.N.*, London 1895, pp. 223, 227-28.

35 Cotton, pp. 271-72.

36 Smyth, p. 393.

37 *United Service Journal* 1836, II, p. 506.

38 Landmann, Vol. II, p. 66.

39 *United Service Journal* 1840, I, p. 364.

40 Wellington, Vol. IV, p. 115, 22 August 1808.

41 'Waterloo, the Day after the Battle', in *With Fife and Drum*, ed. A.H. Miles, London n.d., p. 15.

42 *United Service Journal* 1840, III, pp. 363-64.

43 Cooper, p. 160.

44 Moran of Manton, Lord, *The Anatomy of Courage*, London 1945.

45 *Gentleman's Magazine,* July 1800, p. 687.

46 Wellington, Vol. XI, p. 306, 21 November 1813.

47 Sherer, pp. 84–85.

Chapter 11

1 Smith, Sir Harry, *The Autobiography of Sir Harry Smith*, ed. G.C. Moore Smith, London 1910, p. 17.

2 *Chambers' Edinburgh Journal,* 3 May 1851, p. 288.

3 Wylly, H.C., *The Loyal North Lancashire Regiment,* London 1934, Vol. I, p. 289.

4 Gentleman's Magazine, November 1802, p. 1060.

5 ibid. October 1814, p. 390.

6 ibid. January 1809, p. 87.

7 Quoted in Prebble, J., *The Highland Clearances,* London 1963, p. 321.

8 *London Chronicle,* 31 October 1801.

9 A portrait appears in the second edition of Lagden & Sly, Brightlingsea 1998, p. 206.

10 The author is indebted to Alan Harrison for these details.

11 *Gentleman's Magazine,* October 1800, p. 949.

12 ibid., supplement 1807, p. 628.

13 *Newcastle Courant,* 4 September 1813.

Bibliography

GENERAL WORKS

The following are some of many works that have a bearing upon the ordinary British soldier of the period:

Barthorp, M., *British Cavalry Uniforms*, Poole 1984.

——, *British Infantry Uniforms*, Poole 1982.

Brett-James, A., *Life in Wellington's Army*, London 1972.

Chambers, B., *John Collett and a Company of Foot Guards*, Droitwich 1996-97

Claver, S., *Under the Lash: A History of Corporal Punishment in the British Armed Forces*, London 1954.

Fletcher, I., *Brassey's History of Uniforms: Napoleonic Wars, Wellington's Army*, London 1996.

Fortescue, Hon. Sir John, *The County Lieutenancies and the Army 1803-1814*, London 1909.

Fosten, B., *Wellington's Heavy Cavalry*, London 1982.

——, *Wellington's Infantry I & II*, London 1981-82.

——, *Wellington's Light Cavalry*, London 1982.

Fox, K.O., *Making Life Possible*, Kineton 1982 (military aid to civil power).

Glover, M., *Wellington's Army in the Peninsula*, Newton Abbot 1977.

Glover, R., *Peninsula Preparation: the Reform of the British Army 1795-1809*, Cambridge 1963.

Haythornthwaite, P.J., *The Armies of Wellington*, London 1994.

——, *British Cavalryman 1792-1815*, London 1994.

——, *British Napoleonic Infantry Tactics 1792-1815*, Oxford 2008.

——, *British Rifleman 1797-1815*, Oxford 2002.

——, *Wellington's Army: The Uniforms of the British Soldier*, London 2002.

Holme, N., & Kirby, E.L., *Medal Rolls, 23rd Foot, Royal Welch Fusiliers, Napoleonic Period*, Caernarfon & London 1978.

Ingham, D., *Sudden Death, Sudden Glory; The 59th Regiment 1793-1830*, Oldham 1996.

Lagden, A., & Sly, J., *The 2/73rd at Waterloo*, Brightlingsea 1988.

Oman, Sir Charles, *History of the War in the Peninsula*, Oxford 1902-30. Vol. IX of the reprint, *Modern Studies of the War in Spain and Portugal 1808-1814*, ed. P. Griffith, London 1999, contains a bibliography of memoirs.

——, *Wellington's Army*, London 1912 (contains a bibliography of memoirs).

Page, E.C.G., *Following the Drum: Women in Wellington's Wars*, London 1986.

Palmer, R., *The Rambling Soldier: Military Life through Soldiers' Songs and Writings*, Harmondsworth 1977.

Rogers, H.C.B., *Wellington's Army*, London 1979.

Turner, P., *Soldiers' Accoutrements of the British Army 1750-1900*, Marlborough 2006.

Winstock, L., *Songs and Music of the Redcoats*, London 1970.

MEMOIRS

The following are some of the works written by, or about, members of the rank and file:

Anon., *Jottings from my Sabretasche*, 'by a Chelsea Pensioner' (actually W. Tate), London 1847.

Anon., *Memoirs of a Sergeant late in the 43rd Light Infantry Regiment*, London 1835.

Anon., *Journal of a Soldier of the 71st or Glasgow Regiment, Highland Light Infantry, from 1806 to 1819*, r/p as *A Soldier of the 71st*, ed. C. Hibbert, London 1975.

Anon., *The Personal Narrative of a Private Soldier who served in the 42nd Highlanders, Twelve Years during the Late War*, 1821.

Anton, J., *Retrospect of a Military Life*, Edinburgh 1841.

Blainey, W., *Bonaparte vs. Blainey*, New York 1988.

Brown, W., *The Autobiography, or Narrative of a Soldier, by William Brown, late of the 45th Regiment*, Kilmarnock 1829.

Caldwell, G., *Thomas Plunkett of the 95th Rifles*, Godmanchester 2010.

Cooper, J.S., *Rough Notes of Seven Campaigns in Portugal, Spain, France and America*, Carlisle 1869, r/p 1914.

Costello, E., *Memoirs of Edward Costello*, London 1857; r/p as *The Peninsular and Waterloo Campaigns: Edward Costello*, ed. A. Brett-James, London 1967.

Douglas, J., *Douglas's Tale of the Peninsula and Waterloo*, ed. S. Monick, London 1997.

Eadie, R., *Recollections of Robert Eadie, Private of His Majesty's 79th Regiment of Infantry*, Kincardine 1829.

Farmer, G., *The Light Dragoon*, ed. Revd. G.R. Gleig, London 1844.

Green, J., *Vicissitudes of a Soldier's Life, by John Green, late of the 68th Durham Light Infantry*, Louth 1827.

Green, W., *A Brief Outline of the Travels and Adventures of Wm. Green, Bugler, Rifle Brigade*, Coventry 1857, r/p as *Where Duty Calls Me: the Experiences of William Green of Lutterworth in the Napoleonic Wars*, ed. J. & D. Teague, West Wickham, Kent, 1975.

Hale, J., *Journal of James Hale, late Sergeant 9th Foot*, Cirencester 1826.

Hamilton, A., *Hamilton's Campaign with Moore and Wellington*, ed. J. Colquhoun, Staplehurst 1998.

Harris, B.R., *Recollections of Rifleman Harris*, ed. H. Curling, London 1848.

Jackson, T., *Narrative of the Eventful Life of Thomas Jackson, late Sergeant of the Coldstream Guards*, Birmingham 1847.

Landsheit, N., *The Hussar: the Story of Norbert Landsheit, Sergeant in the York Hussars and the 20th Light Dragoons*, ed. Revd. G.R. Gleig, London 1837.

Lawrence, W., *The Autobiography of Sergeant William Lawrence*, ed. G.N. Bankes, London 1886.

Lindau, F., *A Waterloo Hero: The Reminiscences of Friedrich Lindau*, ed. J. Bogle & A. Uffindell, London 2009.

Low, E.B., & MacBride, M., *With Napoleon at Waterloo*, London 1911 (contains a number of 'other rank' accounts).

Maxwell, W.H., *Peninsular Sketches by Actors on the Scene*, London 1844.

Miller, B., *The Adventures of Serjeant Benjamin Miller*, ed. M.R. Dacombe & B.J.H. Rowe, Sheffield 1928.

Morley, S., *Memoirs of a Serjeant of the 5th Regiment*, Ashford 1842.

Morris, T. (with W. Morris & W. Morris Jnr.), *The Three Serjeants*, London 1858; r/p as *The Napoleonic Wars: Thomas Morris*, ed. J. Selby, London 1967.

O'Neil, C., *Military Adventures of Charles O'Neil under Wellington in the Peninsula and Waterloo*, Staplehurst 1997.

Page, G.A., *The Soldier-Schoolmaster; A Brief Memoir of Christopher Ludlum*, Louth 1874.

Pearson, A., *The Soldier Who Walked Away*, ed. A.H. Haley, Liverpool n.d.

Robertson, D., *Journal of Sergeant D. Robertson, late 92nd Highlanders*, Perth 1842.

Shipp, J., *Memoirs of the Extraordinary Military Career of John Shipp, late a Lieutenant in his Majesty's 87th Regiment*, 1829, r/p as *The Path of Glory*, ed. C.J. Stranks, London 1969.

Smithies, J., *The Life and Recollections of a Peninsular Veteran and Waterloo Hero*, Middleton 1868.

Stevenson, J., *Twenty-One Years in the British Foot Guards*, London 1830.

Surtees, W. , *Twenty-Five Years in the Rifle Brigade*, London 1833.

Thornton, J., *Your Most Obedient Servant: James Thornton, Cook to the Duke of Wellington*, ed. Countess of Longford, Exeter 1985.

Wheeler, W., *The Letters of Private Wheeler 1809-28*, ed. B.H. Liddell Hart, London 1951.

Index